Jews and Anti-Judaism in Esther and the Church

In her clear and thorough analysis, Tricia Miller shows how the book of Esther has been misinterpreted for anti-Semitic purposes. In particular, she demonstrates that hatred of Judaism as an aggressive form of nationalism – a Christian trope in the interpretation of Esther – feeds current attempts to delegitimate the State of Israel.

Bruce Chilton,
Bernard Iddings Bell Professor of Religion,
Bard College, New York

This brilliant work of scholarship is deliberately and sensitively combined with advocacy in support of Israel. Dr. Tricia Miller explores the heart of scholarly debate about the book of Esther: whether there is justification for resistance, in the name of God and by force, to oppression. She argues that this debate is central to understanding the heart and mind of the Hebrew Bible, showing that Jews have a right to defend their existence as individuals, as a community of people, and as a state.

Paul Merkley,
Emeritus Professor of History,
Carleton University, Ottowa

Any theology student can be grateful to have this meticulous study of the origins and historical context of the book of Esther in its Hebrew and Greek versions. Tricia Miller demonstrates the ideological continuity that characterizes attempts to eradicate the Jewish people from Ancient Persia to the modern Middle East.

Malcolm F. Lowe,
Ecumenical Theological Research Fraternity,
Jerusalem

Jews and Anti-Judaism in Esther and the Church

For Elyse,
For the sake of Israel,

Tricia Miller

Tricia Miller

James Clarke & Co

James Clarke & Co
P.O. Box 60
Cambridge
CB1 2NT
United Kingdom

www.jamesclarke.co
publishing@jamesclarke.co

ISBN: 978 0 227 17447 0

British Library Cataloguing in Publication Data
A record is available from the British Library

First published by James Clarke & Co, 2015

CONTENTS

INTRODUCTION

The biblical book of Esther records an account of Jewish resistance to attempted genocide in the setting of the Persian Empire. According to the text, Jews were targeted for annihilation simply because of their Jewish identity. However, the story also reports that they were allowed to defend themselves against anyone who sought to kill them. Particular features included in the original Hebrew and two subsequent Greek versions reveal much about ancient anti-Judaism, as well as the anti-Judaism and anti-Semitism that was yet to come. In the context of attempted genocide, the message of Esther addresses a timeless and universal issue of justice: that humans have the right and responsibility to defend themselves against those who intend to murder. The combination of this message with an exploration of what three versions of Esther reveal about anti-Judaism makes this book profoundly relevant to the contemporary issue of the contested legitimacy of the State of Israel in relation to the ongoing Arab-Israeli conflict.

Israel is a tiny state in the midst of twenty-two vast Arab and Muslim nations, whose populations are comprised of people groups that have more than a millennia-long history of internecine warfare. Since the establishment of the State of Israel in 1948, these nations have finally found something they can agree on: the shared belief that the Jewish State needs to be wiped off the map.[1] And yet, if one

---

1. In 1948, five Arab armies – Egypt, Syria, Transjordan, Lebanon, and Iraq – invaded Israel for the purpose of destroying the fledgling state. Azzam Pasha, Secretary General of the Arab League, made their intentions quite clear: "It will be a war of annihilation. It will be a momentous massacre in history that will be talked about like the massacres of the Mongols or the Crusades." In 1963, the Palestinian Liberation Organization (PLO)

were to accept the perspective of the vast majority of the international media, as well as the belief of significant portions of the modern Church, one would erroneously conclude that the current violence and unrest in the Middle East is due to the existence of Israel and its efforts to defend itself against those who seek its destruction.

Indeed, in the decades since the Holocaust, the very existence of the State of Israel has become the new "Jewish question" troubling the world.[1] Prior to the Holocaust, discussion of the "Jewish question" was most often cloaked in theological garb, and the anti-Semitism that enabled the Holocaust was fed, in part, by an anti-Judaism perpetuated by the Church.[2] After the

---

was formed, and with it, the Palestine National Charter, which called for Israel's destruction. On May 27, 1967, former President Nassar of Egypt declared, "Our basic objective will be the destruction of Israel. The Arab people want to fight." In June 1967, the armies of Egypt, Jordan, Syria, and Lebanon launched joint offensives against Israel, but were defeated in just six days. Another failed attempt on the part of the Arab nations to destroy Israel occurred in 1973 in what is known as the Yom Kippur War. Since 1973, Palestinians have carried out multiple terror attacks and perpetrated intifadas against Israeli citizens. The first intifada lasted from 1987-1993, and the second from 2000-2005. The fact that the Arab Palestinians still intend to destroy the Jewish State is demonstrated by statements contained in the current Palestinian Liberation Organization's Charter, Fatah's Constitution, and Hamas' Charter. For example, Article 15 of the PLO's Charter mentions the need to "repulse the Zionist, imperialist invasion from the great Arab homeland." Article 9 of Fatah's Constitution states that liberating Palestine is a "religious and human obligation." And the Hamas Charter begins with an introduction that calls on Allah for help in its jihad "for the purpose of liberating Palestine."

1. Robert S. Wistrich, *A Lethal Obsession: Anti-Semitism from Antiquity to the Global Jihad* (New York: Random House, 2010), 62.
2. The terms "anti-Semitism" and "anti-Judaism" will be defined in more detail in Chapter Five. However, at this point, "anti-Judaism" can be defined as referring specifically to the opposition to, and persecution of, Jews based on their religion, or the denial of the right of Jews to exist in terms of their own self-understanding. "Anti-Semitism" can be defined as opposition to Jews on the basis of ethnicity, which results from and includes delegitimizing, demonizing, and dehumanizing Jews as a people group. However, in spite of the fact that anti-Judaism is defined in religious terms and anti-Semitism in terms of race, there is essentially no difference between the two on the practical level. An underlying contempt towards Jews is the foundation for both, and opposition to Judaism almost always, if not always, results in opposition to Jews.

Holocaust, much of the Church world seemed to recognize the error of its ways and, in some cases, adopted theoretical positions in opposition to anti-Semitism. However, many of these same members of Christendom are now opposing the existence of the State of Israel and/or the efforts it takes to defend itself against attempted annihilation. As I will demonstrate, this stance is nothing more than a fresh manifestation of anti-Judaism, because it is a stand in opposition to one of the essential identifying features of Judaism – the importance of the Land of Israel to the Jewish people.

Robert Wistrich classifies this relatively new phenomenon as "anti-Zionism," which he identifies as the "offspring and heir" of historical anti-Semitism.[1] Anti-Zionism, or anti-Israel sentiment, has developed in response to the fulfillment of the Jewish people's two-millennia-old dream to return to their ancient homeland. It is the "offspring" of historical anti-Judaism/Semitism because people today justify their anti-Israel sentiments as an appropriate response to actions taken by the government and defense forces of the Jewish State, just as historically people justified their anti-Semitism as an appropriate response to the defining characteristics of Jews or Judaism. To an alarming degree, "critics of Israel and Zionism tend to attribute to them the negative qualities which antisemites were wont to attribute to the Jews in general."[2] In other words, stereotypes and "reviling accusations" against Israel are being employed in "a covert anti-Semitic approach similar to that which claims that the evil quality of the Jews is immutable and is, as it were, a transhistorical factor."[3] As a result of this approach, Israel – the collective Jew – has its right to exist delegitimized, its actions to defend itself against enemies intent on its destruction demonized, and its people dehumanized.

It is indeed sobering that in the last few decades, under the guise of anti-Zionism, substantial parts of the organized Church have succumbed once again to the millennia-old practice of delegitimizing, demonizing, and dehumanizing Jews. However, what is most alarming is that in recent years, those who identify

---

1. Wistrich, *A Lethal Obsession*, 62.
2. Yehoshafat Harkabi, "On Arab Antisemitism Once More," in *Antisemitism Through the Ages* (ed. Shmuel Almog; Oxford: Pergamon Press, 1988), 227-39.
3. *ibid.*, 231.

as Evangelicals – historically the members of Christendom most supportive of Israel – have been targeted with a false pro-Palestinian, anti-Israel narrative specifically designed to turn traditional supporters of Israel away from that support for the purpose of garnering it for Palestinian Christians instead. While the Palestinian Christians' need for support is no doubt genuine, the means being implemented for the sake of this end are disingenuous and blatantly anti-Jewish.

This book has been written in response to this relatively new development within the Evangelical part of the Church in the hope of providing that particular audience with helpful material with which to counter the deceptive narrative being thrust at it. More specifically, this work has been composed for the purpose of exposing the theological and historical errors that form the foundation of the anti-Jewish/Israel narrative Palestinian Christians are promoting with the help of prominent Evangelical leaders in the United States. This volume draws on previous academic work that contributed to the author's PhD dissertation on the story of Esther and anti-Semitism, and research for articles posted on the website of the Committee for Accuracy in Middle East Reporting in America. As a result, extensive footnotes are provided for readers who want to pursue particular topics in more depth. This book is unique in that it uses an academic approach to demonstrate the relationship of historic theology to current events concerning Israel for the purpose of encouraging the Church in general, and Evangelicals in particular, to maintain their position of support for Israel's right to exist and defend itself against those who seek its destruction.

Because the survival of the Jewish people has been threatened by successive empires since before the time of Esther, and because the Hebrew and Greek versions reveal so much about historic anti-Judaism, the book of Esther, with its account of Jewish resistance to attempted genocide, is particularly germane to current events. Indeed, the story of Esther is "surprisingly prophetic about the anti-Judaism that would later come,"[1] and its timeless message of justice has much to say in relation to Israel's right to exist, and to anti-Zionism as a new form of anti-Judaism. Therefore, the majority of this volume is devoted to discussions

---

1. Linda M. Day, *Abingdon Old Testament Commentaries: Esther* (Nashville, TN: Abingdon Press, 2005), 75.

of the message of the Hebrew text, the reality of the danger of annihilation revealed by all three versions, and the unbroken history of anti-Judaism/Semitism from the ancient world to the present, as revealed through the history of interpretation of Esther's story.

In order to establish the relevance of the book of Esther to current events in relation to the contested legitimacy of Israel, one chapter will be devoted to each of the three versions. The first chapter will establish the intent of the author of Hebrew Esther by demonstrating that the account of an attempted genocide of the Jews is purposefully set in a particular historical context within the Persian Period. The historical setting is verifiable through analyses of semantic features and Persian elements in the story, as well as through the establishment of the date of composition of the text. By providing multiple accurate details throughout the account, the author validates the message the audience was intended to hear. Not only was there an attempt to annihilate Jews in a particular time and place, but, when given the means to do so, Jews were able to defend themselves successfully. The identification of this message is a prerequisite for appreciating the significance of later interpretations of the story, and is essential for the purpose of answering the question of whether Esther tells a story of Jewish aggression or one of Jewish resistance. Because the debate over the issue of aggression versus resistance among Esther scholars is almost indistinguishable from ongoing controversy over military actions taken by Israel, the answer to this question is quite applicable to the contested legitimacy of the Jewish State.

Previous statements have already informed the reader that three versions of Esther were written in antiquity. These statements have also inferred that the Hebrew version predates two subsequent Greek renderings, which are known to scholars as Old Greek (OG) Esther – the version preserved in the Septuagint – and Alpha Text (AT) Esther. Chapters Two and Three will focus on OG and AT Esther respectively because they represent the earliest interpretations of the account preserved in the Hebrew version. But, before proceeding to Chapter Two, there will be an Excursus that demonstrates the textual relationships of the three versions of Esther for the purpose of establishing the primacy of Hebrew Esther. It is provided for readers who are interested in the technical work that determined the correlation of the three versions. However, it is not necessary to digest the information provided in order to benefit from the rest of the book, and so readers who are not interested in this material can freely go on to Chapter Two.

Chapter Two will answer the questions of when and why the first Greek version of Esther – OG Esther – was written, and Chapter Three will answer the same questions concerning the second Greek version, AT Esther. These questions will be answered by determining the historical setting of the composition of the texts, and by identifying the intent of their authors. The determination of historical settings will answer the question of when the texts were written, and the identification of the intent of the authors will answer the question of why they were written. The establishment of the context and purpose behind the composition of OG Esther will reveal the reason so many changes and additions were made to the Hebrew version, and the establishment of the same behind the composition of AT Esther will clarify why additional changes were made to the Old Greek. These analyses will provide essential context for the literary comparisons of Greek and Hebrew Esther in Chapter Four.

The fourth chapter will provide an overview of the use of both Greek texts since the time of their composition. A knowledge of *which* version of the story was being read *when, where* and *by whom* is foundational for comprehending how historic understandings of Esther have contributed to anti-Jewish interpretations of the story. Following this survey, literary comparisons of pertinent elements in the Old Greek version with those in the Hebrew will demonstrate that the changes made by the author of OG Esther are the primary source of traditional interpretations and present-day beliefs concerning Jews. Because this rendering of the story is included in the Septuagint, which is still read by significant parts of the Church, interpretations based on OG Esther continue to contribute to a negative perception of Jews that has much in common with the beliefs that feed current Christian anti-Zionism.

Finally, Chapter Five will examine the relationship between historic anti-Judaism and current anti-Zionism by summarizing the development of Christian anti-Judaism, as demonstrated through replacement theology, and the role that erroneous Christian doctrine has played in historic anti-Semitism, even to the point of fueling and justifying the Holocaust. Significant features of Christian anti-Judaism will be identified for the purpose of illustrating how anti-Jewish theology defines Christian identity. Recent statements and activities of certain church leaders in the United States who are promoting a pro-Palestinian, anti-Israel narrative will then be analyzed in order to reveal the doctrine that is at the heart of current Christian anti-Zionism. In short, the same erroneous theology and anti-Jewish features that have defined Christian identity historically appear prominently in the theology of Palestinian Christians and a growing number of Evangelicals. This anti-Jewish theology not only defines their identity, but justifies their anti-Zionist crusade as well.

This work is submitted to the reader in the hope that perspective gained from this study will result in an understanding of the relevance of the message of Esther to the controversy over the contested legitimacy of the State of Israel and the role that anti-Judaism plays in that debate. It is also offered in the hope that knowledge of the theological and historical errors at the root of the anti-Jewish/Israel narrative being promoted by Palestinian Christians will encourage Evangelicals to maintain their position of support for Israel's right to exist and defend itself against those who seek its annihilation.

CHAPTER ONE

Hebrew Esther: Is it a Story of Jewish Aggression or Resistance to Attempted Genocide?

This chapter will answer the question of whether Hebrew Esther tells a story of Jewish aggression or one of Jewish resistance to attempted genocide. The debate over this issue among Esther scholars is remarkably similar to ongoing controversy over military actions taken by the State of Israel. In both cases, the argument is focused on whether Jews initiated an act of war, or whether they took defensive measures in response to enemy aggression. Therefore, the answer to this question is the first step in demonstrating the relevance of the story of Esther to the contemporary issue of the contested legitimacy of the State of Israel.

The question of Jewish aggression or resistance will be answered by establishing what the author of this text intended to say to the original audience. The identification of the message of the text will provide an essential foundation for the following chapters, because an understanding of the author's intent is a prerequisite for appreciating the significance of later interpretations of the story, as well as the applicability of the message to current events in relation to Israel. As has already been stated in the Introduction, the author of Esther purposefully presented the account of an attempted genocide of the Jews in a particular historical context within the Persian period, which is verifiable through analyses of semantic features and Persian elements in the story, as well as through the establishment of the date of composition of the text. The first part of this chapter will demonstrate the author's intent through discussions of these features, and the second part of the chapter will identify the message of Hebrew Esther and answer the crucial question of aggression versus resistance.

Before beginning discussions of the author's intent and identification of the message of this version of Esther, it will be informative to look at a brief overview of the history of interpretation of Esther since the time of Martin Luther. This survey will demonstrate why the question of aggression versus resistance has been pivotal in the interpretation of Esther ever since the time of Luther and how it has profound implications for what the story of Esther has to say in relation to the State of Israel today.

The History of Interpretation of Esther
Since Martin Luther

Esther is the only book in the Hebrew Bible whose primary focus is the recording of an attempted annihilation of the Jews. However, in spite of the clear account it contains of Haman's intent to have all the Jews destroyed, historical interpretations of Esther have contributed to anti-Semitic critique of the book. While it has always been an important book in Jewish tradition, and "the great Jewish medieval scholar Maimonides (1135–1204) ranked Esther immediately after the Pentateuch in importance,"[1] it has had, at best, a marginal status in Christian tradition. It was hardly mentioned in the writings of the Early Church Fathers, but was one of the books Martin Luther despised and wished to exclude from the canon.[2]

In "On the Jews and Their Lies," Martin Luther commented on how much the Jews "love the book of Esther, which so well fits their bloodthirsty, vengeful, murderous greed and hope."[3] He condemned the book, stating that it didn't belong in the canon because it "Judaizes too much and has too much heathen corruption."[4] In his 1908 commentary on Esther, Lewis Bayles Paton wrote that Luther's verdict was "not too severe" and stated,

---

1. Carey A. Moore, "Archaeology and the Book of Esther," in *Studies in the Book of Esther* (ed. C.A. Moore; New York: KTAV Publishing House, 1982), 369-86.
2. Martin Luther, *Table Talk XXIV*, cited in Moore, "Archaeology and the Book of Esther," 369-86.
3. Martin Luther, "On the Jews and Their Lies," in *Luther's Works: Volume 47, The Christian in Society IV* (ed. F. Sherman; Philadelphia, PA: Fortress Press, 1971).
4. Martin Luther, "Table Talk XXIV," in *Luther's Works: Volume 54, Table Talk* (ed. T.G. Tappert; Philadelphia, PA: Fortress Press, 1967).

"there is not one noble character in this book."[1] More specifically, Paton interpreted the actions of the Jews in Esther 8:11, 9:2-10, and 9:13-15 as evidence of aggression rather than resistance. Paton's interpretation not only shows how influential Luther continues to be centuries after he lived, but also provides just one of many examples of how scholarship has interpreted the actions of the Jews of Persia as bloodthirsty and vengeful.

Following Luther, German scholars of the eighteenth and nineteenth centuries accused Esther of "insatiable vindictiveness," and the book of displaying a "blood-thirsty spirit of aggression and persecution," as well as a "very narrow minded and Jewish spirit of aggression."[2] Late in the nineteenth century, Heinrich Ewald commented that "in moving to Esther from the other books of the Hebrew Bible 'we fall as it were, from heaven to earth'."[3] By the end of the nineteenth century, German scholars ranted "against the arrogant nationalism of the book of Esther."[4] This was the same time period in which Otto von Bismarck was establishing the new German Reich, annexing territory, and establishing German colonies in Africa. The contrast between the nationalistic activities of the new German Reich and the book of Esther, in which Esther and Mordecai are portrayed as assimilated and loyal subjects of the king of Persia, with no mention of the nation of Israel or any desire to return to the Land of Israel, makes the German charge of nationalism concerning Esther seem absurd, to say the least. Indeed, there is nothing nationalistic about the book of Esther. Rather, "it is a defense of self-determination in a time of exile."[5]

By the late nineteenth century, anti-Semitic critiques of Esther also became prominent in British scholarship, and then in American scholarship by the beginning of the twentieth century.[6] However, because of the distinct similarities between the threat of

1. Lewis Bayles Paton, *The International Critical Commentary: A Critical and Exegetical Commentary on The Book of Esther* (Edinburgh: T and T Clark, 1908), 96.
2. Elliot Horowitz, *Reckless Rites: Purim and the Legacy of Jewish Violence* (Princeton, NJ: Princeton University Press, 2006), 12-15.
3. Heinrich Ewald quoted in *ibid.*, 15.
4. *ibid.*, 33.
5. Jon D. Levenson, "The Scroll of Esther in Ecumenical Perspective," *JES* XIII (1976): 440-51.
6. For a detailed discussion of the last century of scholarly anti-Semitic interpretation of Esther, see Horowitz, *Reckless Rites*, 23-45.

attempted genocide in the book of Esther and the actual events of twentieth-century Germany, this discussion will remain focused on German scholars' interpretations of Esther. In the 1930s, Otto Eissfeldt saw a "close connection between Jewish religion and the Jewish national spirit,"[1] and Johannes Hempel referred to what he interpreted as vengeance in the book of Esther as "hate-inspired wish-fulfillment."[2] In 1937, Wilhelm Vischer stated that Esther "presents the Jewish question in the sharpest form,"[3] and while Vischer preferred for Jews to be converted rather than murdered, his solution for the "Jewish question" would still have resulted in the end of Judaism. Even in the midst of the Holocaust, "German biblical scholarship saw little reason to reconsider the harsh condemnation of Esther,"[4] as scholars continued to condemn what they saw as "the vengeful spirit of the book of Esther."[5]

While one might think that the events of the Holocaust would have softened scholarly interpretation of the story of Esther, this was not the case. In 1953, Curt Kuhl wrote that the book testified to the Jews' "narrow-minded and fanatical nationalism."[6] As has already been said above, to level a charge of nationalism against the book of Esther, in which there is no identification of Jews with any country except for their country of exile, is, at the very least, absurd. Indeed, "it is a strange nationalism which advocates cooperation with a foreign monarch rather than secession from his control."[7] However, more than just being absurd, a charge of nationalism ignores the facts of the story and betrays a bias on the part of the accuser. Such a bias is perhaps best illustrated by Hermann Gunkel, who said that Esther "cannot be read by a Christian or a non-Jew without great distaste, for it fires up intense Jewish nationalism, celebrates anti-Gentile Jewish vengeance, and

---

1. Otto Eissfeldt, *Einleitung in das Alte Testament* (Tübingen: Mohr, 1964), 566-7.
2. Johannes Hempel, *Das Ethos des Alten Testaments*, 2nd ed. (Berlin: Töpelmann, 1964), 30, 105.
3. Wilhelm Vischer, *Esther* (Munich: Kaiser, 1937), quoted in Levenson, "The Scroll of Esther," 441.
4. Horowitz, *Reckless Rites*, 15.
5. *ibid.*, 37.
6. Curt Kuhl, *The Old Testament: Its Origins and Composition* (trans. C.T.M. Herriot; Edinburgh and London: Oliver and Boyd, 1961), 271.
7. Levenson, "The Scroll of Esther," 444.

promulgates Purim, a festival that means nothing to the church."[1] As a result, some Christian theologians, like Luther before them, "would drop the book from the scriptural canon."[2] Perhaps that is in effect what Walter Eichrodt and Gerhard von Rad did in their Old Testament theologies, which were written in the 1960s. Eichrodt only mentions Esther in footnotes, and then only "as an example of undesirable tendencies," and von Rad doesn't even mention the book in a work of theology that supposedly encompasses the entire Old Testament.[3]

Beginning with Martin Luther and his statement that the book of Esther "Judaizes too much," a common theme throughout all the comments surveyed thus far has been the "Jewishness" of the book. Whether it is reference to the Jewish spirit of revenge, a "close connection between Jewish religion and the Jewish national spirit,"[4] or "the Jewish question in the sharpest form,"[5] the feature that all these comments have in common is the fact that Esther is "Jewish." According to Carl Heinrich Cornill, it would seem that "all the worst and most unpleasing features of Judaism are here displayed without disguise."[6] It is not clear what "features of Judaism" Cornill finds so objectionable, because of all the books in the Hebrew Bible, Esther displays much less "Judaism" than all the rest of the canonical books.

It is significant to note at this point the hypocrisy demonstrated by scholars who gladly appropriate the rest of the Hebrew Bible for Christian use, while at the same time vilifying the book of Esther for being too "Jewish." As David Clines writes, "the undoubted 'Jewishness' of the book is something it shares with the whole of the Old Testament; if that is an 'offence' in Christian eyes, it is a stumbling block that must be surmounted before any part of the Old

---

1. Hermann Gunkel quoted in Edward L. Greenstein, "A Jewish Reading of Esther," in *Judaic Perspectives on Ancient Israel* (ed. Jacob Neusner, Baruch A. Levine, and Ernest S. Frerichs; Philadelphia, PA: Fortress Press, 1987), 225-43.
2. Greenstein, "A Jewish Reading of Esther," 225.
3. Levenson, "The Scroll of Esther," 440-41.
4. Otto Eissfeldt, *Einleitung in das Alte Testament* (Tübingen: Mohr, 1964), 566-7.
5. Wilhelm Vischer, *Esther* (Munich: Kaiser, 1937), quoted in Levenson, "The Scroll of Esther," 441.
6. C.H. Cornill, *Introduction to the Canonical Books of the Old Testament* (trans. G.A. Box; New York: G.P. Putnam's Sons, 1907), 257.

Testament is appropriated for Christian use."[1] Clines' observation is profound in relation to how Christians commandeer the Jewish Scriptures in order to legitimize anti-Judaism and replacement theology, which in turn feed the anti-Zionism to be addressed in Chapter Five. Indeed, the same charges of nationalism, aggression, and Jewishness leveled against the book of Esther are the same allegations made against the State of Israel today.

In contrast to the many theologians and scholars who continued to despise the book of Esther even after the Holocaust, there have been a few who have taken a different approach. Bernhard W. Anderson attempted to counter the position of theologians who would like to exclude Esther from the canon by writing "The Place of the Book of Esther in the Christian Bible."[2] While it is obvious that Anderson was attempting to overcome the well-entrenched heritage of anti-Semitic interpretation as he made his case in favor of Esther's place in the Bible, he still made a number of statements similar to those that fuel anti-Semitic diatribes against Esther. His statements illustrate the ongoing misinterpretation of the message of the text, and they demonstrate common anti-Semitic belief as well. Anderson states that "the book is inspired by fierce nationalism and an unblushing vindictiveness."[3] He also points out that "the barrier of the Law . . . was a wall of separation behind which Jews could maintain their historical identity," and that "by building a wall around its communal life, and thus sharpening the separateness of the Jew from his neighbors, Judaism excited against itself a suspicion and hatred."[4] This argument sounds strangely similar to Haman's justification for his planned annihilation of the Jews of Persia in Esther 3:8.[5] Haman argued that the Jews needed to be destroyed because their laws were different than those of other

---

1. David Clines, *The New Century Bible Commentary: Ezra, Nehemiah, Esther* (Grand Rapids, MI: Wm. B. Eerdmans Publishing Co, 1984), 256.
2. Bernhard W. Anderson, "The Place of the Book of Esther in the Christian Bible," in *Studies in the Book of Esther* (ed. C.A. Moore; New York: KTAV Publishing House, 1982), 130-41.
3. *ibid.*, 130.
4. *ibid.*, 132-3.
5. In Esther 3:8, Haman tells the king that there is a certain people scattered throughout the kingdom who observe different laws than the rest of the people, and that because of this, it is not appropriate for the king to tolerate them.

people, and Anderson concluded that the "barrier of the Law" results in "Judaism inciting persecution and persecution creating Judaism."[1] Anderson's argument is faulty in that it blames Jews for the persecution they receive, and, in so doing, actually offers support for Haman's rationale for genocide.

In answer to all the scholars surveyed above who interpret Esther as displaying "an intense nationalistic spirit and virulent hostility to Gentiles," Frederic Bush states that a careful reading of the book "demonstrates that these points of view are in error."[2] Bush identifies "the dangerous and uncertain character of life for Jews in the diaspora" as "a significant element" in the theme of the book, which is "the deliverance of the diaspora Jewish community from the terrible threat of annihilation."[3] According to Bush, this theme shows "that the book simply cannot be read as a nationalist diatribe."[4] Shemaryahu Talmon also concludes that nationalism does not appear in Esther, and that the message of the book is based on a "non-national wisdom ideology," which is applicable "to any human situation, irrespective of politico-national or religio-national allegiances."[5] In agreement with Bush and Talmon, and in opposition to the conclusions of other scholars, the following work will demonstrate that rather than being a bloodthirsty story of Jewish aggression that promotes a nationalistic spirit, Hebrew Esther presents an account of resistance to attempted genocide, with a message that speaks to the right and responsibility of humans to defend themselves against those who intend to murder.

The Intent of the Author

The Historical Context of Hebrew Esther

The Hebrew text of Esther presents the particulars of the story as events that took place during the reign of Ahashverosh of Persia, a king more commonly known as Xerxes I (486–465 BCE). Events

---

1. Anderson, "The Place of the Book of Esther in the Christian Bible," 133.
2. Frederic W. Bush, *Word Biblical Commentary: Ruth/Esther* (Thomas Nelson Publishers, 1996), 333.
3. *ibid.*, 311, 333.
4. *ibid.*, 333.
5. Shemaryahu Talmon, "Wisdom in the Book of Esther," *VT* 13 (1963): 419-55.

in the book are dated according to the year of the king's reign in which they occurred, and the first date is given in 1:3. After identifying Ahashverosh as the one who ruled over an empire that stretched from India to Ethiopia, it says that in the third year of his reign, the king gave a banquet for all his government officials that lasted for 180 days. According to fifth century BCE Greek historians – including Herodotus, Ctesias, and Photius – Xerxes was a decadent king, particularly known for his lavish banquets.[1] So, it is not surprising that the book of Esther begins with an account of an extensive banquet.

The text reports that the banquet occurred in the third year of the reign of the king. Since his reign began in 486, the third year of that reign would be 484 BCE. According to Herodotus, 484 BCE was the year in which Xerxes finished suppressing a rebellion in Egypt that began before the death of his father, Darius I.[2] However, the rebellion in Egypt was not the only problem facing Xerxes as he began his reign. The biblical book of Ezra testifies to unrest in Judea in the year that Xerxes took the throne when it records in 4:4 and 4:6 that the people of the land sent a letter to the king accusing the inhabitants of Judah and Jerusalem of rebellion against him. In order to deal with unrest and rebellion in both of these regions within his empire, Xerxes went on a military campaign through Judah on his way to Egypt. As a result, Persian power was solidified in Judah and the Egyptian rebellion was successfully extinguished. In light of what Greek historians have to say about Xerxes' fondness for banquets and the date of the banquet described in Esther, it is probable that the lavish banquet described in chapter 1 was a banquet given to celebrate the king's victory over the rebellion in Egypt.[3]

The fact that this feast was given in the third year of his reign also means that it occurred as Xerxes was beginning to prepare for his campaign against Greece. No sooner had he returned

---

1. Pierre Briant, *From Cyrus to Alexander: A History of the Persian Empire* (Winona Lake, IN: Eisenbrauns, 2002), 515-17.

2. *ibid.*, 525.

3. It could also have been a celebration of the completion of the palace in Susa, the construction of which had been left uncompleted by Darius upon his death. "The first pious duty of the new king was to complete at Susa the palace of his father, where a few columns were still to be carved." A.T. Olmstead, *History of the Persian Empire* (Chicago, IL: University of Chicago Press, 1948), 230.

from Egypt than he "instituted a military draft throughout the Empire."[1] Therefore, the gathering of all of his government officials in Susa for the feast described in Esther could also have been for the purpose of planning for the Greek campaign. In fact, we know from Herodotus that upon his return from Egypt, Xerxes convened the highest Persian officials to announce his plans to move against the Greeks.[2] In addition to Xerxes' love of banquets, the length of the feast described by the author of Esther is not unreasonable in light of the fact that armies in the ancient world tended to stay at home during the winter months, and not go to war until the spring. To conclude that Xerxes and his officials may have spent the six months from fall to spring planning for war is also plausible because Herodotus wrote that the preparation for war against the Greeks took four years.[3] In fact, a planning period of six months from the fall of 484 to the spring of 483 is short considering that "to prepare for the final invasion of Greece, Xerxes took temporary residence in Sardis in 481 BCE."[4]

Following the description of the banquet in chapter 1, we read an account of how Queen Vashti was vanquished and was no longer queen because of her refusal to be put on display in front of all the drunken men at the king's feast. As a result of Xerxes being without a queen, a search for a new queen commenced. Chapter 2 details the process for choosing a new queen, a process that culminated with Esther being chosen as the replacement for Vashti. It is significant to note that the time period given in the book between the feast that resulted in the vanquishing of Vashti and the installation of Esther as queen was the third to the seventh year of the reign of Ahashverosh – the same time period as that between the beginning of Xerxes' preparation for war against Greece in 484 and the end of that war in 479.[5] In other words, as the search for the new queen was being undertaken, Xerxes was at war with the Greeks. Following his disastrous

---

1. Briant, *From Cyrus to Alexander*, 526.
2. Herodotus, *The Histories* (Oxford: Oxford University Press, 1998), VII.8.
3. *ibid.*, VII.20.
4. Jon L. Berquist, *Judaism in Persia's Shadow: A Social and Historical Approach* (Eugene, OR: Wipf and Stock, 2003), 91.
5. According to David Clines, "the four years between the deposition of Vashti and the installation of Esther as queen coincide with the four years Xerxes was absent from Persia on the expedition against the Greeks." Clines, *The New Century Bible Commentary*, 261.

defeat at the hands of the Greeks in the summer of 479, he went to his palace at Susa, which he had made "his principal winter residence."[1] According to the biblical account, Esther was taken to the king in the month of Tebeth, or the tenth month, in the seventh year of his reign, or 479. The month of Tebeth falls in the midst of winter, which is consistent with historical accounts that place Xerxes in Susa for the winter. This fact, combined with the fact that the biblical account dates this event in the same year as Xerxes' return from war, indicates that the author's intent to present the account of an attempted genocide of the Jews in a particular historical context within the Persian period was done with an obvious knowledge of events in the reign of King Xerxes. This intent, which is demonstrated through the historical setting of the story, is validated in part through the presence of particular semantic features and Persian elements in the story.

Semantic Features and Persian Elements in the Story

The author's abundant use of ancient Near Eastern names and loan words, as well as accurate descriptions of various aspects of government and life in the Persian court, provides significant support for the accuracy of the historical setting portrayed in the text. The author's historical knowledge is further evidenced by the fact that all of the semantic features and Persian elements in Hebrew Esther are attested by historical and archaeological evidence.[2] This evidence is extensive, as there are a total of fifty-

---

1. Edwin M. Yamauchi, *Persia and the Bible* (Grand Rapids, MI: Baker Books, 1996), 301.
2. For historical and archaeological evidence pertinent to the Persian elements that appear in Hebrew Esther, see Berquist, *Judaism in Persia's Shadow*, 87-104; Briant, *From Cyrus to Alexander*, 515-68; John E. Curtis and Nigel Tallis, eds., *Forgotten Empire: The World of Ancient Persia* (Berkeley, CA: University of California Press, 2005), chapters 1, 2, 4, 5, 9, 10; W.D. Davies and Louis Finkelstein, eds., *The Cambridge History of Judaism, Volume One: The Persian Period* (Cambridge: Cambridge University Press, 1984), 326-58; Prudence O. Harper, Joan Aruz and Francoise Tallon, eds., *The Royal City of Susa: Ancient Near Eastern Treasures in the Louvre* (New York: The Metropolitan Museum of Art, 1992), 215-18, 242-3, 253-7; Amelie Kuhrt, *The Ancient Near East c. 3000–330 BC, Volume Two* (London: Routledge, 1995), 647-701; Olmstead, *History of the Persian Empire*, 214-301; and Yamauchi, *Persia and the Bible*, 187-240, 279-304.

five semantic features that testify to a historical setting within the Persian period. Of these fifty-five features, thirty-eight of them are Persian and Akkadian names for the characters in the story, and seventeen are ancient Near Eastern loan words that describe various aspects of Persian government and life in the Achaemenian court.

The conspicuous number of Persian and other ancient Near Eastern names and loan words used in the Hebrew text makes the presence of these words the most prominent category of Persian elements in the story. Because of the significant number of names and words under consideration, the following discussion will divide these elements into three parts. The first section will discuss the names of the principal characters in the story; the second, the names of the rest of the characters in the story; and the third, the ancient Near Eastern loan words used to tell the story.

Ancient Near Eastern Names of the Principal Characters of the Story

The names of the principal characters in Hebrew Esther are all of ancient Near Eastern origin. The Hebrew name of the king, Ahashverosh, is identified with the Persian name Khshayarsha.[1] Khshayarsha is found in the Persian column of a trilingual inscription from Persepolis and is equivalent to the Babylonian Khishi'arshu. In addition, "in Babylonian tablets such forms occur as *Akhshiyarshu . . . Akhshiyawarshu . . .* and *Akhshiwarshu.* These forms are evidently the etymological equivalents of the Hebrew, `-kh-sh-w-r-sh,* which is the form that appears in Est. 1:16, 2:21, 3:12 and 8:10."[2]

The names of Mordecai, Esther, and Haman are also of ancient Near Eastern origin. Mordechai is of Mesopotamian origin,[3] as evidenced by the many names that incorporate the name of Marduk found in cuneiform documents from the Persian

---

1. See Paton, *The International Critical Commentary*, 53-4; and Ida Fröhlich, *Time and Times and Half a Time: Historical Consciousness in the Jewish Literature of the Persian and Hellenistic Eras* (Sheffield: Sheffield Academic Press, 1996), 132, for the equivalence of Ahashverosh and Khshayarsha, as well as the identification of Ahashverosh with Xerxes.
2. Paton, *The International Critical Commentary*, 53-4.
3. Fröhlich, *Time and Times and Half a Time*, 134.

period.[1] Tablets from Persepolis present variations on the name such as Mar-duk-ka, Mar-du-uka, and Mar-du-kana-sir, and a fifth-century Aramaic inscription contains the name M-r-d-k.[2] Marduka, a government official in Susa, is mentioned in a Persian text from the Persepolis Archives dating from the last years of Darius I or the early years of Xerxes.[3] The mention of a Marduka who was a Persian official is consistent with references to Mordecai in Esther 2:19, 2:21, 5:13, and 6:10, which describe him as "sitting in the gate of the king." In fact, Mordecai's daily presence in the gate of the king indicates his role as an ancient Near Eastern judge as in Ruth 4:11, Job 31:21, and Proverbs 31:23.[4]

Esther's name is from the Persian *stri* for "young woman," or the Persian *stara* for "star." Her name is also related to a Hebrew verb, *str*, which means "to hide." Various forms of this verb are used throughout the Hebrew Bible in connection with the hiding of the face of God. This interpretation of Esther's name is completely appropriate in a book in which Esther's identity was hidden and the presence of God was hidden as well.[5] The Hebrew text also identifies Esther by the name Hadassah, which is from the Akkadian word *hadassatu*, or "bride." Haman's name is from the Persian name Humayun, and according to Hebrew Esther, Haman is the son of Hammedatha, also referred to as "the Agagite." The name of Haman's father is derived from the Elamite name Hamaddadda, and is attested in Persepolis Fortification Tablet 1459.[6] The Old Persian form of this name is amadata.[7]

---

1. Ronald Sack, *Cuneiform Documents from the Chaldean and Persian Periods* (London: Associated University Presses, 1994), 72-3.
2. Robert Gordis, "Religion, Wisdom, and History in the Book of Esther – A New Solution to an Ancient Crux," *JBL* 100/3 (1981): 384.
3. *ibid.*
4. Fröhlich, *Time and Times and Half a Time*, 134, n. 93, 94.
5. Abraham Even-Shoshan, ed., *A New Concordance of the Bible* (Jerusalem: Kiryat Sefer Publishing House, 1996), 816.
6. The Persepolis Fortification Tablets are part of a collection of thousands of clay tablets found in Persepolis (in modern day Iran) that contain administrative archives from the Persian Achaemenid Empire.
7. See A.R. Millard, "The Persian Names in Esther and the Reliability of the Hebrew Text," *JBL* 96/4 (1977): 484; and Fröhlich, *Time and Times and Half a Time*, 134.

Persian Names of the Rest of the Characters in the Story

The names of the rest of the characters in the Hebrew version of Esther are also entirely of ancient Near Eastern origin, and almost all of them are specifically of Persian descent.[1] These names include those of the seven eunuchs who attended the king (1:10);[2] the names of the seven princes of Persia and Media (1:14);[3] Hegai, the keeper of the first house of women (2:8, 2:15); Bigthan and Teresh, the two eunuchs who plotted to kill Ahashverosh (2:21, 6:2); Hathach, the eunuch who attended Esther (4:5, 4:19); Zeresh, the wife of Haman (5:10); and the names of all of Haman's ten sons (9:7-10).[4] The sheer number of Persian names used by the author of Hebrew Esther provides overwhelming evidence that this text

---

1. In the next three footnotes, all names from the Persepolis Fortification Tablets (PF) that are parallel to names in the Hebrew text are from Edwin Yamauchi, "Mordecai, the Persepolis Tablets and the Susa Excavations," *Vetus Testamentum* XLII, 2 (1992): 272-5. All other identifications of names are from Ludwig Koehler and Walter Baumgartner, *The Hebrew and Aramaic Lexicon of the Old Testament* (*HALOT*) (Leiden: Brill, 2001); and Jeremy Black, Andrew George, and Nicholas Postgate, eds., *A Concise Dictionary of Akkadian* (Wiesbaden: Harrassowitz Verlag, 2000).
2. The names of the seven eunuchs are Mehuman, from the Persian Vahuman and attested in Persepolis Fortification (PF) Tablet 455 as Mihimana; Bizzetha, a corrupted form of Old Persian Mazdana; Harbona, the name of a known Persian courtier; Bigtha, a parallel to Bakatanna (PF 1793); Abagtha, the name of a Persian courtier; Zethar, which is related to the name Shethar in 1:14, from the Old Persian *hsatra*; and Carcas, from the Persian *karkās* and attested as Karkis in PF 10.
3. The names of the seven princes of Persia and Media are Carshena, from the Persian *karsna*; Shethar, from the Old Persian *hsatra*; Admatha, from the Persian *adamayita*; Tarshish, related to the neo-Assyrian place name, Tarsisi, as well as *tarsta*, the title of a Persian official; Meres, a Persian name attested as Maraza (PF 522); Marsena, a Persian name attested as Marsena in PF 522; and Memucan, a Persian name attested as Mamakka in PF 1344.
4. The names of Haman's ten sons are Parshandatha, from the Persian *prsndt*; Dalphon, derived from the Babylonian name Dullupu; Aspatha, an attested Persian name; Poratha, an attested Persian name; Adalia, an attested Persian name; Aridatha, a Persian name attested by Hardadda (PF 390); Parmashta, from Old Persian *fara-ma-istha*; Arisai, an attested Persian name; Aridai, a Persian name attested by Irdaya (PF 1475); and Vaizatha, an attested Persian name.

is a reliable source of information concerning the Persian context it seeks to portray. Furthermore, the preservation of authentic Persian names demonstrates the extreme care and accuracy of the Jewish scribes entrusted with the copying of the biblical text. As Millard says, it may be concluded that "the Hebrew text of Esther can be trusted to give non-Hebrew names accurately."[1]

Ancient Near Eastern Loan Words Used to Tell the Story

As with the names of the characters of the story, Hebrew Esther also accurately preserved ancient Near Eastern loan words used to describe various aspects of Persian government and life in the Achaemenian court.[2] Seventeen such terms are used throughout the book, all of which are of Akkadian, Aramaic, or Persian origin. In 1:1, the word that is translated as "province" is *medinah*, which is an Aramaic loan word whose basic meaning is "administrative district." The term used in 1:2 for a fortified city is *birah*, which is a loan word from the Akkadian *birtu*, meaning "fort" or "castle." In 1:3, the Persian word *partemim* is translated as "nobles." The inner part of the palace is called the "bitan" in 1:5, a word that is derived from the Akkadian word *bitanu*, which means "interior of the palace."

These examples are followed by the Persian *karpas* for "cotton" in 1:6; the Aramaic loan word, *dat*, for "law" in 1:8; and the Persian words *keter* for "turban" and *pitgam* for "announcement" found in 1:11, 1:20, 2:17, and 6:8. Other words of Akkadian, Aramaic, or Persian descent are the name of the tenth month, Tebeth (2:16); *ginazim* for "treasuries" (3:9); *ahashdarpenim* for "satraps" and *pachot* for "governors" (3:12, 8:9, 9:3); *haratzim* for "runners" (3:13, 15); *patshegen* for "copy" (3:14, 4:8, 8:13); *ahashteranim* for "royal horses;" *haratzim basusim* for "runners on horses" (8:10, 8:14); and *purim* for "lot" (9:26-32). The use of this many ancient Near Eastern words in the description of various aspects of Persian government and life in the Achaemenian court not only demonstrates that the author of Hebrew Esther could use ancient Near Eastern loan words accurately, but also suggests a familiarity with the historical setting portrayed in the story

1. Millard, "The Persian Names in Esther," 485.
2. All identification of ancient Near Eastern loan words is from Koehler and Baumgartner, *HALOT*, and Black, George and Postgate, *A Concise Dictionary of Akkadian*.

on the part of the author. The combination of the use of these seventeen loan words and thirty-eight Persian and Akkadian names for the characters in the story provides significant evidence in support of the author's informed intent to present an attempted genocide of the Jews in the particular historical context of the Persian period.

However, the fact that the author appears to have been familiar with the historical setting portrayed in the story is not completely conclusive evidence on its own, because it may have been possible for the author to be knowledgeable of Persian names and loan words simply by being a student of history. In order to make a more conclusive case in favor of the proposed intent of the author, it is necessary to determine the date of composition of Hebrew Esther. Not only will a determination of this date contribute to the verification of the author's intent, but it will also serve as an essential foundation for demonstrating the textual relationship of the three versions of Esther in the following Excursus, and for understanding the significance of the literary changes in the Greek versions discussed in Chapter Four.

The Date of Composition of Hebrew Esther

Scholarly consensus regarding the date of composition of Hebrew Esther has changed dramatically in the last one hundred years. An older view was that this version was a product of Hellenistic or Maccabean times in the third or second centuries BCE. However, a consensus of current scholarship now dates the composition of the book to the late Persian period, between the end of the fifth century and the fourth century BCE. Indeed, Hebrew Esther could have been written anytime beginning with the fifth century BCE, based on the dates of the events represented in the story. While the earliest date of composition of the Hebrew version is subject to debate, the latest possible date for its composition is more certain. This is due to a date provided by the colophon[1] at the end of Old Greek (OG) Esther that indicates when this version was written. The date of OG Esther is relevant to this discussion because, as the Excursus on the textual relationships of the three books of Esther will show, OG Esther is dependent on the Hebrew version. Therefore, Hebrew Esther must have been written before OG Esther.

---

1. A colophon is a short statement that gives the name of the author and the year in which the book was written.

Chapter Two will answer the question of when OG Esther was written. Based on the work that will be presented there, and the fact that the Greek version is dependent on the Hebrew, it can be concluded that the latest date the Hebrew version could have been written is early second century BCE. It is also obvious that the earliest date the Hebrew version could have been written is immediately following the date of the events recorded in the story, which would be as early as mid-fifth century. This raises the question: Is it possible to determine a more specific date of composition for Hebrew Esther between the mid-fifth century and the early second century BCE? The answer is yes. A fairly specific date of composition can be determined by taking into account what scholarship has to say concerning the type of Hebrew used in Esther, the complete absence of any Greek vocabulary in Hebrew Esther in contrast to the prevalence of Persian words, the positive attitude Hebrew Esther exhibits towards the Gentile king as opposed to the attitudes displayed towards Gentile kings in the Jewish literature of the Hellenistic period, and the overall worldview of the book. The following survey of scholarship will reveal a very specific date of composition for Hebrew Esther.

The older view concerning the date of composition of Hebrew Esther – that it was a product of Hellenistic or Maccabean times in the third to second century BCE – is typified by Lewis Bayles Paton (1908), who concluded that the book was written in the late Greek period. He considers the use of the Old Greek version by Josephus in the first century CE to be the earliest evidence for Hebrew Esther. He also cites the reference to Purim in 2 Maccabees 15:36, where it is called "the day of Mordecai," as the first mention of Purim. Paton bases his conclusion of a date of composition in the late Greek period on these two points, as well as on his interpretation of data from the text itself.[1] While a detailed discussion of Paton's arguments in favor of this late date of composition is beyond the scope of this chapter, it is sufficient for the sake of discussion regarding the date of composition of Hebrew Esther to note that current scholarship differs significantly with the scholarship of Paton's day.

In contrast to Paton, Carey Moore (1971) suggests a range of dates from 400 to 114 BCE for the composition of Esther, stating that "the first edition probably goes back to the fourth century, or

---

1. Paton, *The International Critical Commentary*. See pages 60-63 for a detailed discussion of Paton's arguments in favor of a date of composition in the late Greek period.

Persian period."[1] The latest possible date of 114 BCE is dependent upon what Moore considers to be the probable date referred to by the colophon at the end of Septuagint Esther. He offers the Hebrew of Esther and the positive attitude towards the Gentile king as evidence in support of the early date of 400 BCE. In agreement with David Noel Freedman's observations regarding Esther's Hebrew, Moore concludes that "the Hebrew of Esther is most like that of the Chronicler, which is now being dated to ca. 400 BCE."[2] He also points out that there is a complete lack of any Greek vocabulary in Hebrew Esther, a point that is especially significant in light of the prevalence of Persian words discussed in the previous section.

Sandra Beth Berg (1979) says that many scholars agree that the book contains material that comes from the Persian period. She also summarizes recent studies as being in agreement that the latest possible date is pre-Maccabean, or pre-second century BCE. While Berg doesn't actually propose a date of composition, some of the factors she points out as important to the discussion of Esther's date of composition include the positive attitude toward the foreign king, the absence of Greek words in the story, and the abundance of Persian terms used.[3]

In contrast to Paton and in agreement with Moore, David Clines (1984) states that "the facts about the date of composition are few and simple."[4] He says that for obvious reasons the book cannot have been written earlier than the fifth century BCE, the time in which the story was set, and it cannot have been written later than the first century BCE due to the date he believes is provided in the colophon of OG Esther. Within this range of dates, Clines suggests that the best clue for the date of Hebrew Esther lies in the favorable attitude it displays towards the Persian king. This attitude indicates authorship during the Persian period, when the king was favorable towards the Jews, and before the Hellenistic period, when the relationship between Jews and their non-Jewish rulers was not as amicable.

---

1. Carey A. Moore, *The Anchor Bible: Esther* (New York: Doubleday, 1971), lviii.
2. *ibid.*, lvii.
3. Sandra Beth Berg, *The Book of Esther: Motifs, Themes and Structure* (Society of Biblical Literature, 1979). For a more complete discussion of all the factors relevant to the discussion of Esther's date of composition, see pages 169-73.
4. Clines, *New Century Bible Commentary*, 271.

Frederic Bush (1996) is in agreement with Clines' and Moore's conclusion that the positive attitude towards the Persian king is indicative of an author who lived in the late Persian or early Hellenistic period (late fourth to early third centuries BCE), and emphasizes that this attitude makes it "highly improbable" that the book was written in the Maccabean period (second century BCE), when Jewish attitudes towards their Greek rulers were anything but positive.[1] Jon Levenson (1997) also concludes that Esther was probably written in the fourth or third century BCE for similar reasons. He then suggests that "the author's focus on Susa suggests that city as the locus of composition" and "if the book of Esther is of Persian origin, it may well be the sole surviving legacy of a Jewish culture very different from those of either Palestine or the rest of the Diaspora."[2]

Levenson is the only author surveyed here who actually suggests the city of Susa as the setting of the author of the text. However, this is not an unreasonable suggestion in light of the number of Persian terms that describe specific aspects of government and life in the court of Susa, as well as the stark contrast between the content of Hebrew Esther and that of every other piece of Second Temple Jewish literature written in either Judea or other places in the Diaspora.[3] At the very least, it is reasonable to propose that Hebrew Esther was written somewhere in the Persian Empire by an author who was quite familiar with verifiable elements particular to an administrative city within that empire, such as Susa.

Adele Berlin (2001) concludes that the date of composition was in the late Persian or early Greek period, and that the book definitely pre-dates the Hellenistic and Maccabean period. She bases this conclusion on linguistic analysis that shows the book to be late biblical Hebrew, like the books of Ezra/Nehemiah and Chronicles, and on the worldview of the book, which portrays the Jews as "ultimately safe and successful in the Diaspora."[4] This

1. Bush, *Word Biblical Commentary*, 296.
2. Jon D. Levenson, *Esther: A Commentary* (Louisville, KY: Westminster John Knox, 1997), 26.
3. Hebrew Esther is unique in the corpus of Second Temple Jewish literature due to the lack of any mention of the God of Israel, the lack of mention of the Temple or the Holy Land, and the lack of mention of forms of piety such as prayer and dietary regulations.
4. Adele Berlin, *The JPS Bible Commentary: Esther* (Philadelphia, PA: The Jewish Publication Society, 2001/5761), xlii.

differs greatly from the worldview of the Maccabean period, when the Jews of Judea were being persecuted by their Greek rulers. In addition, the book does not display any antagonism towards the current culture, in contrast to the antagonism prevalent in Jewish writings from Hellenistic times.

Unlike Bush, Levenson, and Berlin, who allow for the possibility of a date of composition as late as the early Greek period, Michael Heltzer (2008) is convinced that "the story is in fact considerably earlier, dating to sometime in the Achaemenid, i.e. Persian, period" due to "recent advances in the study of Old Persian language and history."[1] He cites examples of Old Persian terms – some of the same ones discussed in the previous section – that "must have gone out of use in the Hellenistic period. . . . [T] hese words were no longer used in the Hellenistic period; they are not found in the Hebrew texts of that time."[2] From this observation, he concludes that the book of Esther must have been written sometime between the reign of Xerxes and the conquest of Alexander, or between 465 and 325 BCE. Heltzer further supports his position that Hebrew Esther is a product of the Persian period by discussing details in the story that reflect a knowledge of Persian administration and life in the royal court. Some of these details include support for the possibility that a Jew could hold a high court office, explanations for why Mordecai would not have been required to bow to Haman, confirmation of the date and length of the banquet described in 1:3-5, historical information from Greek sources concerning the seven advisors of the king, and confirmation from Greek sources that a royal decree could not be revoked.[3]

Like Heltzer, T. Laniak (2003) states that in spite of some uncertainties over some of the events mentioned, the book of Esther "exhibits such a thorough knowledge of Persian names and the details of the Persian court and palace that the book can be dated in the late Persian period."[4] Following a thorough discussion of the potential historical problems in Esther, he enumerates many of the

1. Michael Heltzer, *The Province of Judah and Jews in Persian Times (Some Connected Questions of the Persian Empire)* (Tel Aviv: Archaeological Center Publication, 2008), 147.
2. *ibid.*
3. *ibid.*, 148-51, 219-21.
4. L. Allen and T. Laniak, *New International Biblical Commentary: Ezra, Nehemiah, Esther* (Peabody, MA: Hendrickson Publishers, 2003), 181.

verifiable particulars, concluding that the story "deserves merit as a historical source written close in time and space to the events it describes."[1] Therefore, it is not unreasonable to conclude that the author of Hebrew Esther may not only have had knowledge of the city of Susa, but may also have written the text shortly after the time period described in the story.

As can be seen in this survey of scholarship, it is generally agreed upon that the Hebrew of Esther is like that of Ezra/ Nehemiah and Chronicles; there is a complete lack of any Greek vocabulary in Hebrew Esther in contrast to the prevalence of Persian words; Hebrew Esther exhibits a positive attitude towards the Gentile king contrary to the attitudes displayed towards Gentile kings in the Jewish literature of the Hellenistic period; and the worldview of the book portrays Diaspora Jews as "ultimately safe and successful" as opposed to the worldview of the Maccabean period. Therefore, it seems reasonable to conclude that Hebrew Esther was written in the Persian period around 400 BCE, if not a bit earlier.

This conclusion is not only indicated by the facts summarized above, but is suggested by the historical setting of the story discussed previously. Furthermore, the presence of historically verifiable Persian elements in the story – many of which are particular to an administrative city within the Persian Empire – suggests that Hebrew Esther was written in one of the administrative centers of the empire, if not Susa itself. Levenson comments that "the author's focus on Susa suggests that city as the locus of composition,"[2] and Fox notes that the author may have been a resident of Susa due to the demonstrated knowledge of "Susan geography and his special interest in the date of the holiday in Susa."[3] Indeed, archaeological excavation in Susa has corroborated the descriptions of the palace, the gate of the palace, the throne room, and the palace garden given in the book of Esther.[4] Therefore, the combination of the author's focus on Susa and his/her knowledge of the city's geography and descriptions of various features of the palace not only indicates

1. *ibid.*, 182.
2. Levenson, *Esther*, 26.
3. Michael V. Fox, *Character and Ideology in the Book of Esther* (Columbia, SC: University of South Carolina, 1991), 140.
4. Haim M.I. Gevaryahu, "Esther is a Story of Jewish Defense Not a Story of Jewish Revenge," *Jewish Bible Quarterly* 21/1 (1993): 3-12.

a composition date of 400 BCE at the latest for Hebrew Esther, but suggests that the author could have been physically located in the city of Susa itself.

The combination of all these factors makes a rather strong case in favor of the validity of the intent of the author of Hebrew Esther to present the account of an attempted genocide of the Jews in a particular historical context, which was the Persian Empire during the reign of Ahashverosh, otherwise known in history as Xerxes I. The establishment of the author's intent provides the necessary foundation for the following discussion of the message of Hebrew Esther – a message that was germane to its original audience precisely because of its historical context, and a message that is just as pertinent today because of current events in Israel.

The Message of Hebrew Esther

The identification of the message of Hebrew Esther is foundational for the purpose of this book, which is to demonstrate the relevance of the story of Esther to historic anti-Judaism/Semitism and the contested legitimacy of the State of Israel in the context of the ongoing Arab-Israeli conflict. In light of this purpose, it is essential to answer the aforementioned question: Is Hebrew Esther an account of Jewish aggression or Jewish resistance to attempted genocide? The answer to this question will not only reflect an understanding of the message of Hebrew Esther, but will provide the basis for a subsequent discussion of the history of interpretation of the story – a history that is based on changes made in the Greek versions.

While it is evident that the author of Hebrew Esther intentionally presented the account of an attempted genocide of the Jews in a particular historical context, a careful reading of this text reveals that it "is about more than past history. It calls its readers to reflect and presumably act in the challenges to human dignity that confront us today."[1] In light of Esther's call to reflect and act, the following discussion will reveal that the message of this text expresses a timeless issue of justice, which is "the fundamental responsibility and universal right of self-protection against those who would murder."[2]

1. Alice Ogden Bellis, *Helpmates, Harlots, Heroes: Women's Stories in the Hebrew Bible* (Louisville, KY: John Knox Press, 1994), 216.
2. Marvin A. Sweeney, "Absence of G-d and Human Responsibility in the Book of Esther," in *Reading the Hebrew Bible for a New Millennium*

We can begin to construct a responsible answer to the question of Jewish aggression or Jewish resistance to attempted genocide by carefully comparing the content of Haman's decree calling for annihilation of the Jews found in 3:13 with the content of Esther's decree found in 8:11. Esther's decree in 8:11, which is followed by a description of the subsequent actions of the Jews of Persia, has been a principal proof-text for those who interpret this book as a bloodthirsty story of Jewish aggression. However, a close study of this counter-decree and the actions of the Jews will reveal that the Jews were only allowed to take the same actions against their enemies as those decreed against them in Haman's decree in 3:13. More specifically, the Jews were only allowed to take these actions in self-defense; they were not allowed to initiate them. The following study will demonstrate that the actions of the Jews of Persia were in fact acts of resistance, or self-defense, and that if their enemies had not tried to kill them, the Jews would have had no cause to kill anyone. This study will be divided into three sections: a comparison of the content of the two decrees, a study of four additional statements found in chapters 8 and 9, and a discussion of five features of the story that refute anti-Semitic charges concerning the actions of the Jews.

A Comparison of the Content of the Two Decrees

Esther 3:13 says:

> And letters were sent by the hand of the runners to all the provinces of the king *to exterminate, to kill,* and *to destroy* all the Jews, from young to old, children and women in one day, on the thirteenth of the twelfth month, which is the month of Adar, and *to plunder* their possessions.

Esther 8:11 says:

> Which the king gave to the Jews who were in every city to assemble and to stand for their lives, *to exterminate* and *to kill* and *to destroy* all the army of the people or province, their adversaries, children and women, and *to plunder* their possessions.

(ed. Wonil Kim, Deborah Ellens, Michael Floyd, and Marvin A. Sweeney; Harrisburg, PA: Trinity Press International, 2000), 264-75.

As can be seen, Haman's decree of 3:13 calls for all the people of Persia "*to exterminate, to kill,* and *to destroy* the Jews . . . and *to plunder* their possessions." Esther's counter-decree of 8:11 says that the king *gave,* or "allowed the Jews to assemble and stand for their lives," and "*to exterminate, to kill,* and *to destroy*" anyone who came against them, and "*to plunder* their possessions." Four different verbs used in both of these decrees are in italics because they are identical. Not only are they identical in meaning, but in the Hebrew, they appear in the exact same form as an infinitive construct. The infinitive construct serves to express the idea of purpose, intention, and action in a definite direction. The concentrated use of four infinitives places a significant emphasis on the extent of the actions Haman intended to be taken against the Jews in 3:13, as well as on the reciprocal actions the king allowed the Jews to take against their attackers in 8:11. These four verbs all describe hostile actions taken against an enemy. The use of three different verbs that all bring about the same intended result – the annihilation of the objects of those verbs – emphasizes the severity of the intended actions.

In addition to the use of the same four verbs found in 3:13, the decree of 8:11 allows the Jews "to assemble and to stand for their lives." The form of the verb "to assemble" is a passive infinitive, which also appears in Esther 9:2, 9:15-16, and 9:18, as well as in 2 Samuel 20:14. In each of these cases, the use of this form refers to an act of assembling for conflict or war. The verb "to assemble" is connected to the next verb, "to stand," by a conjunction, which indicates that these two actions are to be done together. Therefore, the purpose of the Jews in assembling for war was "to stand for their lives", which is "to take a position of defense and resistance."[1] In this position of defense and resistance, the Jews were then allowed to exterminate, to kill, and to destroy "all the army of the people and province" who took offensive actions against them, in accordance with the decree of 3:13. "The idea of the king is not that the Jews may attack anyone who is supposed to be unfriendly disposed toward the Jews; they only receive permission to resist any attack."[2] The action taken by the Jews in assembling "to stand for their lives" "is that of a body forming for defense, not a mob hunting down individuals it considers

1. Paul Haupt, "Critical Notes on Esther," in *Studies in the Book of Esther* (ed. Carey A. Moore; New York: KTAV Publishing House, 1982), 1-79.
2. *ibid.*, 62.

hostile."[1] In other words, the counter-decree of 8:11 only allowed for acts of self-defense against aggressors, while the decree of 3:13 ordered the annihilation of the whole Jewish population, including women and children.

A Study of Four Additional Statements
Found in Chapters 8 and 9

Esther's decree of 8:11 is quite clear concerning the provision of resistance, or self-defense, that the king gave to the Jews. However, this is not the only verse in the book that counters the erroneous charge of Jewish aggression made by critics of the story. There are four statements found in chapters 8 and 9 that provide additional insight into the content and intent of the decree of 8:11, and into the kind of action the Jews took in response to that decree. Therefore, it will be quite informative to take a look at what Esther 8:13b, 9:2a, 9:5, and 9:16a have to say.

In 8:13b, it says, "and the Jews were to be ready on that day to avenge themselves against their enemies." This verse is often interpreted as evidence in favor of the alleged theme of bloodthirsty vengeance demonstrated in the story. However, this is a faulty interpretation due to an inaccurate translation of the form of the word whose root means "to take aggression," or "to avenge." The word that appears in this verse is most often translated into English as "to take aggression."[2] "To take aggression" implies an active act of aggression or vengeance. However, in the case of 8:13b, the word appears in a passive form, which indicates an act done by the Jews for themselves in response to aggressive acts from their enemies. In other words, the sense communicated through the use of the passive form of the word is one of inflicting punishment on those who attacked first. This interpretation is certainly consistent with the context in which the verse appears. Just two verses earlier, the counter-decree allowed the Jews "to assemble" and "to stand for their lives," an action defined as taking a position of resistance or defense.

Esther 9:2a reports that the Jews throughout all the provinces "gathered themselves together, to send – or to stretch out a hand – against those who sought their evil, injury or calamity." It is

---

1. Michael V. Fox, *The Redaction of the Books of Esther* (Atlanta, GA: Scholars Press, 1991), 111.
2. For example, see the New Revised Standard Version translation.

quite clear from the form of the words in the Hebrew that the Jews are only taking action against those who seek to do them harm. The actions of the Jews in this verse are again in keeping with an act of resistance to acts of aggression against them, rather than an initiation of an act of aggression.

A summary of the action in all the provinces is provided in 9:5a, which reports that the Jews "smote" all their enemies with the sword and "killed and destroyed them." This action on the part of the Jews is described by the use of two of the same verbs that were used in both decrees found in 3:13 and 8:11. The actions "to kill" and "to destroy," which the original decree intended to be taken against the Jews, have now been carried out by the Jews against their enemies according to the provisions allowed by the king in the counter-decree of 8:11.

However, the second part of 9:5 includes some additional information. It says that the Jews did to those who hated them "as they pleased." In the context of the first part of the verse, which makes the connection to both of the decrees by the use of the verbs, "to kill" and "to destroy," "the Jews were now following the king's law to do *as they pleased* with their enemies."[1] Gerleman interprets this to mean that the Jews "had free hand without being hindered by the Persian bureaucracy,"[2] meaning that the government would not prevent the Jews from taking action against those who sought to do them harm. In 1:8, the same form of the word meaning to do "as they pleased" is used in the context of each man drinking "as he pleased," according to orders given by the king. In both cases, the use of the term "as they/he pleased" was a sign of imperial favor. As such, the ability to do as one pleased was a freedom that was restricted by limits established by the king. Therefore, in 9:5b, the Jews were not free to do whatever they wanted to their hearts' content,[3] but rather were free to defend themselves against their enemies within the confines of the king's law as stated in the decree written by Esther in 8:11.

9:16a states that the Jews "gathered themselves together and stood for their lives and then rested from their enemies." The rest

---

1. Allen and Laniak, *New International Biblical Commentary*, 256.
2. Gillis Gerleman, *Biblischer Kommentar Altes Testament: Esther* (Neukirchen-Vluyn: Neukirchener Verlag Des Erziehungsvereins GMBH, 1973), 132.
3. Gerleman states specifically that the word used here does not mean "nach Herzenslust," or "to one's heart's content." *ibid.*

they had from their enemies was a direct result of the fact that they had killed a rather large number of "those who hated them." The following verse reports that on the next day the Jews "rested" and made that day "a day of feasting and rejoicing." The fact that the Jews had a day of celebration after they killed their enemies has been used to support the accusation that the story of Esther is a bloodthirsty story of Jewish aggression. However, the celebration was "not to the memory of the victory" but "to the memory of the day of silence after the victory."[1] Contrary to the accusation that 9:17 is an account of a celebration of the bloodshed in 9:16a, "the celebration was for the deliverance of the Jewish people from destruction, not for the opportunity to destroy others."[2]

The fact that the celebration was to "the memory of the day of silence" is evidenced by the use of the word meaning "to rest" in 9:17 to describe what followed the day of fighting in the provinces, in 9:18 to describe what followed the two days of fighting in Susa, and in 9:22 in which the celebration of two days of Purim is instituted as the days on which the Jews "rested, or gained rest, from their enemies." What is being stressed here is the rest that followed the fighting, not the opportunity to kill. As its literature shows, "to be allowed to live in peace" is "the ultimate dream of diaspora Judaism."[3] In the case of the Persian Jews, rest was only possible when their enemies were defeated, and the celebration of Purim celebrates "the month which was turned for them from grief to joy and from mourning to a good day [or holiday]."

Five Features of the Story that Refute Anti-Semitic Charges

Critics of the story of Esther use the account of bloodshed that follows the counter-decree of 8:11 to support the charge that Esther in particular and the Jews in general were bloodthirsty killers of Gentiles motivated by a nationalistic spirit. However, this conclusion can only be reached by ignoring the significance of the two additional verbs found in 8:11 that were discussed above, and by ignoring five features of the story that clearly refute anti-Semitic charges concerning the actions of the Jews. The first

---

1. *ibid.,* 134.
2. Sweeney, "Absence of G-d and Human Responsibility in the Book of Esther," 267.
3. Clines, *Ezra, Nehemiah, Esther,* 324.

feature of the story that is often ignored has to do with *what it was* that Esther requested when she went before the king for the purpose of saving her people. It is frequently charged that Esther asked the king for permission to attack and kill the enemies of the Jews. However, in the Hebrew version of the story, she did not request bloodshed or permission for aggression.

According to 8:5, what Esther did request was that the decree written by Haman ordering the annihilation of the Jews be revoked. While this appeal is an excellent example of a human taking personal responsibility to act in response to evil, Esther's knowledge of the difficulty of this request is reflected in the fact that she prefaced her request with four conditional clauses. Before telling the king what it was that she wanted, she said "if it is good to the king," "if I have found favor before him," "if the proposal is right before the king," and "if I am pleasing in his eyes." This excessive use of conditional clauses indicates an awareness of the fact that it was quite unusual to suggest that a decree be revoked. However, this was the extent of Esther's request – that the original decree be revoked. She did not ask permission to kill the enemies of the Jews. The counter-decree, which the king authorized Esther and Mordecai to write, allowed the Jews to stand for their lives and kill those who attacked them. Permission for the Jews to defend themselves was the king's solution for the situation, not Esther's.

Secondly, Esther's request of the king in 9:13 for a second day of fighting in Susa and the public hanging of Haman's ten sons has been cited as evidence of bloodthirsty aggression on the part of Esther and the Jews. While it is often charged that what Esther requested was a second day of killing, what she actually requested was that the Jews in Susa be able "to do according to the law of this day." In other words, she was asking for a second day of self-defense in the city of Susa according to the "law of that day," implying that while the danger was over in the rest of the empire according to 9:16, she "saw a need for an additional day to win a clear victory for the Jews"[1] of Susa. The request for a second day of fighting did not mean that the Jews would be killing randomly; it simply meant that according to the provisions outlined in the counter-decree, the Jews would still be allowed to defend themselves against those who sought their destruction. The Jews' killing of those who were seeking

---

1. Gevaryahu, "Esther is a Story of Jewish Defense," 10.

to destroy them is "entirely in keeping with the Bible's various expressions of corporate punishment and salvation. . . . [T]he issue is not vengeance. . . . [I]t is a matter of justice, that is, the fundamental responsibility and universal right of self-protection against those who would murder."[1]

Just as the request for a second day of self-defense is not evidence of bloodthirsty aggression, neither is the public hanging of Haman's sons. In fact, Esther's request in 9:13 that Haman's sons be hung in public does not mean that they were executed in public. Rather, according to 9:5-10, these sons were killed in the context of Jews killing those who came against them, implying that Haman's sons were among the attackers. The hanging of the sons of Haman in 9:14 was therefore the hanging of dead bodies; the bodies of those who had sought to murder Jews. "The public display – and thus, disgrace – of an enemy's body was not all unusual in the ancient world. . . . [S]uch was the fate of Saul and his sons, for instance, in I Samuel 31:8-10."[2] The public display of the bodies of Haman's sons would not only demonstrate that the enemies of the Jews were defeated and disgraced, but would serve to discourage others from following the actions of those hung as well. Esther's request for the hanging of the sons of Haman is completely in line with her request for a second day of fighting in Susa, as both requests demonstrate her concern for the defense of the Jews and illustrate a particular principle of justice, which is the responsibility and right to resist attempted genocide.

The third feature in the text that negates the charge that Esther in particular and the Jews in general were aggressive killers of Gentiles motivated by a nationalistic spirit has to do with the fact that the Jews only received permission to resist armed people who came against them. Gillis Gerleman points out that the difference between the original decree in 3:13 and the counter-decree in 8:11 is that the decree of 3:13 contains the command to kill, whereas the counter-decree of 8:11 only contains permission for the Jews to defend themselves, as indicated by the phrase, "which the king gave [or allowed] to the Jews."[3] In other words, in 8:11, the

1. Sweeney, "Absence of G-d and Human Responsibility in the Book of Esther," 273.
2. Carol M. Bechtel, *Interpretation: A Bible Commentary for Teaching and Preaching: Esther* (Louisville, KY: John Knox Press, 2002), 80.
3. Gerleman, *Esther*, 129.

Jews were not being commanded to kill, but were being given permission to resist being killed. As a result, "the killing was limited to those who sought to kill Jews."[1]

It is reported in 9:3 that all the princes of the provinces, the satraps, governors, and royal officials "supported" and "assisted" the Jews because the fear of Mordecai fell upon them following the counter-edict of 8:11. If all of the royal officials could figure out that it was not a good idea to attack the Jews once they had been given the right to resist, one has to wonder how much less bloodshed there might have been if more people had decided not to attack. One of the unanswerable questions in this story is "why so very many people dislike the Jews so much that they risk their own lives to attack them."[2] Perhaps the only answer to this question is the fact that "the explanation for anti-Semitism resides within the anti-Semite's soul, and the narrator's refraining from giving further motivation for this irrational behavior is realistic."[3]

A fourth feature in the story that negates the accusation of bloodthirstiness on the part of the Jews is revealed by what the text *doesn't* say concerning their actions. The permission given to the Jews in 8:11 "to assemble" and "to stand for their lives" allowed them to kill "all the army of the people and province," along with their "children and women." However, in spite of this allowance, the text does not record any killing of women and children by the Jews. In fact, when the text reports the number of casualties from the two days of fighting in 9:6, 9:12, 9:15, and 9:16, it uses the word "men" in the first three instances, and the phrases "their enemies" and "those who hated them" in the last instance. In other words, all who were killed were either "men," "enemies," or "those who hated them." Therefore, women and children were not targeted for killing and the only possible killing of women and children by the Jews would be those who may have been among the attacking "army of the people and province" in 8:11, or the "enemies" and "those who hated them" in 9:16. The condition of the counter-decree in 8:11, which only allowed the Jews to resist an armed force coming against them, stands in stark contrast therefore to the original decree of 3:13, which ordered armed, offensive actions against all Jews, from

1. Sweeney, "Absence of G-d and Human Responsibility in the Book of Esther," 267.
2. Day, *Esther*, 155.
3. Fox, *Character and Ideology in the Book of Esther*, 111.

the young to the old, the children, and the women. The fact
that women and children were not targeted for killing, and the
fact that Jews only resisted those who came against them, is
particularly poignant in relation to the precautions taken by the
Israeli military to prevent civilian casualties as it takes necessary
steps to eliminate rocket launching sites and weapons targeting
Jewish civilians.

And finally, the fifth feature of the story that refutes common
criticisms of the story of Esther is the fact that the Jews did not
take any plunder from those they killed. Three times, in 9:10, 9:15,
and 9:16, the text reports that the Jews "did not stretch out their
hands on the plunder," in spite of the fact that they were allowed
to do so according to 8:11. The report in 9:10 refers to the first
day of fighting in Susa, 9:15 refers to the second day of fighting
in Susa, and 9:16 refers to the fighting in the provinces. In other
words, in every instance where they would have had occasion to
take plunder, they did not. The repetition of this phrase after each
occasion of fighting emphasizes that the Jews were not motivated
by a desire to acquire goods, but were motivated solely by the
need for self-preservation. In fact, "such self-restraint as the Jews
expressed here is quite prudent in a situation where a minority is
essentially defending itself from its enemies rather than initiating
the conflict."[1] Not only is refraining from taking plunder an
indication of self-restraint, but it is further evidence that the
Jewish action stopped at self-defense and "never degenerated
into aggression."[2]

A detailed study of the counter-decree in 8:11 has demonstrated
that the Jews of Persia were given the right to assemble themselves
together for the purpose of standing for their lives in resistance
to those who would attack them according to the original decree
of 3:13. The study of the statements made in 8:13b, 9:2a, 9:5, and
9:16a provides additional insight into the content and intent of
the counter-decree in 8:11, and into the kind of action the Jews
took in response to that decree as well. The preceding discussion
of five features that appear in the context of the counter-decree
clearly refutes the charge that Esther in particular and the Jews
in general were aggressive killers of Gentiles motivated by a
nationalistic spirit. In every case, it has been demonstrated that
rather than being motivated by a nationalistic spirit or by a desire

---

1. Moore, *Esther*, 88.
2. Gevaryahu, "Esther is a Story of Jewish Defense," 3.

to kill, the Jews simply took actions that were necessary for self-defense due to a decree that called for their annihilation. As acts of self-defense, the military actions carried out by the Jews of Persia may be described as "acts of resistance . . . motivated by the intention to thwart, limit or end the exercise of power of the oppressor over the oppressed."[1] The obvious conclusion of this study is that if their enemies had not tried to kill them, the Jews would have had no cause to kill anyone.

Conclusions

After validating the author of Esther's intent to present the account of an attempted genocide of the Jews in the particular historical context of the Persian Empire during the reign of Ahashverosh, this chapter identified the message of Hebrew Esther and answered the question of whether it is a story of Jewish aggression or Jewish resistance to attempted genocide. It has been demonstrated that rather than being a story of Jewish aggression that promotes a nationalistic spirit, this text presents an account of resistance to attempted genocide, with a message that expresses a timeless issue of justice: "the fundamental responsibility and universal right of self-protection against those who would murder."[2] In light of this issue of justice, and of the fact that the story of Esther is "surprisingly prophetic about the anti-Judaism that would later come,"[3] the message of Hebrew Esther has serious implications in relation to how historic interpretations of Esther have contributed to Christian anti-Semitic interpretation of the story, and how they influence current Christian anti-Zionism as well. Ultimately, the timeless issue of responsibility and right in relation to self-defense has profound ramifications vis-à-vis ongoing critique of actions the State of Israel takes to protect its citizens against those who seek to kill Jews.

---

1. Nechama Tec, "Jewish Resistance: Facts, Omissions and Distortions," (Nechama Tec: Assigned to the United States Holocaust Memorial Council, 1997; Third Printing, September 2001), 4.
2. Sweeney, "Absence of G-d and Human Responsibility in the Book of Esther," 264-75.
3. Day, *Esther*, 75.

EXCURSUS

The Textual Relationships of the Three Books of Esther

The previous chapter demonstrated the authorial intent behind the composition of Hebrew Esther, which was to tell a story of Jewish resistance to attempted genocide in a particular historical context. The next two chapters will reveal the motivation for the many changes and additions made to the Hebrew (MT) version by the authors of Old Greek (OG) Esther and Alpha Text (AT) Esther.[1]

However, before beginning these next two chapters, it is necessary to support the preceding statement that the Greek versions have made changes and additions to the Hebrew version. In other words, it is necessary to establish the primacy of Hebrew Esther. In order to verify that the Hebrew version preceded the two Greek versions, and then to show the relationship of the two Greek versions to one other, this Excursus will reveal how the three versions of Esther are related to each other by providing a summary of their textual relationships.

For the purpose of determining the textual relationships between MT, OG, and AT Esther, Esther 4:14 in the Hebrew version was divided into ten short phrases and compared with comparable phrases from OG Esther, AT Esther, Josephus' version of Esther, and the Latin version found in the Vetus Latina (VL). Six different comparisons of these versions were made: 1) a comparison of the MT and the OG; 2) a comparison of the OG and the AT; 3) a comparison of the MT and the AT; 4) a comparison of Josephus with the AT and the OG; 5) a comparison of the VL with the AT and the OG; and 6) a comparison of the AT, Josephus, and the VL.

---

1. The designation of MT for the Hebrew version stands for Masoretic Text, which is the authoritative Hebrew text of the Hebrew Scriptures.

Josephus and the VL are included in this analysis of the relationships between MT, OG, and AT Esther because comparisons of Josephus with the AT and OG; the VL with the AT and OG; and the AT, Josephus, and the VL are all necessary for determining the relationship of the AT to the MT. This is due to the fact that Josephus and the VL demonstrate a dependence on both the AT and the OG. An understanding of how these four texts are related is essential for discerning how AT Esther is related to the Hebrew version.

The dependency of Josephus on the AT is indicated by the fact that his version of Esther "contains some typical AT readings," and the VL's dependency is confirmed by the fact that the VL "has variants in common with the AT."[1] Josephus' dependency on the OG is evidenced by the fact that he included material found in the additions of the OG, that his version of Esther is even longer than the OG, and that he used the Hebrew "only very selectively."[2] And the dependency of the VL on OG Esther is obvious since the Septuagint "served as the basis . . . for the oldest Latin translations."[3]

The comparison of MT and OG Esther (1) demonstrated that in six of the ten phrases, the author of the OG made changes in syntax, semantics, or style, while the remaining four phrases were literal translations of the MT. Changes in syntax, semantics, or style are evidence of interpretation on the part of the author of OG Esther, rather than an attempt to translate the text literally from the Hebrew. The fact that the author of OG Esther chose to interpret the majority of the phrases in this verse rather than translate them literally indicates that OG Esther is not a literal translation, but a rewritten version of MT Esther.

The comparison of OG and AT Esther (2) revealed that the author of AT Esther made changes in syntax, semantics, or style in six of the ten phrases, while the remaining four phrases are

---

1. Kristin De Troyer, *Rewriting the Sacred Text: What the Old Greek Texts Tell Us About the Literary Growth of the Bible* (Atlanta, GA: Society of Biblical Literature, 2003), 66.

2. Louis H. Feldman, *Studies in Josephus' Rewritten Bible* (Atlanta, GA: SBL, 1998), 513. Feldman points out that Josephus' version of Esther is 643 lines in comparison to the 621 lines found in the OG version.

3. Abraham Wasserstein and David J. Wasserstein, *The Legend of the Septuagint from Classical Antiquity to Today* (Cambridge: Cambridge University Press, 2006), 14.

identical to the OG. As before, the changes in syntax, semantics, or style in a majority of the phrases indicate an interpretative rewriting of the OG by the author of AT Esther.

The comparison of MT and AT Esther (3) had similar results. In six of the ten phrases, the author of AT Esther made changes in syntax, semantics, or style. Only four remaining phrases were similar to the MT. The fact that the majority of the phrases in this verse in the AT are different to those in the MT suggests that there is no direct relationship between the AT and a different Hebrew text, a possibility proposed by some Esther scholars. Furthermore, in two phrases, the AT omitted what was in the MT, and in two other phrases, the AT added to what was in the MT. The omission and addition of material in the AT in comparison to the MT makes it unreasonable to suggest that the AT is directly related to a Hebrew version. This conclusion is further strengthened by the fact that of the four phrases in the AT that are similar to the MT, three of these phrases are identical to the OG. In light of the many differences between the MT and AT exhibited in the other six phrases, it is not reasonable to conclude that the four phrases in which the MT and AT are similar provide evidence of a relationship between the AT and a Hebrew text. Rather, the equality of three of those phrases to the OG suggests a dependency of AT Esther on the OG.

The comparison of Josephus with the AT and the OG (4) demonstrated that in every one of the ten phrases of Esther 4:14, Josephus differs from the AT and OG in syntax, semantics, or style. These differences indicate that Josephus was involved in his own interpretive rewriting of the texts he had in front of him.

The comparison of the VL with the AT and the OG (5) revealed that in seven of the ten phrases, the VL differs in syntax, semantics, or style from the AT, and that in seven phrases, it is equal to the OG. When combined with the rest of the data, the fact that the VL is not equal to the AT in seven of the phrases contributes further to the preliminary conclusion that the AT is not based on a pre-existing Hebrew version of Esther. The agreement of the VL with the OG in seven phrases not only supports this conclusion, but confirms the dependency of the VL on OG Esther as well.

And finally, the comparison of the AT, Josephus, and the VL (6) showed that these three texts are not all equal in any of the phrases of Esther 4:14. As a result, these three texts are never simultaneously similar to the MT. Therefore, there is no indication that these versions are dependent on the Hebrew. The comparison of these three texts also demonstrated that they are never all unequal to the OG. Thus, it may be concluded that these three versions are more closely related to the Old Greek version of Esther than the Hebrew one.

In conclusion, the comparison of the AT with OG Esther suggested that the AT is an interpretive rewriting of the Old Greek version. Because the comparison of the MT and the AT demonstrated that AT Esther is not dependent on a Hebrew version, it can be concluded that the Alpha Text is in fact a rewritten version of OG Esther. Likewise, the comparison of MT and OG Esther provided evidence of interpretation in the Old Greek. The fact that the author of OG Esther chose to interpret the majority of the phrases in this verse rather than translate them literally proves that OG Esther is not a literal translation, but a rewritten version of MT Esther.

The verification of dependency of the OG on the MT and the AT on the OG allows for the conclusion that MT Esther was in use before OG Esther, and that the OG was in use before the AT. As a result, the primacy of Hebrew Esther has been established and the statement that the Greek versions have made changes and additions to the Hebrew versions has been supported. An essential foundation has been laid for the following two chapters, which will reveal the motivation behind the many changes and additions the authors of the Greek versions made to the Hebrew version of Esther.

CHAPTER TWO

Old Greek Esther:
When and Why Was It Written?

This chapter will answer the questions of when and why Old Greek (OG) Esther – the version preserved in the Septuagint – was written by determining the historical setting of its composition, and by identifying the intent of its author. The establishment of the context and purpose behind the composition of OG Esther will reveal the reason so many changes and additions were made to the Hebrew version. This understanding will provide necessary background for the discussion in Chapter Four of how historic interpretations based on this version continue to contribute to negative perceptions of Jews. It is significant to note that similar conceptions of Jews and the Jewish State feed current Christian anti-Zionism in much the same way.

The Historical Setting of Old Greek Esther

Of all the books included in the Septuagint, Old Greek Esther is unique in the fact that it includes a colophon at the end of the book, providing information concerning the author of the book and the date it arrived in Alexandria. This information gives a starting place for determining an approximate date of composition for OG Esther, which in turn will shed light on the historical setting in which it was written. Because several interpretations of the date referenced in the colophon are possible, the information it contains needs to be analyzed in order to determine the most probable year the book was taken to Alexandria. This determination will then allow a proposal to be made as to the relative date of composition, due to the fact that its date of composition must precede its arrival in Alexandria.

The year in which this version of Esther was taken to Alexandria and its relative date of composition will be confirmed through comparisons with Jewish and Greek literature from the same time period, as well as the historical context of the date indicated by the colophon and the proposed date of composition. These discussions will demonstrate that the author of OG Esther made dramatic changes and additions to the Hebrew version for the purpose of addressing specific issues in the particular historical setting in which the book was written.

Information Provided by the Colophon

The colophon states that in the fourth year of the reign of Ptolemy and Cleopatra, Dositheus took the book of Purim from Jerusalem to Alexandria. Dositheus is identified as a priest and a Levite, and the translation is said to be the work of Lysimachus, a resident of Jerusalem.[1] This information is pertinent to this discussion in several ways. First of all, the latest possible date for the composition of Old Greek Esther is provided, as it must have been written by the year Dositheus took it to Alexandria. Second, the information shows that the book was written by a Jewish author. The fact that the translator and the priest who took the book to Alexandria both have Greek names does not mean that these men were not Jewish. Instead, the names are evidence of the Hellenization that had occurred among the Jews of Judea, a reality that was present in Alexandria as well. As John Collins says, "The early embrace of Greek culture, reflected in the choice of names, did not imply a loss of Jewish identity."[2] And finally, the fact that the translation was done by a resident of Jerusalem and taken to Alexandria by someone identified as a priest and a Levite indicates that the intended audience was Jewish. Because Jewish communities in the Diaspora developed libraries organized like the Greek libraries of the time, it is likely that Old Greek Esther was "deposited" in Jewish archives in Alexandria.[3]

---

1. See OG Esther, Addition F, verse 11 as it appears in the Septuagint or the Apocrypha.
2. John J. Collins, *Between Athens and Jerusalem: Jewish Identity in the Hellenistic Diaspora* (Grand Rapids, MI: Eerdmans, 2000), 67.
3. Elias J. Bickerman, "The Colophon of the Greek Book of Esther," in *Studies in the Book of Esther* (ed. Carey A. Moore; New York: KTAV Publishing House, 1982), 529-52.

The colophon is much less clear when it comes to the date the book of Purim was taken to Alexandria. The year in which this event occurred was undoubtedly obvious to the author of the colophon, but it is not as apparent to interpreters separated in time by over 2,000 years. This is because there are multiple possibilities for the date of this event due to the number of Ptolemies and Cleopatras who ruled over Ptolemaic Egypt. Beginning with the reign of Ptolemy V Epiphanes (203–181 BCE) and Cleopatra I, there were a total of seven Ptolemies who reigned with a Cleopatra for at least four years. Because the colophon specifies the fourth year of the reign of these two monarchs, all seven of these must be considered in order to determine the most probable year the colophon is referring to.

Following is a chart that summarizes the regnal years of seven Ptolemies, the regnal years of seven Cleopatras and their relationship to their particular Ptolemy, and the corresponding possible date for the arrival of Old Greek Esther in Alexandria.[1]

The Regnal Years of the Ptolemies	The Regnal Years of the Cleopatras and Relationships to the Ptolemies	Possible Date of Arrival of Old Greek Esther in Alexandria
Ptolemy V Epiphanes 204–180 BCE	Cleopatra I Married in 193 BCE	The fourth year of the reign of both of them would be 190 BCE
Ptolemy VI Philometor 180–145 BCE	Was co-regent with his mother, Cleopatra I until her death in 176 Cleopatra II (his sister) Married c. 175 BCE	Ptolemy was only five in 180, so Cleopatra I was actually the ruler The fourth year of the reign with Cleopatra II would be 172 BCE

1. The regnal years are based on those found in Sandra Gambetti, "Ptolemies," in *The Eerdmans Dictionary of Early Judaism* (ed. John J. Collins and Daniel C. Harlow; Grand Rapids, MI: Eerdmans Publishing Company, 2010), 1117-21; and Günther Hölbl, *A History of the Ptolemaic Empire* (trans. Tina Saavedra; London and New York: Routledge, 2001), 134-256. The content of this chart and the following analysis are taken from the author's dissertation, "Three Versions of Esther."

The Regnal Years of the Ptolemies	The Regnal Years of the Cleopatras and Relationships to the Ptolemies	Possible Date of Arrival of Old Greek Esther in Alexandria
Ptolemy VIII Euergetes II Physcon 170–163 BCE, 145–116 BCE	Cleopatra II (his sister) Married in 145 BCE upon the death of Ptolemy VI Married Cleopatra III (his niece) in 142 without divorcing Cleopatra II	The fourth year of their reign would be 142 BCE After 142, there were two Cleopatras on the throne
Ptolemy IX Soter II Lathyros 116–107 BCE	Married Cleopatra IV (his sister) in 119 while he was still a prince, but ruled jointly with his mother Cleopatra III throughout his reign	The fourth year of the co-regency of Ptolemy IX with his mother would be 114/113 BCE
Ptolemy X Alexander I 107–88 BCE	Married to a Cleopatra (his sister) but like his brother, Ptolemy IX, he shared the throne with his mother, Cleopatra III	The fourth year of the co-regency of Ptolemy X with his mother would be 104 BCE
Ptolemy XII Neos Dionysos 80–51 BCE	Married Cleopatra V or VI	The fourth year of their reign would be 78/77 BCE
Ptolemy XIII 51–47 BCE	Ruled with Cleopatra VII (51–30), his older sister, for the first five years of her reign	The fourth year of the reign would be 48 BCE, but Ptolemy was only co-regent with his older sister

As this chart demonstrates, the colophon could be referring to any one of seven possible dates for the arrival of Old Greek Esther in Alexandria. However, when other factors are taken into consideration, such as how the colophon is worded, how a document of this type was recorded in the Ptolemaic period, and how the phrase "in the fourth year of the reign of Ptolemy and Cleopatra" is to be interpreted, five of the seven dates can be eliminated as possibilities. Before determining how five of the dates are not possible when other factors are considered, the probability of the two most commonly accepted dates, 114/113 BCE and 78/77 BCE, will be analyzed.

Scholarship is somewhat divided between the two most commonly accepted dates of 114/113 BCE, the fourth year of Ptolemy IX, and 78/77 BCE, the fourth year of Ptolemy XII. James VanderKam simply states that these two dates are the most likely, without giving a reason for either.[1] In the context of arguing that "the uniqueness of the colophon among canonical books argues for its authenticity," Carey Moore states that while either date is compatible with Esther's Greek literary style, he prefers the date of 114 BCE.[2] In contrast to Moore, Elias J. Bickerman argued that 114/113 was not a possible date because of how the colophon is worded in comparison with documents from the time of Ptolemy IX.[3] In the colophon, the word for "reign" is in the *singular* and the name of Ptolemy comes before that of Cleopatra. Bickerman points out that in documents from the time of Ptolemy IX, the word for "reign" is in the *plural* and the name of Cleopatra preceded that of Ptolemy. Not only does the use of the plural indicate a joint rule, but the appearance of Cleopatra's name first indicates that "the Queen acted as regent for her son."[4]

Bickerman's argument is consistent with the historical data. Ptolemy IX married Cleopatra IV in 119 while he was still a prince, but when he became king in 116, his mother Cleopatra III was still on the throne as well. As a result, Ptolemy IX ruled with his mother as regent throughout his reign. Therefore, the date referenced by the colophon cannot be 114/113 BCE because the form of the word for "reign" and the order of the names are inconsistent with the wording of documents from the reign of Ptolemy IX and his mother, Cleopatra III.

---

1. James C. VanderKam, *An Introduction to Early Judaism* (Grand Rapids, MI: Eerdmans, 2001), 85.
2. Carey A. Moore, "On the Origins of the LXX Additions to the Book of Esther," *JBL* 92:3 (1973): 382-93.
3. Bickerman, "The Colophon of the Greek Book of Esther," 529-52.
4. *ibid.*

The majority of scholars accept Bickerman's argument concerning the date of 114/113 BCE and conclude with him that the colophon of OG Esther refers to 78/77 BCE. According to John Collins, Bickerman "has shown decisively that the date in question was the fourth year of Ptolemy XII and Cleopatra V, that is, 78/77 BCE."[1] David deSilva references Bickerman's argument in favor of 78/77 BCE in the context of acknowledging that there are "two lively possibilities for the date of the translation" without indicating which of the two dates he prefers.[2] George Nickelsburg simply states that the colophon indicates that OG Esther was taken to Egypt in 77 BCE and makes reference in a footnote to the work of Bickerman and Moore for a discussion of the alternate date of 114 BCE.[3] Kristin De Troyer also suggests the date of 78 BCE "based entirely on the study of E. Bickerman," but she differs from all the rest of the scholars in that she suggests that date as a *terminus ante quem*.[4] The use of this term simply means that 78 BCE is the *latest* date referred to by the colophon, meaning that it is possible that OG Esther could have been taken to Alexandria at an earlier date.

With the elimination of the date of 114/113 BCE, there are still five other dates in addition to the year 78/77 that the colophon of OG Esther could be referring to. These are 190, 172, 142, 104, and 48 BCE. 190 BCE was the fourth year of the reign of Ptolemy V and Cleopatra I after they were married in 193. However, 190 was not the fourth year of the reign of Ptolemy V, as he began ruling in 203. The problem with 190 being the date indicated by the colophon has to do with how the phrase "in the fourth year of the reign of Ptolemy and Cleopatra" is to be interpreted. If the colophon is to be interpreted literally to mean that there was a Cleopatra on the throne all of the first four years of the reign of Ptolemy, then 190 BCE is not a possible date for the event described in the colophon, since Ptolemy V ruled for ten years before marrying Cleopatra I.

1. Collins, *Between Athens and Jerusalem*, 110-11.
2. David A. deSilva, *Introducing the Apocrypha: Message, Context and Significance* (Grand Rapids, MI: Baker Academic, 2002), 117.
3. George W.E. Nickelsburg, *Jewish Literature between the Bible and the Mishnah* (Minneapolis, MN: Fortress Press, 2005), 203.
4. Kristin De Troyer, *The End of the Alpha Text of Esther: Translation and Narrative Technique in MT 8:1-17, LXX 8:1-17, and AT 7:14-41* (Atlanta, GA: Society of Biblical Literature, 2000), 398.

The same conclusion also applies to 172 BCE, which was the fourth year of the reign of Ptolemy VI and Cleopatra II but the ninth year that Ptolemy VI was on the throne. For the first five years of the reign of Ptolemy VI, he was co-regent with his mother, Cleopatra I. According to Bickerman's argument, which was cited in relation to the discussion of the date of 114/113, Cleopatra's name would have been listed first when she acted as regent for her son. Therefore, neither the fourth year of the reign of Ptolemy VI when he was co-regent with his mother, nor the fourth year of his joint reign with Cleopatra II, allow for the possibility that Ptolemy VI is the one referred to in the colophon.

142 BCE was the fourth year of the reign of Ptolemy VIII and Cleopatra II. Ptolemy VIII had been a co-regent with his brother Ptolemy VI and Cleopatra II from 170–163 BCE, but was removed from the throne in Alexandria in 163 as the result of a partitioning of the kingdom that left Ptolemy VIII in charge of Cyrenaica. However, upon the death of Ptolemy VI in 145, Ptolemy VIII returned to Alexandria, claimed the throne, and married Cleopatra II. Therefore, the fourth year of the reign of both Ptolemy VIII and Cleopatra II would be 142 BCE. Like the date of 78/77 BCE, the date of 142 BCE is a valid possibility because it meets the requirements of the various factors that need to be considered in light of how the colophon is worded. When Ptolemy VIII took the throne in 145, it was as the primary ruler. Furthermore, he married Cleopatra II at the same time, which means that their reign began in the same year. Therefore the colophon, which lists the name of Ptolemy before that of Cleopatra and uses the singular form of "reign," could very well be referring to the fourth year of the reign of Ptolemy VIII and Cleopatra II.

There are two final dates to be considered: 104 BCE and 48 BCE. 104 BCE was the fourth year of the reign of Ptolemy X and his mother, Cleopatra III. Ptolemy X was also married to a Cleopatra (his sister) but like his brother, Ptolemy IX, he ruled with his mother as regent until he had her killed in 101. Therefore, just as with Ptolemy IX, this joint reign of mother and son would be described by the plural form of "reign" and the name of Cleopatra would precede that of Ptolemy. Since this wording is inconsistent with the wording of the colophon, 104 BCE cannot be the date referred to by the colophon. 48 BCE was the fourth year of the reign of Ptolemy XIII and Cleopatra VII. Just as in the reigns of Ptolemy IX and Ptolemy X, Ptolemy XIII ruled with Cleopatra as regent. In the case of Ptolemy XIII, Cleopatra VII was his older sister and he ruled with her for the first five years of her reign. As with the reigns of Ptolemy IX and X, the plural form of "reign" would be used to describe the reign of Ptolemy XIII and Cleopatra VII, and Cleopatra's name would be listed first since she acted as regent for her younger brother. Therefore, 48 BCE cannot be the date referred to by the colophon of Old Greek Esther.

The preceding analysis of seven possible dates for the arrival of the book of Purim in Alexandria has eliminated five of them. When factors such as how the colophon is worded, how a document of this type was recorded in the Ptolemaic period, and how the phrase "in the fourth year of the reign of Ptolemy and Cleopatra" is to be interpreted are taken into consideration, there are only two remaining dates the colophon could be referring to. These dates are 142 and 78/77 BCE. The scholarly debate over the dates of 114/113 and 78/77 BCE for the arrival of Old Greek Esther in Alexandria makes it obvious that the information provided in the colophon is not enough to determine the actual date of this event. In order to do so, the historical contexts of the two remaining dates and common themes in comparative literature from the same time period will have to be added to the discussion.

The fact that this rewritten story was taken from Jerusalem to Alexandria in either 142 or 78/77 BCE suggests a composition date in the context of the Maccabean/Hasmonean period, which lasted from 164 to 63 BCE. In order to understand the authorial intent behind the changes and additions to this book, it will be helpful to look at common themes found in other Jewish literature written during this hundred-year time frame. And in order to appreciate the significance of, and reasons for, the common themes expressed in this corpus, it will be necessary to know what contemporary Greek authors wrote about Jews and Judaism. A comparison of themes found in this version of Esther with those found in other Jewish literature written between 164 and 63 BCE will demonstrate Maccabean/Hasmonean influence on the entire corpus, and will reveal a relationship between Jewish and Greek literature as well.

The Relationship Between
Jewish and Greek Literature

Jewish literature from the Maccabean/Hasmonean period is extremely valuable for its insight into second and first century

BCE Judaism, as well as for how it exhibits Hellenistic thought concerning Jews and Judaism. In fact, Jewish literature from this time period cannot be fully understood without knowledge of what Greek authors wrote about Jews, because to a large extent, Jewish authors wrote in response to prevalent Hellenistic thought. The following survey of what Greek authors wrote about Jews and Judaism prior to, and during, the Maccabean/Hasmonean period will expose beliefs that are overtly anti-Jewish and anti-Semitic.

Greek Authors on Jews and Judaism

Beginning in the fifth century BCE, Greek authors showed an awareness of Jews and the practices of Judaism. Herodotus (fifth century BCE) knew of a people group that came out of Egypt who practiced circumcision.[1] Theophrastus (372–288 BCE) exhibited a complete misunderstanding of Jewish ritual that resulted in a strong disgust towards the practice of animal sacrifice because he believed that the animals were burned alive. According to Bezalel Bar-Kochva, Theophrastus' misunderstanding of animal sacrifice was the result of confusing the verb "to sacrifice animals" with the verb "to sacrifice a victim alive." This confusion was the result of bad transmission in a source used by Theophrastus.[2] Not only did he mistakenly believe that the victims were burned alive, but everything he wrote about Jewish sacrificial customs was erroneous. Because "Theophrastus is known to have used Egyptian sources," Bar-Kochva suggests that the source of information concerning Jewish sacrifices was Egyptian, and as a result, Theophrastus "is a witness to the beginnings of Egyptian anti-Judaism."[3] Hecataeus (c. 300 BCE) wrote a detailed excursus concerning the Jews that was written in Alexandria and is known from the fortieth book of Diodorus (first century BCE). According to Josephus, Hecataeus displayed a significant lack of knowledge of Jewish history before the Persian period, a deficiency that is undoubtedly a reflection of the anti-Jewish Egyptian priestly

---

1. Herodotus, *The Histories* (trans. Robin Waterfield; Oxford: Oxford University Press, 1998), II:104.
2. Bezalel Bar-Kochva, *The Image of the Jews in Greek Literature: The Hellenistic Period* (Berkeley and Los Angeles, CA: University of California Press, 2010), 24-34.
3. *ibid.*

sources he used.[1] Hecataeus' misunderstanding of Jewish history is exhibited by his belief that Moses went to Judea, founded Jerusalem, and wrote the Jewish constitution there.[2] In addition to Hecataeus, Josephus acknowledged numerous Greek writers, eight of whom he named, who he said made distinct mention of the Jews in their writings.[3] However, like Hecataeus, these early authors made many mistakes concerning the history and practices of the Jews.[4]

While these writers reveal an early awareness of Jews and Judaism among the Greeks, their lack of knowledge concerning Jewish history and ritual reflects the anti-Jewish Egyptian sources they used. According to Rosemary Ruether, these classical writers provide evidence of "a special strain of anti-Judaism that has a specifically Egyptian provenance."[5] She credits this to the fact that the Egyptians are on the wrong side in the Jewish salvation story, a fact that was not only pointed out by Celsus, but was responsible for "a literary tradition of Egyptian anti-Jewish polemic" and the creation of alternate versions of the Exodus story.[6] These erroneous beliefs were preserved in the work of later Greek, Roman, and Christian authors, thereby contributing to the continuity of theologically based anti-Judaism/Semitism from the time of the Egyptians to the present day.

Following Theophrastus' (372–288 BCE) disapproval of animal sacrifice, the next most obvious example of anti-Jewish writing appeared in the third century BCE in the work of

---

1. Josephus, *Contra Apion*, I:183-205. From *The New Complete Works of Josephus* (trans. William Whiston; Grand Rapids, MI: Kregel Publications, 1999), 948-9. For further discussion of Hecataeus' excursus on the Jews, his Egyptian sources, and how the excursus was used in the anti-Jewish writings of Diodorus, see Bar-Kochva, *The Image of the Jews in Greek Literature*, 99-123; and Elias J Bickerman, *The Jews in the Greek Age* (Cambridge and London: Harvard University Press, 1988), 16-17.
2. Menahem Stern, *Greek and Latin Authors on Jews and Judaism: Volume I, From Herodotus to Plutarch* (Jerusalem: The Israel Academy of Sciences and Humanities, 1976), 21.
3. Josephus, *Contra Apion*, I:215-16.
4. *ibid.*, I:217.
5. Rosemary Radford Ruether, *Faith and Fratricide: The Theological Roots of Anti-Semitism* (Eugene, OR: Wipf and Stock Publishers, 1997), 24.
6. *ibid.*

Manetho, a priest in Heliopolis, Egypt. Manetho's work exposed the anti-Jewish trend in Hellenistic Egypt, but, even more significantly, it helped to popularize those already existing, recurring anti-Semitic themes.[1] Josephus not only quoted from him directly, but displayed familiarity with previous Hellenistic Jewish refutations of Manetho and their polemic against Greco-Egyptian anti-Semites. In *Contra Apion* I:73-105, Josephus discredited Manetho's version of the origin of the Jews as descendants of the Hyksos who burned the cities of Egypt, destroyed temples, were cruel towards the native population, and then built a city in Judea and named it Jerusalem after being expelled from Egypt. This account of the founding of Jerusalem indicates, among other things, a lack of knowledge of the pre-Jewish history of Jerusalem. In addition to Manetho's account of the founding of Jerusalem, Josephus refuted other claims of his, such as: Moses was originally a priest in Heliopolis who instigated war against the Egyptian king; the Jews were guilty of great brutality against the Egyptians; and Moses was expelled from Egypt because he had leprosy.[2] Josephus concluded that Manetho either "forged" his accounts of the Jews "without any probability, or else gave credit to some men who spoke so out of their ill-will to us."[3]

Following his refutation of Manetho, Josephus addressed the allegations of Lysimachus of Alexandria, a Greco-Egyptian writer whose precise date of birth is unknown, but who probably lived in the second or first century BCE.[4] According to Josephus, Lysimachus "has taken the same topic of falsehood [as Manetho] . . . but has gone far beyond them in the incredible nature of his forgeries; which plainly demonstrates that he contrived them out of his virulent hatred of our nation."[5] In *Contra Apion* I:305-311, Josephus quoted Lysimachus' belief that the Jews were expelled from Egypt because they were leprous. According to Lysimachus, they were then sent into the desert to be destroyed by exposure, but Moses appeared and led them on a journey. Moses commanded them that while they were on that journey, they were not to do any good to anyone and they were

---

1. Stern, *Greek and Latin Authors on Jews and Judaism: Volume I*, 62.
2. Josephus, *Contra Apion*, I: 228-87.
3. *ibid.*, I: 287.
4. Stern, *Greek and Latin Authors on Jews and Judaism*, 382.
5. Josephus, *Contra Apion*, I: 304.

to destroy all temples and altars to any other gods. And finally, according to Lysimachus, after abusing everyone they came in contact with, they entered Judea and built a city and called it Jerusalem.[1]

As either a contemporary or a close follower of Lysimachus, Diodorus (first century BCE) is of tremendous value because he preserved the contents and views of earlier writers who would otherwise be lost in his *Bibliotheca Historica*.[2] As a result, he reflects the views expressed in at least 200 years of anti-Jewish writing. He stated that his authority on the Jews was Hecataeus (300 BCE) and in fact, "there is a striking similarity of content" between the writings of Diodorus and references to Jews in Hecataeus' *Aegyptiaca*.[3] Diodorus repeated the commonly accepted history of the Jews as a leprous people who were driven out of Egypt because they were "impious and detested by the gods," and who then occupied the territory around Jerusalem.[4] From there, they were said to have organized a nation that made their hatred of mankind into a tradition and, as a result, introduced laws that prohibited eating with any other race or extending good will towards others. This belief is specifically dependent on Hecataeus, who wrote that "the Jewish way of life was 'unsociable and hostile to strangers.'"[5] Diodorus went on to say that the reason Antiochus Epiphanes decided to prohibit their practices and destroy the books containing their xenophobic laws was because he was so shocked by their "hatred directed against all mankind."[6] This explanation presents Antiochus as a "magnanimous and mild-mannered person" (in contrast to the hateful Jews), who was lenient towards the Jews in spite of encouragement from his friends "to make an end of the race completely."[7]

---

1. For a more thorough discussion of Lysimachus and his "hostile accounts of the Exodus," as well as the Egyptian sources for those accounts, see Bar-Kochva, *The Image of the Jews in Greek Literature*, 306-33.
2. Stern, *Greek and Latin Authors on Jews and Judaism*, 167.
3. Bar-Kochva, *The Image of the Jews in Greek Literature*, 103.
4. Diodorus, *Bibliotheca Historica*, XXXIV-XXXV, 1:1. Quoted in Stern, *Greek and Latin Authors on Jews and Judaism*, 182-3.
5. Bickerman, *The Jews in the Greek Age*, 18.
6. Diodorus, *Bibliotheca Historica*, XXXIV-XXXV, 1:3.
7. *ibid.*, XXXIV-XXXV, 1:5.

In addition to the recurring anti-Semitic themes concerning the history of the Jews and their actions towards others that were popularized by Manetho in the third century and expanded upon by Lysimachus and Diodorus in the second and first centuries, topics related to the religion of the Jews were also common in the works of Greek authors. The Jewish belief in one God who was unique, who was above all other gods, and who was not to be represented by any image, drew reactions from Hellenistic authors that included disapproval, contempt, and hostility. As early as 300 BCE, Hecataeus related Jewish monotheism, aniconism, and their expulsion from Egypt to their way of life which, according to him, was "an unsocial and intolerant mode of life."[1] The third century Egyptian priest Manetho concluded that the Jews were actually godless because they had no image of their God. Like Hecataeus, Manetho connected the refusal of the Jews to worship the same gods everyone else worshiped with their refusal to have contact with any other people.[2] The fact that Jewish belief did result in an observable difference in how Jews lived lead to a "special polemic against the Jews. . . . [I]t was a reaction caused by the special social consequences of Jewish religious law."[3] The connection made by Manetho and Hecataeus between the Jewish religion and the Jews' "unsocial and intolerant mode of life" is a clear example of how anti-Judaism contributes to anti-Semitism, and how anti-Semitism tends to include anti-Judaism. The early Hellenistic disapproval and contempt for Jewish monotheism and aniconism continued to be associated by subsequent Greek authors with what they believed to be was a hostile way of life on the part of Jews. Because of this association, the German historians of the nineteenth century were not in error when they applied their new term, "anti-Semitism," to the anti-Judaism that occurred in antiquity.

Along with the Jewish belief in one God, the practices of abstinence from pork, observation of the Sabbath, and circumcision were the most popular topics of discussion among Greek authors. They were also the practices prohibited by Antiochus IV when he issued his decrees against Judaism in 167 BCE. According to Diodorus, it was the "misanthropic and lawless customs" ordained by Moses that caused Antiochus to be so "shocked by such hatred

---

1. Hecataeus is preserved by Diodorus in *Bibliotheca Historica*, XL, 3:4. Quoted in Stern, *Greek and Latin Authors on Jews and Judaism*, 26-8.
2. Josephus, *Contra Apion*, I:239.
3. Ruether, *Faith and Fratricide*, 24.

directed against all mankind [that] he set himself to break down their traditional practices."[1] Accordingly, he sacrificed a pig in the Temple, poured its blood on the altar, prepared its flesh, and poured the broth of the meat on "their holy books, containing the xenophobic laws."[2] In other words, Diodorus explained the profaning of the Temple by Antiochus as a justifiable action done for the purpose of destroying the hated religious practices of the Jews. When Antiochus profaned the Temple, he also decreed the sacrifice of pigs and other unclean animals and the profaning of the Sabbath, and forbade the practice of circumcision. Antiochus' acts to prohibit the practices of observant Jews, Hellenistic contempt for Jewish monotheism and aniconism, and recurring anti-Semitic themes concerning the history of the Jews and their actions towards others found in all the Greek authors surveyed clearly demonstrate how anti-Judaism was related to anti-Semitic themes in Hellenistic writings about Jews and Judaism.

Discussions concerning the religion of the Jews became particularly anti-Semitic when accusations involving Jewish worship of the head of an ass and human sacrifice became prominent topics. Mnaseas of Patara (c. 200 BCE) is the first known writer to refer to the worship of the golden head of an ass in the Temple in Jerusalem, a theme that is perpetuated by later writers such as Diodorus (first century BCE), Damocritus (first century BCE), and Apion (first half of first century CE). Diodorus' version is a little different in that, according to him, what was found in the Temple was a statue of Moses seated on an ass holding a book.[3] The story first seen in Mnaseas originated in Hellenistic Egypt in an atmosphere hostile to the Jews and was probably taken by Mnaseas from earlier sources, "in accordance with his usual procedure."[4] In fact, "Mnaseas did not invent stories but merely preserved and reworked what he found elsewhere."[5] As Parkes says, "it is perhaps natural that Egypt, with its animal-headed deities, should have evolved the story of the worship of an ass-headed deity by the Jews. The choice of an ass is significantly Egyptian."[6] Posidonius, who

---

1. Diodorus, *Bibliotheca Historica*, XXXIV-XXXV, 1:3.

2. *ibid.*, 1:4.

3. Bar-Kochva, *The Image of the Jews in Greek Literature*, 443.

4. Stern, *Greek and Latin Authors on Jews and Judaism*, 97-8.

5. Bar-Kochva, *The Image of the Jews in Greek Literature*, 216.

6. James Parkes, *The Conflict of the Church and the Synagogue: A Study in the Origins of Antisemitism* (New York: Atheneum, 1969), 16.

wrote c. 151–135 BCE, repeated the story of the worship of a head of an ass, and described the Jews as sorcerers using incantations who worshiped the same gods worshiped by others. Furthermore, he added to the accusation of the worship of the head of an ass and made popular an account of an annual sacrifice of a Greek in the Temple in Jerusalem, a story that was perpetuated in various forms by later writers such as Damocritus and Apollonius Molon in the first century BCE, and Apion in the early first century CE.[1]

The writings of Apion show dependence on the work of Apollonius Molon, who in turn was dependent on Posidonius.[2] In particular, Apion claimed he found the story of human sacrifice, or "Hellenistic blood libel," in the writings of Posidonius and Apollonius Molon. The term "Hellenistic blood libel" is borrowed from Bar-Kochva, who defines the term "blood libel" as one that "denotes a slander concerning ritual murder of any kind."[3] Apion's account of the ritual sacrifice of a Greek is known from Josephus, who documents the story and then refutes it in *Contra Apion* II:89-111. According to Josephus, Apion said that the Jewish practice of sacrificing a Greek was revealed when Antiochus Epiphanes entered the Temple in 168 BCE and discovered the Greek, who was being held against his will in preparation for being sacrificed. Judging from Josephus' comments to the contrary found in *Contra Apion* II:97, Apion must have used this supposed discovery on the part of Antiochus to justify Antiochus' desecration of the Temple and the subsequent religious persecution of the Jews. This would be consistent with the justification of the profaning of the Temple found in Diodorus (first century BCE) where, upon Antiochus' discovery of Jewish practices and xenophobic laws, the friends of Antiochus urged him "to make an end of the race completely."[4]

---

1. Hans Conzelmann, *Gentiles, Jews, Christians: Polemics and Apologetics in the Greco-Roman Era* (trans. M. Eugene Boring; Minneapolis, MN: Fortress Press, 1992), 47.

2. Stern, *Greek and Latin Authors on Jews and Judaism*, 141. For a more detailed discussion of the anti-Jewish writings of Apollonius Molon, see Bar-Kochva, *The Image of the Jews in Greek Literature,* 469-516. For a more detailed discussion of the relationship between the writings of Apion, Apollonius Molon, and Posidonius, see Bar-Kochva, *The Image of the Jews in Greek Literature,* 440-44.

3. Bar-Kochva, *The Image of the Jews in Greek Literature,* 253.

4. Diodorus, *Bibliotheca Historica,* XXXIV-XXXV, 1:5.

In addition to Apion, Damocritus (first century BCE) also maintained that the Jews practiced the ritual sacrifice of a foreigner.[1] His version of this "Hellenistic blood libel" is found in his *Peri Ioudaion*, a work preserved in the *Suda*, a Byzantine lexicon of the tenth century CE.[2] However, there are obvious differences in the story when the account of Damocritus is compared to that of Apion. Damocritus only refers to the victim as a foreigner, whereas Apion stresses that the identity of the victim was specifically Greek. According to Damocritus, the human sacrifice took place once in seven years, while Apion maintains that it was an annual occurrence. These differences, as well as differences in the descriptions of how and where the victim was killed, indicate that there is not a close interdependence between these two writers. This suggests that Apion and Damocritus relied on different sources for this story, which indicates that it was more widely believed than if there was only one source.

The introduction of the "Hellenistic blood libel" by Posidonius c. 151–135 BCE, the perpetuation of that libel by Apollonius Molon in the first century BCE and Apion early in the first century CE, and the introduction of what appears to be another version of the blood libel by Damocritus in the first century BCE, are overt examples of anti-Jewish themes in Hellenistic writings about Jews and Judaism. So too are the examples given concerning the commonly accepted history of the Jews as a people descended from the Hyksos who burned the cities of Egypt, destroyed temples, and were cruel towards the native population; and/or a people who were driven out of Egypt because they were impious, detested by the gods, leprous, and under a curse. A further example is the Greek belief that when the Jews settled in Jerusalem, they organized a nation that made their hatred of humanity into a tradition and introduced laws that prohibited showing any good will towards any others. In short, the Greek writers surveyed here described the Jews as

1. Peter Schäfer, *Judeophobia: Attitudes toward the Jews in the Ancient World* (Cambridge, MA: Harvard University Press, 1997), 61.
2. There is a remarkable similarity between this "Hellenistic blood libel" – preserved in a Byzantine lexicon that would have been referenced in the Middle Ages – and the well-known medieval blood libel. There is also an alarming resemblance between ancient blood libels and various libels believed in the Arab world to this day.

"the 'evil incarnate,' denying and perverting in their xenophobic and misanthropic hatred all cherished values of humankind, conspiring against the civilized world."[1]

The Greeks' conclusion that a hatred of humanity is the natural result of the relationship between Jewish religion and the alleged "intolerant" Jewish way of life is a graphic illustration of how anti-Judaism fuels anti-Semitism. Indeed, anti-Judaism becomes anti-Semitism with this charge of "a deeply rooted, essential misanthropy."[2] Anti-Judaism/Semitism then becomes genocidal when accompanied by the belief that the only way to deal with those accused of conspiring against the world is through the elimination of the entire race. The story of Esther, the European Holocaust, and repeated Arab attempts to eradicate the Jewish State reveal that the relationship between anti-Judaism, anti-Semitism, and the perceived need to rid the world of Jews has been consistent throughout history. Not only is the chilling similarity between ancient and modern forms of anti-Judaism/Semitism observable throughout the world today, but the intent to wipe Israel off the map is made abundantly clear through the statements and actions of the enemies of the Jews.

The Jewish Response:
I, II, III Maccabees and Old Greek Esther

An overview of Jewish literature from the Maccabean/Hasmonean period will demonstrate that Jewish authors addressed the anti-Judaism of the time by incorporating popular Greek beliefs about Jews and Judaism and then answering them by extolling Jewish law and piety. According to Conzelmann, the texts found in the Septuagint "were composed (primarily or secondarily) for apologetic purposes," and "were, at the minimum, intended to contribute to Jewish self-edification while defending against the objections of non-Jews."[3] Collins also describes this corpus as "apologetic," since it "is seen as defending a view of Judaism" in response to "the assessments and polemics of the Gentiles."[4]

---

1. Schäfer, *Judeophobia*, 206.
2. *ibid.*, 207.
3. Conzelmann, *Gentiles, Jews, Christians*, 139-40.
4. Collins, *Between Athens and Jerusalem*, 14-15.

These writings were also polemic in that they advocated for the rights of Jews to live by their own laws and exposed the violence and threat of genocide that so easily resulted from the anti-Judaism/Semitism of the time. The books of I, II, and III Maccabees (included in the Greek Septuagint but not in the Hebrew canon) all provide clear examples of Jewish apologetics and polemics written in this historical context. Because these books were written during the same time period proposed for the composition of Old Greek Esther, the following discussions of dates and purpose for their composition will provide insight into the historical setting of the composition of this version of Esther.

I Maccabees

The book of I Maccabees covers a period of forty years from the accession of Antiochus Epiphanes in 175 BCE to the death of Simon Maccabee in 135 BCE. It gives an account of how Mattathias and his five sons refused to conform to Greek religion, how they delivered the Jews from the religious persecution of Antiochus, and how they ultimately restored political independence to Israel. Since the death of Simon is the last event recorded in the book, it must have been written after 135. Because the book emphasizes good relations between Rome and the Jews and Rome's faithfulness as an ally, it must have been written before the conquest of Jerusalem by Pompey in 63 BCE, when relations between Rome and the Jews became hostile.

The author was obviously a devout Jew and a loyal supporter of the Hasmonean dynasty, as evidenced by the many positive references to Jewish law, the piety of the people, and the heroic deeds of the Maccabees/Hasmoneans throughout the book.[1] Furthermore, the author "was a person of means (or at least well supported by literary patrons) . . . with access to the official archives in Jerusalem."[2] The internal evidence that indicates the author's access to official archives, combined with the clear

1. For examples of the emphasis on piety and zeal for the law, see 1:62, 2:20-22, 2:27, 2:50, 3:46-53, 4:38-58. For examples of the emphasis on the heroic deeds of the Maccabees, see 3:1-9, 3:23-25, 3:58-59, 4:36-37, 5:16-68.

2. J.R. Bartlett, *I Maccabees* (Sheffield: Sheffield Academic Press, 1998), 33.

pro-Hasmonean stance of the book, suggests that the book was not written solely for the apologetic purpose of exalting Jewish law and the piety of all those who resisted the religious edicts of Antiochus. The same features also indicate that this text was not written solely for the polemic purpose of glorifying how the Maccabees restored the practice of Jewish law. Rather, the combined evidence indicates that I Maccabees was also written as Hasmonean propaganda designed to justify the actions of the Maccabees and give legitimacy to their dynasty.

II Maccabees

II Maccabees covers a period of less than twenty years, from the last years of the reign of Seleucus IV, who was succeeded by Antiochus IV in 175, to the victory of Judas Maccabeus over Nicanor, the governor of Judea, in 161 BCE. Because the book ends with the celebration of Judas' victory and the decree to celebrate that victory annually, the book must have been written after 161. As in I Maccabees, there is a positive portrayal of relations with Rome (4:11 and 11:34-36), indicating that it was composed before the conquest of Jerusalem by Pompey in 63 BCE. Additional evidence from the text suggests a later date within the range of 161–63 BCE, as the author of the book claims it is a condensation of a five-volume history of the Maccabean revolt written by Jason of Cyrene (2:23). Since deSilva concludes that Jason would have completed his work by 124, this book must have been written later than 124 BCE.[1]

II Maccabees extols the importance of Jewish law and piety and the purification of the Jerusalem Temple, and makes heroes of the Jerusalem martyrs who stood against the anti-Jewish edicts of Antiochus Epiphanes.[2] The practices of Sabbath observance, circumcision, and dietary regulations were of great interest to the Greeks and were specifically targeted for extinction by Antiochus IV. The author of II Maccabees documented Antiochus' anti-Jewish edicts and his sacrilege of the Temple in a detailed account in chapters 6-7. These chapters also glorify the martyrs as heroes

---

1. deSilva, *Introducing the Apocrypha*, 270.
2. For examples of the importance on Jewish law, piety, and the purification of the Temple, see 2:19-22, 3:1-3, 3:10:1-8. For examples of the importance of Jerusalem martyrs as heroes, see 6:7-11, 18-31, 7:1-42.

who would rather die than violate the laws of God.[1] Through the examples of the martyrs, who take their place alongside Judas Maccabeus as the heroes of this book, II Maccabees is not only apologetic in its exaltation of Jewish law and the piety of all those who resisted the religious edicts of Antiochus, but is polemic in its emphasis on the superiority of the Jewish way of life over any other, and the need to maintain the distinctiveness of that way of life at any cost.

III Maccabees

III Maccabees gives an account of the persecution and attempted genocide of the Jews in Alexandria during the reign of Ptolemy IV Philopator (222–204 BCE). This is consistent with internal evidence, which indicates that the composition of the book should be dated to the Ptolemaic period based on the comparison of technical language used by the author with that used in Egyptian papyri.[2] In addition, III Maccabees exhibits a "command of Ptolemaic court procedure," and uses a greeting formula that was only used for a century beginning at the end of the second century BCE.[3] Furthermore, the similarity of vocabulary and parallels with the plot of II Maccabees "suggest a conscious literary imitation of 2 Maccabees."[4] Therefore, the linguistic and literary evidence suggests a composition date after that of II Maccabees, or sometime in the late second century or

---

1. The sacrilege of the Temple is documented in 6:2-5; the persecution resulting from the edicts of Antiochus is documented in 6:6 ff; and accounts of martyrs who would rather die than violate the laws of God begin in 6:10. Women were killed for circumcising their sons (6:10); others who had assembled to observe the Sabbath were burned (6:11); Eleazar had swine's flesh forced into his mouth but chose to die rather than swallow it (6:18-31); and a mother and her seven sons endured horrible tortures and death rather than eat swine's flesh (7:1-42).

2. deSilva, *Introducing the Apocrypha*, 308.

3. Sara Raup Johnson, *Historical Fictions and Hellenistic Jewish Identity: Third Maccabees in Its Cultural Context* (Berkeley and Los Angeles, CA: University of California Press, 2004), 138-9.

4. deSilva, *Introducing the Apocrypha*, 312. For a detailed outline of the parallels in the plots of II and III Maccabees, see the discussion by deSilva, pp. 311-12.

early first century BCE. According to Johnson, it is "universally agreed that 3 Maccabees cannot have been composed before the end of the second century B.C.E."[1]

As in the case of I and II Maccabees, the author is an observant Jew who obviously wrote for the benefit of a Jewish audience. Indeed, this book could not have been intended for a Gentile audience, as the Ptolemaic king and Gentiles in general are referred to rather negatively throughout the book.[2] While the story is set in Egypt and has nothing to do with the Maccabees of Judea, III Maccabees has much in common with the apologetics and polemics of the books of I and II Maccabees in relation to the exaltation of Jewish law and piety, the connection of all Jews to the Temple, and the anti-Judaism of the Greek period. All of these writings show the "need felt by the Jews to defend their culture and religion" in the context of Greek culture, and specifically include a defense against anti-Semitism.[3] These parallels, in addition to the fact that III Maccabees tells a story so similar to that of II Maccabees in terms of the theme of religious persecution, probably explain the association of this book with the previous two. The account of accusations of Jewish xenophobia, misanthropy, and political seditiousness, and the resulting persecution that culminated in attempted genocide, provides an invaluable reflection of the anti-Semitism expressed by the Greek writers of this time period, and a dramatic illustration of the violence that so easily results from that sentiment.[4]

This brief overview of the books of I, II, and III Maccabees has demonstrated that I Maccabees was written between 135 and 63 BCE, II Maccabees was written after 124 BCE, and III Maccabees was written sometime in the late second century or early first century BCE. Therefore, all three of these books were written in the context of what Greek authors wrote about Jews and

---

1. Johnson, *Historical Fictions and Hellenistic Jewish Identity*, 131.
2. For example, see Simon's prayer in 2:2-20 and Eleazar's prayer in 6:1-15.
3. Johnson, *Historical Fictions and Hellenistic Jewish Identity*, 171.
4. See 3:2-7 and 3:12-30 for accusations of Jewish xenophobia, misanthropy, and political seditiousness, as well as the command to kill all the Jews – young and old – for the purpose of establishing the government "in good order." See 2:25-30, 3:1, 4:14, and 5:1-2 for accounts of religious persecution that culminated in Ptolemy's attempt to annihilate all the Jews by having them trampled to death in the hippodrome by drunken elephants.

Judaism, and during the time of Maccabean/Hasmonean rule in Judea as well. As examples of Jewish literature from this period, the books of I, II and III Maccabees address the anti-Judaism of the time by incorporating popular Hellenistic beliefs and then answering them by extolling Jewish law and piety. In addition to their apologetic purpose, all three books have a polemic message as well. I Maccabees appears to have been written to justify the actions of the Maccabees and give legitimacy to their dynasty; II Maccabees presents a strong message on the superiority of the Jewish way of life and the need to maintain the distinctiveness of that way of life at any cost; and III Maccabees testifies to the threat of genocide that so easily resulted from the anti-Jewish/Semitic sentiment of the period. As the following section will establish, Old Greek Esther has much in common with the books of the Maccabees in the way it incorporates Hellenistic beliefs concerning the Jews and then responds to them. Furthermore, the story of Esther is amazingly similar to that of III Maccabees in respect to the Gentile government's perceived need to annihilate all Jews for the sake of preserving that government. The following discussion of the historical setting of the composition of Greek Esther will indicate that the approximate dates of composition and purpose behind the writing of the books of the Maccabees are particularly relevant to the process of answering the questions of when and why Old Greek Esther was written.

Old Greek Esther

With the exception of the lack of reference to the Temple, all the apologetic and polemic content of the additions in OG Esther, as well as the inclusion of Hellenistic beliefs concerning the Jews, corresponds directly to that of the three books of Maccabees. A significant example of common Greek beliefs about the Jews appears in addition B:4-5, in which the author has written an expanded version of Haman's charge against the Jews found in 3:8-9a of the Hebrew text. In the Hebrew version of this accusation, Haman informs the king that there is a certain people "scattered" and "dispersed" throughout his kingdom whose laws are "different" from those of every other nation, and who do not keep the king's laws. Because their laws are different, Haman advises the king that these people need to be destroyed. In 3:8-9a of the Old Greek text, the Jews are also referred to as a "scattered people" who observe "special or distinguishing" laws, who do not keep the king's laws, and who therefore need to be destroyed.

However – possibly because it is difficult to imagine how an exiled people that was involuntarily dispersed among many other peoples could be considered a serious enough threat that annihilation was necessary – the author of OG Addition B felt the need to embellish Haman's accusation. As a result, additional information is provided that echoes Hellenistic beliefs concerning the Jews. In contrast to Haman's charge in 3:8 that the Jews are a "scattered" people who observe "special or distinguishing" laws and do not keep the laws of the king, Addition B:4-5 identifies the Jews as a "hostile people" who "in their laws are opposed to other people." Furthermore, it states that they are ready to "lead an army against everyone" and commit the "worst evil deeds." Not only have the Jews been changed from being a "scattered people" to being a "hostile people," and from being a people who observe "special or distinguishing" laws to people having laws that "are opposed to other people," but the charges now include their readiness to "lead an army against everyone" and commit the "worst evil deeds." As a result, the amplified version of Haman's accusation against the Jews in Addition B:4-5 emphasizes charges of xenophobia and misanthropy, just like the ones found in Hellenistic writings about the Jews. Because of these charges, Haman declares that the Jews need to be destroyed. Haman's insistence is very similar to that of Diodorus, who stated that the Greeks should "make an end of the race completely," and to the situation in III Maccabees, where the government believed it needed to destroy the Jews in order to protect that government.

But the additions found in OG Esther don't just reflect common Greek accusations against the Jews – they include apologetic and polemic answers to those charges as well. The answer to the accusations against the Jews in Addition B:4-5 is found in Addition E:13, in which the king extols the piety of Mordecai and Esther and refers to Mordecai as the "savior" of the kingdom and to Esther as its "blameless partner." This statement refutes Greek perceptions of xenophobia and misanthropy by emphasizing the special relationship between Esther, Mordecai, and the Persian king. In so doing, E:13 not only offers an apologetic response to Greek charges against the Jews, but also makes a polemic statement that testifies to the importance of the roles Esther and Mordecai played in the kingdom.

OG Addition E:13 is only one example of many in which an apologetic and/or polemic response is made to Hellenistic beliefs concerning the Jews. As was mentioned previously, the Greeks believed the Jews were atheistic because they would not worship Greek gods. In response to this charge, the author of this version emphasized the presence of the God of Israel and the relationship of Mordecai and Esther to their God from the very beginning of the book. In contrast to the Hebrew version, in which the words "God" and "Lord" do not appear even once, "God" and "Lord" appear more than fifty times, both in the additions and in the canonical portions of Esther. For example, in Addition A:1-11, Mordecai has a dream that not only mentions God, but is attributed to God (A:11). In Addition C, Mordecai and Esther pray to the Lord concerning the edict that called for the destruction of the entire Jewish people. In both of their prayers, numerous statements are made that provide clear intertextual connections to belief in the God of Israel, the Jews' relationship to Abraham, and their identity as God's inheritance. In Addition D:8, God is credited with changing the spirit of the king from anger to gentleness in response to Esther appearing before him uninvited. When the Persian king writes a letter to counteract the edict calling for the annihilation of the Jews in Addition E, even he is made to appear as if he believes in the God of the Jews. In F:6, Mordecai states that the Lord has saved his people, and in F:9-10, the people of Israel are referred to as the people of God and the inheritance of God.

Addition C – in which Mordecai and Esther pray concerning the decree that called for the destruction of the entire Jewish people – has already been mentioned above in terms of what it says about the relationship of Mordecai and Esther to the God of Israel. However, it is worthy of more discussion in that it also serves as an excellent example of multiple features of Maccabean/ Hasmonean piety. Not only is prayer and dependence on the Lord emphasized, but the importance of humility in prayer, circumcision, and dietary regulations are as well. Esther's prayer takes place only after she has taken off her queenly apparel, put on garments of mourning, covered her head with ashes, and completely humbled her entire body. Then, in the context of her desperate prayer, Esther reminds the Lord how much she hates the splendor of the wicked and the bed of the uncircumcised (verse 26), and how she has not eaten at Haman's table or partaken of the king's feast or drunk the wine of libation (verse 28). In this way, Esther's actions exhibit aspects of Maccabean/Hasmonean piety for the purpose of providing an answer to Greek beliefs concerning the Jews. Through these additions to the original Hebrew version, the author of Old Greek Esther answered Greek accusations concerning the relationship of the Jews to their God, and effectively proved that the Jews were anything but atheistic.

In addition to the preceding examples of apologetics that demonstrate the relationship of the Jews to their God and extol Jewish piety, several of the additions make polemic statements concerning the chosenness of the Jewish people, the right of the Jews to live by their own laws, and their right to defend themselves in the face of attempted genocide. In Addition C, both Mordecai and Esther refer to the Jewish people as God's people and inheritance in the context of their prayers for deliverance from annihilation. In Addition F, in which Mordecai interprets his dream that was recorded in Addition A, the identification of Israel as the people of God and the inheritance of God is further emphasized. But it is in Addition E:13-20, in which the king explains his reversal of the decree of annihilation, that brilliant apologetic answers to Greek accusations are combined with powerful polemics. In verses 15-16, the king declares that the Jews are not evildoers, but instead are governed by righteous laws and are children of the greatest God. Then in verses 19-20, the king decrees that because of their piety, righteous laws, and chosenness, the Jews are to be allowed to live by their own laws and they are to defend themselves against those who attack them. In this way, the author of Old Greek Esther countered the perceptions of Jewish xenophobia and misanthropy found in the writings of Greek authors, while simultaneously making a strong case in favor of the Jewish way of life and the right to self-defense.

This obvious intent on the part of the author undoubtedly reflects at least part of the purpose for which this book was written, as well as the probable purpose of sending it to Alexandria. The next step in understanding the significance of the additions and the purpose behind the composition of OG Esther is to determine the historical setting of its composition in Jerusalem and its arrival in Alexandria.

Dates for the Arrival of OG Esther in Alexandria and Its Composition in Jerusalem

Earlier in this chapter, an analysis of seven possible dates for the arrival of Old Greek Esther in Alexandria eliminated five of them based on various factors, such as how the colophon is worded, how a document of this type was recorded in the Ptolemaic period, and how the phrase "in the fourth year of the reign of Ptolemy and Cleopatra" is to be interpreted. As a result, there are only two possible dates that OG Esther could have been taken to Alexandria: 142 or 78/77 BCE. The conclusion was then made that, regardless of which of these two dates OG Esther arrived in Alexandria, this rewritten story of Esther was most probably composed during the Maccabean/Hasmonean period, which lasted from 164 to 63 BCE. The preceding discussions of Greek and Jewish literature from this period have established that, like I, II, and III Maccabees, the additions in Old Greek Esther provide multiple examples of how the author incorporated common accusations of Jewish xenophobia and misanthropy found in Hellenistic literature and answered them through apologetics and polemics. In order to determine whether 142 or 78/77 BCE is the more likely date for the arrival of OG Esther in Alexandria, it will be necessary to consider the historical setting in Jerusalem and Alexandria for both of those years. An analysis of current events will not only provide further insight into why Lysimachus wrote what he did in Jerusalem, but will suggest the most probable date that Dositheus took the book to Alexandria as well.

In the previous discussion of possible dates referenced by the colophon, it was noted that the majority of scholars accept the argument of Elias Bickerman and conclude with him that the colophon refers to 78/77 BCE. Bickerman's reasons for choosing this date are explained in two different articles written in 1944 and 1950, in which he discussed his interpretation of the historical events surrounding the composition of OG Esther and its arrival in Alexandria. In addition to concluding that the book was taken to Alexandria in 78/77 BCE in the fourth year of the reign of Ptolemy XII and Cleopatra V, he dated its composition in Jerusalem to the time of Alexander Janneus (103–76 BCE).[1] These dates are the

---

1. Elias J. Bickerman, "Notes on the Greek Book of Esther," in *Studies in the Book of Esther* (ed. Carey A. Moore; New York: KTAV Publishing

result of his view that the content of the additions reflect anti-Jewish writings and historical events of the late second century and early first century BCE. In particular, he stated that the two edicts in Additions B and E present the anti- and pro-Jewish arguments that were circulated around 100 BCE.[1] Furthermore, he believed that the historical background of the composition of this version of Esther was the "violent and implacable war between the Maccabees and the Greek cities in Palestine, which developed since c. 110 BC."[2] Bickerman then associated the delivery of the book in Alexandria with the publication of the pamphlet, *Against the Jews,* written by Apollonius Molon (first century BCE), which not only charged the Jews with xenophobia and exclusiveness, but repeated the story told by Posidonius concerning the annual ritualistic murder of a Greek. Bickerman also wrote that "the first anti-Jewish riots in Alexandria . . . of which we have a record" occurred in 88–87 BCE, suggesting that the combination of these riots and the pamphlet by Apollonius Molon might have set the context for the arrival of OG Esther.[3]

While Bickerman's reasons for concluding that the colophon refers to 78/77 BCE are reasonable, his understanding of the historical context for the composition of OG Esther and its arrival in Alexandria is not the only possible interpretation of the relationship of the content of the additions to anti-Jewish writings or to the historical events in Alexandria and "Palestine."[4] In contrast to his conclusion that the additions reflect anti-Jewish writings of the late second century and early first century BCE, the previous discussion of what Greek writers wrote about Jews and Judaism revealed that anti-Jewish sentiment was quite strong much earlier than 100 BCE, as evidenced by the writings

---

House, 1982), 488-520; Bickerman, "The Colophon of the Greek Book of Esther," 529-52.

1. Bickerman, "Notes on the Greek Book of Esther," 513.
2. Bickerman, "The Colophon of the Greek Book of Esther," 551.
3. *ibid.*
4. Bickerman (along with other scholars) refers to the land of Israel in the time of the Maccabees as "Palestine." However, in the time of the Maccabees and throughout the Hasmonean dynasty, the Land of Israel was referred to as "Judea" or "Israel." It was not called "Palestine" until the Romans renamed it after the revolt of Bar Kokhba in 132-135 CE. Therefore, in keeping with the historically accurate name for the land during the time of the Hasmoneans, this book will refer to the Land of Israel as "Judea" or "Israel."

of Manetho in the third century BCE. While Bickerman is not in error to observe that anti-Jewish sentiment was quite prevalent around 100 BCE, it could be erroneous to conclude that 100 BCE was the primary time period in which both anti- and pro-Jewish arguments were written. To the contrary, the survey of Greek literature demonstrated strong anti-Jewish beliefs by at least the third century, beliefs that are reflected in the books of I, II, and III Maccabees from the second century BCE as well.

Bickerman also concluded that the historical background for the composition of Old Greek Esther was the ongoing war between the Maccabees and the Greek cities in Judea and Israel, which was at its height by the time of Alexander Janneus (103–76 BCE). However, this proposed historical setting for the composition of the additions to Esther misses the point concerning the primary message of the book. The story of Esther – even the Greek version with all of its additions – emphasizes the fact that the actions of the Jews of Persia were those of self-defense in the face of attempted genocide. In contrast, the war between the Hasmoneans and the Greek cities throughout Israel by the time of Alexander Janneus was a war of aggression on the part of the Hasmoneans, waged for the purpose of extending the Hasmonean dynasty established under Simon Maccabeus in 142.

In other words, the Hasmonean war against the Greek cities "was internally bound up with the foundation of the Jewish state and with its economic development."[1] It is therefore hard to reconcile these historical realities with Bickerman's claim that the wars waged by the Hasmoneans in the late second century and early first century BCE in the Land of Israel provided the historical background for Old Greek Esther, in which the only battles the Jews were involved in were as exiles in a foreign land, and were battles of self-defense against those who attempted to annihilate them.

As has been said previously, Bickerman associated the arrival of this book in Alexandria with the publication of Apollonius Molon's pamphlet, *Against the Jews,* and the Alexandrian riots of 88–87 BCE. While the writings of Apollonius Molon were certainly quite anti-Jewish and could have motivated the sending of Old Greek Esther to Alexandria, his pamphlet was not the only anti-Jewish literature that could have had the same effect, as has been

---

1. Victor Tcherikover, *Hellenistic Civilization and the Jews,* (Grand Rapids, MI: Baker Academic, 1999), 247.

demonstrated previously in the section on Greek authors on Jews and Judaism. In addition, the riots that occurred in Alexandria in 88–87 are not the first anti-Jewish riots we have a record of, and they were not for the sole purpose of persecuting the Jews, but were part of a general revolt against Ptolemy X. The riots were related to anti-Jewish sentiment in that the Alexandrians were incensed with Ptolemy X's friendliness towards the Jews, and as such they provide evidence that "Alexandria was rife with anti-Semitism at the beginning of the first century BC."[1] However, in spite of the fact that the riots were motivated in part by Alexandrian anti-Semitism, the ultimate purpose of the riots was the removal of Ptolemy X from the throne. There is no literary record of direct actions taken against the Jews in the riots of 88–87, in contrast to accounts of Jewish persecution that occurred prior to the first century BCE.

Contrary to Bickerman, other scholars give a significant amount of attention to accounts of a dramatic persecution of the Jews that included direct actions specifically directed against the Jews early in the reign of Ptolemy VIII Physcon (145–116 BCE). According to deSilva, "The Jews in Diaspora Egypt appear . . . to have enjoyed good relations with their Ptolemaic overlords. The one notable exception appears to be a short period of persecution under Ptolemy VIII."[2] Collins says, "In view of Physcon's notorious cruelty and the opposition of the Jews in his civil war with Cleopatra II, Tcherikover and others have argued that the story [III Maccabees] is a melodramatic dramatization of the real threat to the Jews in his reign."[3] Specifically, Tcherikover has written that the "historical nucleus" of III Maccabees is "the persecution of the Jews by Ptolemy VIII."[4] And Barclay points out that not only did the Jewish opposition to Ptolemy VIII "expose the Jews of Alexandria to the wrath of the new king . . . but more than two centuries later Apion still cast this episode against the Alexandrian Jews, using it to fuel his charge that they were disloyal to the city."[5]

1. Hölbl, *A History of the Ptolemaic Empire*, 211.
2. deSilva, *Introducing the Apocrypha*, 59.
3. Collins, *Between Athens and Jerusalem*, 123.
4. Tcherikover, *Hellenistic Civilization and the Jews*, 274-5, 282.
5. John M.G. Barclay, *Jews in the Mediterranean Diaspora: From Alexander to Trajan (323 BCE-117 CE)* (Berkeley, CA: University of California Press, 1996), 38.

The young Ptolemy VIII had actually been a co-ruler with his older brother Ptolemy VI Philometor and Philometor's sister/wife Cleopatra II as early as 170 BCE, when he was installed on the throne by Antiochus Epiphanes after Antiochus invaded Egypt. However, this co-regency simply did not work and in 163 BCE, Philometor and Physcon agreed to a partition of the kingdom that left Ptolemy VIII in charge of Cyrenaica. This agreement lasted until the death of Ptolemy VI in 145, which provided Ptolemy VIII wth the opportunity to return to Alexandria and fight Cleopatra for the throne. According to Josephus in *Contra Apion* II:49-52, Ptolemy VI and Cleopatra II had appointed two Jews, Onias and Dositheus, as generals of their army. This is not surprising, because not only were Jews found in every level of the military throughout the Ptolemaic period, "they were at their most prominent under Ptolemy VI Philometor" because "he was by far the most philosemitic member of the dynasty."[1] So, when Ptolemy VIII returned to claim the throne, it was Onias who was responsible for saving Cleopatra and her sons from being exiled by Ptolemy VIII. As a result of the fact that the fight against his accession to the throne was led by a Jewish general, Ptolemy VIII instituted severe actions against all the Jews of Alexandria. After having himself proclaimed Pharaoh in 144, he instituted mass purges and expulsions of the Jews from Alexandria, actions that, according to Josephus, were followed up by an attempted annihilation of all remaining Jews.

In *Contra Apion* II:53-55, Josephus reports how Ptolemy VIII had the Jews rounded up and exposed naked and in bonds to intoxicated elephants, so that they would be trampled to death by those elephants. However, the elephants turned and killed Physcon's friends instead and the Jews instituted a day of celebration. This account of the attempted annihilation of the Jews of Alexandria is very similar to the story found in III Maccabees. In both cases, all the Jews were to be destroyed in one day by being trampled to death by intoxicated elephants; in both cases, the Jews were miraculously saved from death when the elephants turned and trampled those trying to kill the Jews; and in both cases, a yearly festival was instituted to celebrate the Jews' deliverance from destruction. The primary difference in the two

---

1. Margaret Williams, *The Jews among the Greeks and Romans: A Diasporan Sourcebook* (Baltimore, MD: Johns Hopkins University Press, 1998), 88-9.

stories is that the book of III Maccabees sets these events in the reign of Ptolemy IV Philopator (221–203 BCE), rather than that of Ptolemy VIII. As was mentioned above, Tcherikover believes that "the historical nucleus" of the story found in III Maccabees is Ptolemy VIII's persecution of the Jews, as he was the Ptolemy who "had sufficient grounds not to love his Jewish subjects."[1] This is a reasonable conclusion in the light of the fact that he was said to be "harsh in his persecution of those who opposed his accession to the throne," and the fact that "literary sources indicate that Ptolemy VIII began his rule with brutality and injustice."[2]

Not only does the story of an attempted annihilation of the Jews found in III Maccabees and Josephus fit in with the known historical context of Ptolemy VIII, but it also does not fit in with known relationships between any other Ptolemies and the Jews. With the exception of Ptolemy VIII, the rest of the Ptolemies were actually quite favorable towards the Jews. Under Ptolemaic rule in Judea from 319–198 BCE, "the Judeans enjoyed relative freedom and peace" and the Jews had the legal right to "self-regulation under the Torah."[3] In addition, "The Jews in Diaspora Egypt appear . . . to have enjoyed good relations with their Ptolemaic overlords."[4] Therefore, contrary to the conclusions of Bickerman, and in light of the known persecution of Jews in Alexandria early in the reign of Ptolemy VIII, it seems reasonable to suggest that Old Greek Esther – the story of Jews living in a foreign land who had victory over those who attempted to annihilate them – would have been a most appropriate book to send to Jews living in a foreign city in a time of intense persecution by a king who attempted to annihilate them. The combination of this historical setting and the information provided by the colophon indicates that 142 BCE is the most probable year for OG Esther to have been sent to Alexandria. If OG Esther was in fact sent to Alexandria in 142, it must have been written prior to that date. A previous discussion of some of the content of the Greek additions highlighted multiple examples of apologetics and polemics written in the context of Maccabean/Hasmonean rule. This evidence indicates that this rewritten version of Esther was composed after 164 BCE, the year the Maccabees gained control

---

1. Tcherikover, *Hellenistic Civilization and the Jews*, 275.
2. Hölbl, *A History of the Ptolemaic Empire*, 194-5.
3. deSilva, *Introducing the Apocrypha*, 46-7.
4. *ibid.*, 59.

of Jerusalem. The following discussion of relevant information from the three books of the Maccabees will provide additional support for a composition date of OG Esther between 164 and 142 BCE.

I Maccabees and the Composition of Old Greek Esther

To summarize what was written previously: the book of I Maccabees covers a period of forty years from the accession of Antiochus Epiphanes in 175 BCE to the death of Simon Maccabee in 135 BCE and gives an account of how Mattathias and his five sons refused to conform to Greek religion, how they delivered the Jews from the religious persecution of Antiochus, and how they ultimately restored political independence to Israel. The events that took place in the years between 164, when the Maccabees took control of Jerusalem and the Temple, and 143/142, when Judea was officially recognized by the Seleucid king as an independent nation, are particularly significant for this discussion because this is the proposed time period for the composition of Old Greek Esther.

According to I Maccabees 10:25-46 and 11:19 ff, the Seleucid king, Demetrius, made multiple concessions to Jonathan Maccabeus (160–143 BCE) at different times, including the confirmation of Jonathan's previous appointment as high priest by King Alexander in 152 and his consent to Jonathan's request to release Judea and three districts of Samaria from royal taxes in 145. However, Demetrius broke his word to Jonathan, prompting Jonathan and his brother Simon to wage war against numerous Greek cities throughout Judea, Samaria, and Galilee. After Jonathan was killed at Ptolemais (Akko) in 143, Simon took his place as the leader of the Maccabees. King Demetrius then made peace with Simon as he had with Jonathan, releasing him from taxes and granting him all the strongholds he had built (13:36-40). Demetrius' letter of concession to Simon is followed by the statement that "the yoke of the Gentiles was removed from Israel" in the "one hundred seventieth year" (13:41), or 143/142 BCE.[1]

---

1. In the books of the Maccabees, dates are given according to the number of years from the time of the Macedonian conquest. Therefore the "one hundred seventieth year" was 170 years since the beginning of Greek rule over Israel, or 143/142 BCE.

I Maccabees 14:35-38 then reports how Simon was made leader and high priest by the people and how he was confirmed as high priest by Demetrius. Immediately after these events, the Jews and their priests issued a decree that essentially gave absolute power to Simon (14:41-49). Not only was Simon high priest and commander – in charge of the sanctuary as well as the weapons and strongholds – but the decree specified that Simon was to be obeyed by all, that all contracts were to be written in his name, that none of the people or priests could nullify or oppose anything he said, that no assembly could be convened without his permission, and that anyone who acted contrary to anything in the decree would be punished. It is this decree that "allows one to speak formally of the Hasmonean dynasty and Judah as an independent nation."[1]

From the time the Maccabees revolted against the Seleucids and regained Jerusalem and the Temple in 164 until 143/142, when "the yoke of the Gentiles was removed from Israel," the Maccabees and all those who supported them were in a state of almost constant war against an enemy who attempted to destroy their religious observance, their identity as Jews, and even their lives.[2] Therefore, it is not surprising that the story of Esther would be particularly meaningful at this point in history. It is also not surprising that additions would be written for the purpose of countering Greek perceptions of Jewish xenophobia and misanthropy, as well as for the purpose of promoting Maccabean/Hasmonean apologetics and polemics that argued in favor of the Jewish way of life and the right to self-defense when their way of life, as well as their lives, were threatened with annihilation. Consequently, it seems probable that, as in the case of I Maccabees, the composition of OG Esther may have been sanctioned or even commissioned by the Maccabean/Hasmonean dynasty in Jerusalem sometime after they gained power in 164 BCE. As Collins says, the "emphasis on the separatist piety of Esther may be taken to reflect the Hasmonean milieu in which the translation was made" and "the Greek translation of Esther may, in a sense, be regarded as Hasmonean propaganda."[3]

---

1. Lester L. Grabbe, *An Introduction to Second Temple Judaism: History and Religion of the Jews in the Time of Nehemiah, The Maccabees, Hillel and Jesus* (London: T and T Clark, 2010), 18.
2. An exception to this might be the years between 158 and 152 BCE, when according to I Maccabees 9:73, "the sword ceased from Israel."
3. Collins, *Between Athens and Jerusalem*, 111-12.

This suggestion seems especially likely in light of the contents of the decree recorded in I Maccabees 14:41-49, in which the Jews and their priests gave what was essentially absolute power to Simon. This decree is quite informative, not only because of what it says about the power given to Simon, but because of the insight it gives into the power of the Maccabean leaders in general. A reading of I Maccabees 9-12 makes it clear that Jonathan, Simon's predecessor, held the same level of authority as Simon.[1] Therefore, whether Old Greek Esther was written during the reign of Jonathan (160–143 BCE) or at the beginning of the reign of Simon (143–135 BCE), it is reasonable to conclude that it was sanctioned or commissioned by the high priest and leader of the Hasmoneans for the purpose of promoting Hasmonean piety and observance of the law, their right to live by their own laws, and their right to defend themselves and their way of life from attempted annihilation.

Regardless of who commissioned its composition, it can be assumed that the book was sent to Alexandria under Simon's authority based on the previous conclusion that it arrived in Alexandria in 142, and based on what is known of how Simon controlled virtually every aspect of life in Judea. The fact that Simon held the position of high priest implies that Dositheus, the priest and Levite who took Old Greek Esther to Alexandria, was under the direct authority of Simon. A Levite was a sub-category of clergy within the broader category of priests, an office that was often responsible for scribal duties associated with the operation of the Temple.[2] As a priest and Levite, Dositheus was therefore an appropriate person to be given the responsibility of delivering the book to the Jewish community in Alexandria. The conclusion that this version of Esther was most probably sent to Alexandria under the authority of the high priest in Jerusalem at a time when the Jews of Alexandria were experiencing severe persecution is quite likely, as the Hasmonean apologetics and polemics contained in the book would have been applicable and meaningful to a Jewish audience facing persecution and attempted annihilation.

---

1. See in particular 9:28-31, 10:18-21, 10:25-34, 10:88, 11:20-37, 12:1-6.

2. Grabbe, *An Introduction to Second Temple Judaism*, 44.

II Maccabees and the Composition
of Old Greek Esther

The book of II Maccabees contains three features in particular that contribute to a further understanding of the historical setting of the composition of OG Esther. The first of these features is the mention of the celebration of the "feast of Mordecai" in 15:36. The reference to the celebration on the fourteenth of Adar as the "feast of Mordecai" indicates that the annual observance of Purim was established before the date of composition of II Maccabees. Furthermore, the fact that II Maccabees was written in Greek suggests that the author may have been more familiar with the Greek version than with Hebrew Esther, especially since the feast was referred to as the "feast of Mordecai," rather than "Purim," as it is named in the Hebrew text. This way of referring to the holiday reveals that the author of II Maccabees knew Old Greek Esther, which means that this version of Esther must have been written before II Maccabees. The previous conclusion that II Maccabees was written after 124 BCE confirms that Old Greek Esther must have been written prior to 124 BCE, in contrast to Bickerman's conclusion that it was composed in the time of Alexander Janneus (103–76 BCE).

The second feature of II Maccabees that contributes to a further understanding of the date of composition of Old Greek Esther is the use of letters to establish the observance of a festival. II Maccabees begins with two letters, found in 1:1-9 and 1:10-2:18, which serve as prefixes to the story that follows. Both letters were sent from the Jews in Jerusalem to the Jews in Egypt, and both letters encouraged the Jews of Egypt to keep the festival of Hanukkah, which is referred to as "the festival of booths" in both letters. The identification of Hanukkah with the festival of booths at this point in history was due to fact that both are celebrated for eight days.[1] By prefixing these two letters to the beginning of the book, it is obvious that in addition to recording Judas' victory over the Seleucids, a significant purpose for the book was to encourage Egyptian Jews to observe a festival that was important to the Jews in Jerusalem. This was accomplished through the sending of letters. According to deSilva, the second letter (1:10-2:18) was written with the intent to legitimize the

---

1. deSilva, *Introducing the Apocrypha*, 270 fn #7.

observance of the new festival, and the first letter (1:1-9), which appears to have been written later than the second, was written as a reminder to keep that festival.[1] And as Philip Alexander observes, "It is hard not to detect Hasmonean political ambition behind this tireless promotion of Hanukkah. Hanukkah and the Hasmoneans cannot be divorced; the rededication of the Temple was their finest hour. Hanukkah was a potent vehicle of Hasmonean propaganda."[2]

The use of letters by those in authority to establish a festival as demonstrated in II Maccabees has some striking parallels to the story of Esther, as well as its distribution. In Hebrew and Greek Esther, the observance of Purim is established by the sending of letters by those in authority – the letters of Mordecai and Esther in chapter 9, and the letter of the king in Greek Addition E. Furthermore, in the colophon attached to the OG version, what Dositheus took to Alexandria is referred to as the "letter" of Purim. The use of the word "letter" suggests a similarity in timing and purpose in the sending of Old Greek Esther and II Maccabees from Jerusalem to Egypt. Further similarity can be inferred from the fact that the second letter in II Maccabees begins by stating who it was from: "the people of Jerusalem and of Judea and the senate and Judas" (1:10). The inclusion of the name of Judas as one of the senders of the letter to the Jews in Egypt is evidence of how the Maccabees used their positions of authority to promote Jewish observance. This is consistent with what has already been noted concerning the authority of both Jonathan and Simon, one of whom sanctioned or commissioned the rewriting of the story of Esther, and of Simon specifically, under whose authority that story was sent to Alexandria. The fact that II Maccabees was sent to the Jews in Egypt to encourage the observance of the festival of dedication within years of the sending of the letter of Purim to the Jews in Alexandria helps to illuminate the historical setting of the composition of Old Greek Esther as well as its arrival in Alexandria. Both books serve as examples of how letters were sent from Jerusalem by those in authority to encourage Egyptian Jews to celebrate the

---

1. *ibid.*, 270.
2. Philip S. Alexander, "3 Maccabees, Hanukkah and Purim," in *Biblical Hebrews, Biblical Texts: Essays in Memory of Michael P. Weitzman* (ed. Ada Rapoport-Albert and Gillian Greenberg; London: Sheffield Academic Press, 2001), 321-39.

festivals. Indeed, "The promotion of Purim in Egypt seems to have had the backing of the Jerusalem authorities."[1]

And finally, the third feature of II Maccabees that contributes to a further understanding of the date of composition of OG Esther is the letters of Antiochus IV and V in 9:19-27 and 11:27-33, in which both kings write to the Jews to express greetings and good wishes for their health and prosperity. The letter of Antiochus V in 11:27-33, which is dated to the year 164 BCE, gives permission to the Jews to look after their own affairs, eat their own food, and observe their own laws. In addition, the king states that they shall not be persecuted as they were in the past. These provisions are quite similar to those in the letter of the Persian king in Addition E of Greek Esther, in which the Jews and their laws were exonerated, they were to be allowed to live under their own laws, and they were to be given help as they defended themselves against those who attacked them. According to Kristin De Troyer, the letters of Antiochus IV and his successor Antiochus V "constitute a primary source of inspiration for the LXX translator of Esther," and "the LXX translated and interpreted the Esther narrative in light of the events of the year 164 BCE."[2] As a result, De Troyer dates the composition of OG Esther to sometime after the death of Antiochus IV in 164 BCE. This conclusion is consistent with the evidence for Maccabean/Hasmonean influence on the additions revealed throughout this chapter, and with the conclusion that OG Esther was written between 164 and 142 BCE for the purpose of promoting Hasmonean piety and observance of the law, the right of Jews to live by their own laws, and their right to defend themselves and their way of life from attempted annihilation.

III Maccabees and the Composition of Old Greek Esther

The relevance of the book of III Maccabees to a more complete understanding of the date of composition of Old Greek Esther is indicated through features common to both books. Not only do "verbatim parallels" exist between the two stories, but "the Greek Esther constructs a model of Hellenistic Jewish identity virtually indistinguishable from that promoted by 3 Maccabees."[3]

---

1. Alexander, "3 Maccabees, Hanukkah, and Purim," 336-7.
2. De Troyer, *The End of the Alpha Text of Esther*, 398.
3. Johnson, *Historical Fictions and Hellenistic Jewish Identity*, 137, 51.

III Maccabees and the additions to Esther both incorporate the most popular accusations of Jewish xenophobia and misanthropy found in the writings of Greek authors. Haman's accusations against the Jews in Addition B:4-5 of Esther are virtually identical to III Maccabees 3:2-7, which reports how rumors were circulated against the Jews accusing them of being hateful and hostile to the government because of their separateness and special laws concerning worship and food. All of the Greek additions to Esther (except Addition B) and chapters 6 and 7 of III Maccabees respond to those accusations with apologetics and polemics that extol Jewish law and piety, the chosenness of the Jewish people, and the right of the Jews to live by their own laws. Furthermore, OG Esther and III Maccabees both provide glaring examples of Diodorus' first century BCE belief – that the need "to make an end of the race completely" was, according to the respective authorities, the result of "Jewish practices and xenophobic laws."[1] Consequently, both books establish how easily anti-Judaism becomes anti-Semitism, and how easily false accusations against the Jews develop into the perceived need to eliminate an entire people.

Conclusions

In order to determine the historical setting in which OG Esther was written, the preceding discussions have analyzed the information provided by the colophon, and then confirmed an approximate date of composition in light of information gained from Greek and Jewish literature from the same time period, and the historical events surrounding the date indicated by the colophon. The survey of Greek literature revealed overt anti-Jewish and anti-Semitic beliefs from at least 300 BCE, beliefs that were addressed by the apologetics and polemics in the additions of OG Esther, as well as those found in the books of I, II, and III Maccabees. In addition to having been written in the context of what Greek authors wrote about Jews and Judaism and in the time period of Maccabean/Hasmonean rule in Judea, the books of the Maccabees are relevant to this study because they provide information that further illuminates the historical setting in which Old Greek Esther was composed and taken to Alexandria.

---

1. Diodorus, *Bibliotheca Historica*, XXXIV-XXXV, 1:5.

It has been determined that this book was written between 164 BCE, when the Maccabees gained control of Jerusalem, and 142 BCE, the fourth year of the reign of Ptolemy VIII. The author rewrote the story of Esther for the purpose of countering Greek perceptions of Jewish xenophobia and misanthropy, and in order to promote the Jewish way of life and the right to self-defense when this way of life, as well as their lives, was threatened with annihilation.

In light of the bigger picture under consideration in this book, it is significant to note at this point that the apologetic and polemic motivation behind the changes and additions to Hebrew Esther resulted in what were certainly unintended consequences in terms of how this rewritten version would be interpreted in the future. First of all, in spite of the fact that OG Esther maintains the Hebrew version's message concerning the right to self-defense, the emphasis in the original message is changed by the predominant presence and activity of the God of Israel in OG Esther. Whereas Hebrew Esther highlights human resistance against those who intend to murder, the OG version establishes the God of Israel as the one responsible for the deliverance of the Jews. As a result, the importance of human action in response to evil is diminished. Second, as the work in Chapter Four will demonstrate, the rewriting of the Hebrew version altered the character of Esther and the actions of the Jews of Persia. These changes invite anti-Semitic critique of the story, and have significant consequences, both in terms of how this account has been interpreted historically, and in relation to the relevance of the message of Hebrew Esther to the contested legitimacy of Israel.

CHAPTER THREE

Alpha Text Esther:
When and Why Was It Written?

This chapter will answer the questions of when and why the second Greek version of Esther, known as the Alpha Text (AT), was written.[1] As with OG Esther, the determination of its historical setting will answer the question of when it was written, and the identification of the intent of the author will answer the question of why it was written. The establishment of the context and purpose behind the composition of AT Esther will reveal why additional changes were made to the Old Greek version. This information will provide further background for subsequent discussions of how historic interpretations of Esther have contributed to anti-Semitic interpretations of the story and inherited perceptions of Jews.

The Historical Setting of the Composition
of Alpha Text Esther

The historical setting in which the Alpha Text of Esther was written needs to be determined in order to identify the intent of the author, and to understand the significance of the changes made to the first Greek version of the story. Unlike Old Greek Esther, the Alpha Text does not include a colophon with information that can be used to determine even an approximate date of composition. However, a range of dates in which AT Esther was composed can be deduced from the previous conclusions concerning the date of composition of OG Esther and the textual relationships of all three versions presented in the Excursus. The combination of a date of

---

1. For the Greek text and translation of Alpha Text Esther, see David J.A. Clines, *The Esther Scroll: The Story of the Story* (Sheffield: JSOT Press, 1984).

composition for OG Esther between 164 and 142 BCE, and the fact that AT Esther is dependent on OG Esther, as demonstrated in the Excursus, means that the earliest probable date for the composition of AT Esther is 142 BCE, the year OG Esther was taken to Alexandria. The Excursus also established the fact that Josephus was dependent on the Alpha Text because his version of Esther contains some typical AT readings. Therefore, AT Esther must have been written before the work of Josephus in the late first century CE, but after 142 BCE, the latest possible date for the composition of OG Esther.

In order to determine a more specific date for the composition of the AT between 142 BCE and the late first century CE, as well as the reason AT Esther was written, it will be useful to summarize what Greek, Latin, and Jewish authors from that time period wrote about Jews and Judaism. The content of these writings can then be compared with the changes the author of AT Esther made to the story. Following the discussions of what Greek, Latin, and Jewish authors wrote between 142 BCE and the late first century CE, relevant historical events that may have inspired the author of the AT to make the changes that were made will be discussed. By looking at common themes in the literature from this time period in combination with historical events from the same era, it will be possible to identify the purpose for which AT Esther was written. As with OG Esther, these discussions will demonstrate that the author of AT Esther made significant changes for the purpose of addressing specific issues in the particular historical setting in which the book was written.

Common Themes on Jews and Judaism in Greek and Latin Authors

The survey of what Greek authors wrote about Jews and Judaism presented in Chapter Two demonstrated that beginning in the fifth century BCE with Herodotus, Greek authors showed an awareness of Jews and the practices of Judaism. However, this awareness was based on erroneous Egyptian sources. In particular, Theophrastus (372–288 BCE) demonstrated a complete misunderstanding of, and disgust for, Jewish ritual. Because "Theophrastus is known to have used Egyptian sources," Bezalel Bar-Kochva suggests that the source of information concerning

Jewish sacrifices was Egyptian, and as a result, Theophrastus "is a witness to the beginnings of Egyptian anti-Judaism."[1] Hecataeus (c. 300 BCE) wrote a detailed excursus concerning the Jews that, according to Josephus, demonstrated a significant lack of knowledge of Jewish history before the Persian period, which was undoubtedly a reflection of the anti-Jewish Egyptian priestly sources he used.[2] The work of Manetho, a priest in Heliopolis, Egypt, in the third century BCE, provides ample examples of obvious anti-Jewish writing; his work not only reveals the anti-Jewish trend in Hellenistic Egypt, but also helped to popularize already existing, recurring anti-Semitic themes.[3] Lysimachus, writing in the second or first century BCE, took "the same topic of falsehood [as Manetho] . . . but has gone far beyond them in the incredible nature of his forgeries; which plainly demonstrates that he contrived them out of his virulent hatred of our nation."[4] Diodorus (first century BCE) used Hecataeus as his authority on the Jews and preserved the contents and views of other earlier writers who would otherwise be lost in his *Bibliotheca Historica*, thereby reflecting at least 200 years of anti-Jewish writing.[5] In *Contra Apion*, Josephus acknowledged numerous Greek writers, eight of whom he named, who made many mistakes concerning the history and practices of the Jews.[6]

In addition to the recurring anti-Semitic themes concerning Jewish history and ritual that were popularized by these authors, we have seen that a "Hellenistic blood libel" was introduced by

1. Bezalel Bar-Kochva, *The Image of the Jews in Greek Literature: The Hellenistic Period* (Berkeley and Los Angeles, CA: University of California Press, 2010), 24-34.

2. Josephus, *Contra Apion*, I:183-205. From *The New Complete Works of Josephus* (trans. William Whiston; Grand Rapids, MI: Kregel Publications, 1999), 948-9. For further discussion of Hecataeus' excursus on the Jews, his Egyptian sources, and how the excursus was used in the anti-Jewish writings of Diodorus, see Bar-Kochva, *The Image of the Jews in Greek Literature*, 99-123; and Elias J Bickerman, *The Jews in the Greek Age* (Cambridge and London: Harvard University Press, 1988), 16-17.

3. Menahem Stern, *Greek and Latin Authors on Jews and Judaism: Volume I, From Herodotus to Plutarch* (Jerusalem: The Israel Academy of Sciences and Humanities, 1976), 62.

4. Josephus, *Contra Apion*, I: 304.

5. Stern, *Greek and Latin Authors on Jews and Judaism: Volume I*, 167.

6. Josephus, *Contra Apion*, I:217.

Posidonius c. 151–135 BCE. The perpetuation of this blood libel by Apollonius Molon in the first century BCE and Apion early in the first century CE, and the introduction of what appears to be another version of the blood libel by Damocritus in the first century BCE, provide further evidence of anti-Judaism in Hellenistic writings. As was said previously, the Greek writers surveyed described the Jews as "the 'evil incarnate,' denying and perverting in their xenophobic and misanthropic hatred all cherished values of humankind, conspiring against the civilized world."[1] The perception of Jewish history and ritual demonstrated by Hellenistic authors was a reflection of the anti-Jewish Egyptian sources used by these writers. However, what Greek authors wrote about Jews and Judaism then became the source of information for subsequent Roman authors as well.

Latin Authors on Jews and Judaism

Latin authors who wrote about Jews and Judaism between the composition of OG Esther and the work of Josephus – the time period in which AT Esther was composed – include Cicero, Pompeius Trogus, Seneca, and Tacitus. Cicero (106–43 BCE) is known as the greatest orator of Rome and as a writer who had significant influence over his contemporaries, as well as his successors. Negative references to Jews appear in his speeches *Pro Flacco* and *De Provinciis Consularibus*, which were given in 59 BCE and 56 BCE. In his speech in defense of Flaccus against the Jews, Cicero cast various dispersions on the Jews, and described the religion of the Jews as a "barbarae superstitioni" in contrast to Roman religion.[2] In the second speech, he identified the Jews as enemies and described them as a people "born to be slaves."[3]

Following Cicero, Pompeius Trogus (end of first century BCE to beginning of first century CE) wrote a history of the Macedonian-Hellenistic states in which he surveyed the history of the Jews in the thirty-sixth book.[4] While his work has not been preserved on its own, it is known from the *Epitome* of Justin, which was

---

1. Peter Schäfer, *Judeophobia: Attitudes toward the Jews in the Ancient World* (Cambridge, MA: Harvard University Press, 1997), 206.
2. Stern, *Greek and Latin Authors on Jews and Judaism: Volume I*, 193-201.
3. *ibid.*, 202-4.
4. *ibid.*, 332-43.

composed in the third and fourth century CE. From the *Epitome*, it appears that Pompeius Trogus' account of Jewish antiquity included the Greco-Egyptian version in which the ancestors of the Jews were lepers who were expelled from Egypt. Like other Greek and Roman writers, Trogus demonstrated a complete ignorance of Jewish history between the time of Moses and the Persians, and referred to Xerxes, king of Persia, as the first who conquered the Jews.[1] Since, as Stern points out, Trogus does not seem to have known of the Assyrian or Babylonian rule over Israel, and he "hardly knew the details of the political history of the Hasmonean revolt," "it is hard to account for the supreme importance given to Xerxes." One wants to question, along with Stern, if the importance given to Xerxes is "because this Persian king is connected with Greece," "or is it because Trogus echoes a tradition that knew something about a collision between the Jews and the Persian government under Xerxes?"[2] Whether or not Trogus knew something about an interaction between Jews and Xerxes, what he wrote about the Jews demonstrates how the Greco-Egyptian version of the early history of the Jews was perpetuated by Latin authors, who, like the Greek authors before them, were virtually ignorant of the actual origin or religion of the Jews.

Two of Cicero's Latin successors were Seneca and Tacitus, both of whom "adopted a clearly hostile stand towards Judaism."[3] Seneca (end of first century BCE to 65 CE) was the first Latin writer to explicitly write against the Jewish religion due to its impact on Roman society. In contrast to Cicero, who denigrated Jews in the context of speeches written to defend others against the Jews, and Trogus, who simply perpetuated what had been written by those who preceded him, Seneca criticized Jews and Judaism because of Jewish proselytizing and the perceived threat of the spread of Jewish customs throughout the Mediterranean world. He identified Jewish customs as superstitions, opposed Jewish monotheism, and particularly criticized the observance of the Sabbath as a lost day spent in idleness.[4]

Tacitus (56 CE–120 CE), the best known Roman historian, refers to Jews several times in his *Annals* and *Histories*, and he

---

1. *ibid.*, 338.
2. *ibid.*, 342.
3. *ibid.*, 193.
4. *ibid.*, 429-31.

gives the most detailed account of the history and religion of the Jews found in classical Latin literature in book V, sections 2-13 of *Histories*, written in the first decade of the second century CE.[1] His work is particularly significant because it "reflects the feelings of influential circles of Roman society."[2] Even though his writings post-date those of Josephus, which is the latest possible date for the composition of AT Esther, the views expressed by Tacitus are relevant to this discussion because he not only reflects the thoughts of Roman society, but reflects Hellenistic belief concerning the Jews and Judaism as well. His work, which "seems to be echoing the writings of the provincial Apion," reflects prominent themes found in the works of Greek writers.[3]

Tacitus repeated the anti-Jewish Greco-Roman account of the ancestors of the Jews as lepers who were expelled from Egypt (V:3), demonstrating that this particular view of Jewish history was not only well-entrenched, but was quite normative by the first and second centuries CE. In reference to Jewish religion, he also echoed the authors who preceded him, writing that "things sacred with us, with them have no sanctity, while they allow what with us is forbidden" (V:4). Tacitus attributed the "rest of the seventh day" to "the charm of indolence" (V:4), declared that "all their other customs, which are at once perverse and disgusting, owe their strength to their very badness", and claimed that "they regard the rest of mankind with all the hatred of enemies" (V:5). This open hostility to Jews and Judaism not only reflects the feelings of influential circles of Roman society, but is in obvious continuity with four centuries of Greek authors who preceded him as well. Because of his status in Roman society, Tacitus simultaneously reflected and influenced that society, as well as influencing future thought concerning Jews and Judaism. Views like those of Tacitus are also found in other writers of the period, such as Quintilian, Plutarch, and Apuleius. When education in Latin

1. Moses Hadas, ed., *The Complete Works of Tacitus* (New York: Random House, 1942).
2. Menachem Stern, *Greek and Latin Authors on Jews and Judaism: Volume II, From Tacitus to Simplicius* (Jerusalem: The Israel Academy of Sciences and Humanities, 1980), 1.
3. Avi Avidov, *Not Reckoned among Nations: The Origin of the so-called "Jewish Question" in Roman Antiquity* (Tübingen: Mohr Siebeck, 2009), 6.

became widespread from the sixteenth century on, there was, in particular, a revival of interest in Tacitus. As a result, the opinions of Tacitus continue to be influential today.[1]

Philo and Josephus on Jews and Judaism

The analysis of Jewish literature from the Maccabean/Hasmonean period in Chapter Two demonstrated that Jewish authors addressed the anti-Judaism of the time by incorporating popular Greek beliefs about Jews and Judaism and then answering them by extolling Jewish law and piety. This literature was apologetic as it promoted the Jewish way of life while countering Greek perceptions of Jewish xenophobia and misanthropy, and it was polemic in that it advocated for the rights of Jews to live by their own laws, and their right to self-defense when their way of life and their lives themselves were threatened with annihilation. Jewish authors who wrote later than the authors of OG Esther and the books of the Maccabees followed a very similar methodology in the face of ongoing anti-Judaism. The two most significant authors whose work is relevant to the discussion of the composition of AT Esther are Philo (20 BC–50 CE) and Josephus (37 CE–c. 100 CE). As was the case with Jewish literature from the Hasmonean period, the work of Philo and Josephus addressed anti-Judaism expressed by Greek and Latin authors through brilliant apologetics and polemics. Because the work of Philo predates that of Josephus, his work will be discussed first.

The work of Philo is significant because he lived and wrote in Alexandria, the largest Jewish community outside Judea in the Second Temple period. As a result, he is an important witness to first century CE Hellenistic Judaism, and to events that affected the Jews of Alexandria. Indeed, as "the main surviving literary figure of the Hellenized Judaism of the Second Temple period of ancient Judaism," Philo "is critical for understanding many of the currents, themes, and interpretive traditions which existed in Diaspora and Hellenistic Judaism."[2] Most of his writings

---

1. *ibid.*; Stern, *Greek and Latin Authors on Jews and Judaism: Volume II*, 1. For an excellent discussion of Latin authors from Tacitus to Simplicius (first half of the sixth century CE), see Stern, *Greek and Latin Authors on Jews and Judaism: Volume II.*
2. C.D. Yonge, *The Works of Philo: Complete and Unabridged, New Updated Version* (Peabody, MA: Hendrickson Publishers, 1993), xiii.

paraphrase and expand the biblical books of Moses and include his own philosophical commentaries on various subjects as well. His commentaries reflect Greek influence because, while his "commitment to and passion for the law of Moses was genuine," Philo also "drank deeply at the philosophical well of the Platonic tradition."[1] This was not unusual, because in his time, "much of Judaism was significantly Hellenized."[2]

In addition to all he wrote that was of a "philosophical and exegetical nature," Philo wrote "two treatises that are commonly dubbed his 'historical' treatises."[3] "Historical" is put in quotation marks because Philo's primary concern is theological or pastoral, rather than historiographical. But in spite of the fact that these compositions contain theological content, *On the Embassy to Gaius* and *Flaccus* are considered "historical," as Philo was obviously intending to record history. The fact that these two treatises differ from all his other works focusing solely on philosophical and theological subjects raises the question of why Philo wrote them. "The reason for this deviation must be sought in the historical circumstances of the Jewish community in Alexandria in the years 38–41 CE," since in these two writings, Philo gives an account of what happened, as well as his involvement in those events.[4]

By the summer of 38 CE, already existing tensions between Jews and Greeks in Alexandria reached a climax as a result of the arrival in Alexandria of the Jewish king Agrippa, who had just been appointed king of Judea by the emperor Gaius Caligula and was on his way from Rome to Judea.[5] According to Philo in *Flaccus* 21-35, violence against the Jews broke out as a result of a combination of the envy of the Alexandrians due to the fact that the Jews had a king, the Egyptians' "ancient and, in a sense, innate enmity towards the Jews," and the fact that Flaccus, the Roman governor of Egypt, had already begun persecuting the Jews. First the Alexandrians put on a play that ridiculed Agrippa, a play that, according to Philo, Flaccus failed to stop. Then they erected statues of the emperor in the synagogues and, according

---

1. *ibid.*
2. *ibid.*
3. Pieter W. van der Horst, *Philo's Flaccus: The First Pogrom, Introduction, Translation and Commentary* (Atlanta, GA: Society of Biblical Literature, 2003), 1.
4. *ibid.*, 2.
5. Agrippa was the grandson of Herod the Great.

to Philo, Flaccus was complicit in this act. In *Flaccus* 45-52, Philo expressed the concern that the desecration of the synagogues of Alexandria would be an example to others "everywhere," and in fact, the synagogue in the city of Dora was similarly desecrated in 41 CE. Claudius, who was emperor after Gaius Caligula from 41–54 CE, did seem "to have sensed a certain danger in the Alexandrian tensions that was of wider significance than just for this city,"[1] because according to Josephus, Claudius restored the rights of the Alexandrian Jews to live according to their own laws[2] and then extended those rights to all Jews in the Roman Empire.[3]

Following the desecration of the synagogues, Flaccus issued a decree that designated the Jews as "foreigners and aliens" in *Flaccus* 54. Since "Philo often employs these terms to refer to a social status distinctly less than that of a citizen," this designation indicates that whatever their citizenship status was before Flaccus issued this decree, the Alexandrian Jews were now only "second rank residents."[4] As a result, the Jews were no longer allowed to live according to their own laws and permission was given "to those who wanted to plunder the Jews" (54). There then ensued the plundering and burning of Jewish homes, synagogues, and shops, and the creation of an overcrowded ghetto (55). Not only were Jews rounded up and forced to live in one quarter of the city where many died from disease and famine (55-63), but unchecked violence was perpetrated upon the Jews at every opportunity. If the they left the ghetto to find food, they were killed by mobs with swords, burned to death, suffocated by smoke, dragged through town by ropes until they were dead, tortured, and crucified (64-72). The council of Jewish elders was arrested, paraded through town, stripped, scourged, and executed as well (74).

As a result of these events in the summer and fall of 38 CE, Philo was commissioned to lead a Jewish delegation to Rome to intercede for the Jews with the emperor, Gaius Caligula, in the spring of 39 CE. In addition to the Jewish delegation, a delegation of Alexandrian Greeks headed by Apion also went to Rome for the

---

1. Van der Horst, *Philo's Flaccus*, 144.
2. Josephus, *Jewish Antiquities*, 19.284-6. From *The New Complete Works of Josephus* (trans. William Whiston; Grand Rapids, MI: Kregel Publications, 1999).
3. *ibid.*, 19.287-91.
4. Van der Horst, *Philo's Flaccus*, 155.

purpose of arguing against the Jews before Gaius. Philo's account of this trip and his role in the events is described in his *On the Embassy to Gaius*.[1] After being kept waiting for months, they were finally given an audience with the emperor. The Jews' primary argument was that they should be allowed to live according to their own laws, while the Greeks pointed out that the Jews refused to sacrifice to the emperor. After what Philo describes as a long, exhausting, and terrifying interaction with the emperor, in which their "pleadings on behalf of justice were thus broken up, and cut short, and interrupted, and crushed as one may almost say,"[2] Gaius finally commanded the Jews to depart without having given any decision as to whether the Jews would be allowed to live by their laws or whether other states would also "overturn every principle of justice in respect of those of their countrymen who arrayed themselves in opposition to the national laws and customs of the Jews."[3] As it turned out, the petition of the Jews would never be answered by Gaius Caligula. The reinstatement of the rights of the Jews of Alexandria did not happen until 41 CE, when, following the death of Gaius, the new emperor, Claudius, sent an edict to the Alexandrians in which he confirmed the right of the Jews to live by their laws.

At this point, it is appropriate to discuss some of the writings of Josephus, as he not only mentions the events that took place in Alexandria and Rome, but is also the source of our knowledge of not just one, but two edicts from Claudius that gave Jews the right to live according to their own laws. This discussion will draw from parts of *Jewish Antiquities* and *Contra Apion* that are relevant to the historical context of the composition of AT Esther. [4] *Jewish Antiquities* was written c. 93–94 CE, and presents all of Jewish history from the book of Genesis to events in the lifetime of Josephus. *Contra Apion* was written c. 100 CE as a defense against all the anti-Jewish writings of the preceding four centuries.

As a first century CE Jew from Judea, Josephus is an important witness to the history of the Jews of Judea through his own lifetime, as well as to first-century Judaism. His *Jewish Antiquities* is "the oldest systematic commentary on the historical books of the Bible

---

1. See *On the Embassy to Gaius* in Yonge, *The Works of Philo*, 757-90.
2. Philo, *On the Embassy to Gaius*, 366.
3. *ibid.*, 371.
4. *Jewish Antiquities* and *Contra Apion* are found in Whiston, *The New Complete Works of Josephus*, 47-661 and 937-81.

that has come down to us,"[1] and a source of Jewish history for the time period following that which is covered by the biblical books as well. Josephus' rewritten Bible in the form of the *Antiquities* is an excellent example of apologetics and polemics, defending the history and religion of the Jews while advocating for their right live by their own laws. Since we know that by the time Josephus wrote the *Antiquities* he was living in Rome and writing for a local audience,[2] the intentionality of the apologetics and polemics is obvious as "every sentence is a calculated transaction between this author and his Roman audience."[3]

In *Jewish Antiquities* 18.257-260, Josephus mentions the events in Alexandria and Rome in 38–39 CE by recording what he called a "disturbance" between the Jews and the Greeks of Alexandria. As a result of this "disturbance," "ambassadors were chosen out of each party that were at variance, who came to Gaius" in Rome. The leader of the Greek embassy was Apion, "who uttered many blasphemies against the Jews, and among other things he said, he charged them with neglecting the honors that belonged to Caesar . . . by which he hoped to provoke Gaius to anger at the Jews." "But Philo . . . a man eminent on all accounts . . . and one not unskillful in philosophy was ready to . . . make his defense against those accusations."[4] However, in agreement with what Philo wrote in *On the Embassy to Gaius*, Josephus reported that Gaius prevented Philo from making a complete defense, and commanded the Jews to leave without giving any ruling concerning the rights of the Jews.

As has been said previously, the petition of the Jews would never be answered by Gaius Caligula. But following the death of Gaius in 41 CE, the new emperor, Claudius, issued two edicts that gave Jews the right to live according to their own laws. According to Josephus, the emperor restored the rights of the Alexandrian Jews, which had been deprived them "on account of the madness of Gaius,"[5] and then extended those same rights to all Jews in the Roman Empire, because he judged them "worthy of such a favor,

---

1. Louis H. Feldman, *Studies in Josephus' Rewritten Bible* (Atlanta, GA: Society of Biblical Literature, 1998), xix.
2. Whiston, *The New Complete Works of Josephus*, 12.
3. Steve Mason, *Josephus, Judea and Christian Origins: Methods and Categories* (Peabody, MA: Hendrickson Publishers, 2009), 43.
4. Josephus, *Jewish Antiquities*, 18.259.
5. *ibid.*, 19.279-85.

on account of their faithfulness and friendship to the Romans."[1] It is interesting to note that these two edicts were issued after there was "an insurrection of the Jews against the Greeks" following the death of Gaius.[2] In order to "quiet that disturbance," Claudius sent the first of the edicts giving Alexandrian Jews the right to live by their own laws,[3] followed by the second edict granting the same rights to all Jews in the empire.[4]

As we know from both Philo and Josephus, Apion was the leader of the Greek delegation to Rome in opposition to the Jewish delegation led by Philo. It is obvious from Josephus' account of the events in his *Antiquities* that he considered Apion a serious enemy "who uttered many blasphemies against the Jews."[5] However, Josephus had much more to say about Apion than the role he played in opposing Philo in Rome. His final work, *Contra Apion* – which is actually composed of two books – provides abundant evidence of how much of a threat Josephus considered Apion. In book two, Josephus responds specifically to the attacks of Apion, answering all of Apion's slanders of the Jews by arguing in favor of the superiority of Jewish law and culture. This work follows book one, which is directed against all writers who wrote against the history and/or the religion of the Jews, and is a dramatic example of a Jewish apologetic response to widespread anti-Jewish writings demonstrated in the work of Greek and Latin authors through the time of Tacitus. As Hans Conzelmann has written, "In this writing Josephus has preserved the traditional forms of apologetic in their purest state."[6]

Contra Apion as a whole is such an articulate defense of Judaism against centuries of anti-Jewish writing that "the book remains one of the most brilliant defenses of Judaism extant."[7] The combination of the works of Josephus and Philo demonstrates the continuing need in the first century CE to provide a thorough

---

1. *ibid.*, 19.287-91.
2. *ibid.*, 19.278.
3. *ibid.*, 19.279.
4. *ibid.*, 19.288.
5. *ibid.*, 18.257.
6. For an in-depth discussion of the apologetic content of *Contra Apion*, see Hans Conzelmann, *Gentiles, Jews, Christians: Polemics and Apologetics in the Greco-Roman Era* (trans. M. Eugene Boring; Minneapolis, MN: Fortress Press, 1992), 219-25.
7. Whiston, *The New Complete Works of Josephus*, 14.

Jewish response to on-going anti-Judaism expressed by Latin authors and the Greek authors on whom they were dependent, something that Philo and Josephus succeeded in doing through brilliant apologetics and polemics.

Common Themes in Philo, Josephus, Maccabees, OG, and AT Esther

Relevant material found in AT Esther is remarkably similar to that of the apologetics and polemics of Philo and Josephus. It is also quite similar to that of OG Esther which, as was discussed in Chapter Two, is much like that of the three books of Maccabees. In spite of multiple changes, it is obvious that the author of the AT echoed the apologetics and polemics of the author of the OG. In so doing, the author demonstrated the need to answer the same issues addressed by the authors of OG Esther and the books of the Maccabees, as well as those addressed by Philo and Josephus.

For example, in AT Addition B:16-17, the author incorporated popular beliefs about Jews and Judaism by using the identical terms found in OG Addition B:4-5 that identify the Jews as a "hostile people" who "in their laws are opposed to other people," who are ready to "lead an army against everyone," who commit the "worst evil deeds," and who oppose all people because of their "perverse laws." As in OG Addition E:13, the author of the AT countered these charges in AT Addition E:26-27 by having the king refer to Mordecai as the "savior" of the kingdom, to Esther as his "blameless partner," and to the Jews as those governed by "most righteous laws." The king's statement refutes the perceptions of xenophobia and misanthropy reflected in AT Addition B:16-17 by demonstrating the importance of Esther and Mordecai to the Persian king, and exalting the laws of the Jews as righteous at the same time as identifying the Jews as the "sons of the only true God."

In addition to this refutation of charges of xenophobia and misanthropy, the AT joins the OG and other Jewish authors in including a broader defense of Jews and Judaism. Much like OG Esther, the AT emphasizes the relationship of Mordecai and Esther to the God of Israel from the very beginning of the book. Addition A includes Mordecai's dream, which is attributed to God, and Addition C portrays Mordecai and Esther praying to the Lord concerning the edict that called for the destruction of the entire Jewish people. In their prayers, numerous statements are made that remind the reader of intertextual connections to belief in the God of Israel, the Jews' relationship to Abraham, their redemption from Egypt, and their identity as God's inheritance. When Esther goes before the king uninvited in AT 6:7, God is credited with changing the spirit of the king from anger to gentleness. In Addition E, when the king writes the letter to counteract the edict calling for the annihilation of the Jews, even the Persian king is made to sound as if he believes in the God of the Jews. And finally, in Addition F, Mordecai credits God with what has happened in the context of the interpretation of his dream from Addition A.

Addition C – in which Mordecai and Esther pray concerning the decree that called for the destruction of the entire Jewish people – serves as an excellent example of how the author answered popular beliefs about Jews and Judaism by extolling Jewish law and piety. Just as in OG Esther, prayer and dependence on the Lord is emphasized, as well as the importance of humility in prayer, circumcision, and dietary regulations. And like OG Esther, AT Esther's prayer takes place only after she has taken off her queenly apparel, put on garments of mourning, covered her head with ashes, and completely humbled her entire body. In C:26 and C:28, Esther reminds the Lord how much she hates the splendor of the wicked and the bed of the uncircumcised, and how she has not honored the king's feasts or drunk the wine of libation.

Likewise, several of the additions include polemic statements concerning the chosenness of the Jewish people, the right of the Jews to live by their own laws, and their right to defend themselves in the face of attempted genocide. Just as in OG Esther, both Mordecai and Esther refer to the Jewish people as God's people and inheritance, and Mordecai's interpretation of his dream emphasizes the identification of Israel as the people of God.

But it is in Addition E, in which the king explains his reversal of the decree of annihilation, that brilliant apologetic answers to common accusations are combined with powerful polemics. In verse 27, the king declares that the Jews are not evildoers, but instead are governed by most righteous laws and are sons of the only true God. Then in verse 29, the king decrees that because of their piety, righteous laws, and chosenness, the Jews are to be allowed to live by their own laws and are to be given reinforcements so that they can defend themselves against those who attack them. In this way, the author of AT Esther countered the perceptions of Jewish xenophobia and misanthropy found in the writings of non-Jewish authors, while simultaneously making a strong case in favor of the Jewish way of life and the right to self-defense.

The fact that the author of the AT made use of the apologetic and polemic material written by the author of OG Esther, combined with the fact that the apologetics and polemics of Philo and Josephus are so similar to those of the Maccabees, demonstrates that the Greek perceptions of Jews and Judaism (and their reflection of the anti-Jewish Egyptian sources they used) continued to influence subsequent Roman authors. Whenever AT Esther was written, it is evident that it was written for the purpose of addressing anti-Judaism, as well as for the purpose of advocating for the rights of Jews to defend themselves and live by their own laws.

A Date of Composition for AT Esther

Because the apologetic and polemic material in AT Esther is so much like that of OG Esther, the books of the Maccabees, Philo, and Josephus, it is not possible to determine a specific date of composition for AT Esther between 142 BCE and the work of Josephus based on its content alone. Since this corpus of Jewish literature addresses issues that confronted Jews in Judea and Alexandria within this time period, it is necessary to look at historical events in both of these centers of Jewish life. This discussion will demonstrate that just as in the case of OG Esther, the Alpha Text was written for the purpose of addressing specific issues in a particular historical context.

The preceding discussion of the historical setting of OG Esther demonstrated that it was taken to Alexandria in response to a particular time of crisis for the Jews of Alexandria. Contrary to Bickerman's conclusion that the historical background for the composition of OG Esther was the ongoing war between the Maccabees and Greek cities in Judea and Israel, the analysis in Chapter Two revealed that this setting for the composition of the additions to Esther misses the point concerning the primary message of the book. The story of Esther emphasizes self-defense in the face of attempted genocide, whereas the war between the Hasmoneans and the Greeks was a war of aggression on the part of the Hasmoneans, waged for the purposes of extending the dynasty first established under Simon Maccabeus in 142 BCE.

In other words, the Maccabean war against the Greeks "was internally bound up with the foundation of the Jewish state."[1] It is therefore hard to reconcile these historical realities with Bickerman's claim that the wars waged by the Hasmoneans in the late second century and early first century BCE in the Land of Israel provided the historical background for OG Esther, in which the only battles the Jews were involved in were as exiles in a foreign land and were battles of self-defense against those who were attempting to annihilate them. Since AT Esther preserves so much of the content of the additions in OG Esther, including the polemics concerning the right of the Jews to defend themselves against attempted annihilation in a foreign land, there was no need for AT Esther to be written in the context of late second or early first century BCE Judea when the Hasmoneans were in control and Jews were not threatened with annihilation by the Greeks.

Hasmonean control of Judea essentially ended in 63 BCE, when Judea was conquered by Roman legions under the leadership of Pompey. When Pompey reached Jerusalem, he entered the Temple and the Holy of Holies, thus profaning it. This sacrilege resulted in the emergence of apocalyptic anti-Roman literature such as *The Psalms of Solomon,* the *Kittim* from Qumran, and the *Third Sibyl.*[2] This literature was written between 48 BCE and 40 CE in Judea, and expresses the Jewish hope that Rome would be defeated by divine justice in retribution for the profaning of the Temple. However, in spite of Pompey's lack of respect for the Temple and the Holy of Holies, "between Pompey's capture of Jerusalem in 63 BCE and the destruction of the Temple after the Judean War in 70 CE, there is no evidence of excessively harsh regulations coming directly from Rome and aimed directly at the Jewish cult."[3]

---

1. Victor Tcherikover, *Hellenistic Civilization and the Jews* (Grand Rapids, MI: Baker Academic, 1999), 247.
2. For a detailed discussion of this literature, see Mireille Hadas-Lebel, *Jerusalem Against Rome* (Leuven: Peeters, 2006), 22-39.
3. *ibid.,* 42.

Not only is there no evidence of excessive Roman regulations prohibiting Jewish practice prior to the war of 66–70 CE, there is also no evidence that the Jews were in danger of attempted annihilation simply because they were Jews. The destruction of the Temple in 70 CE and the subsequent prohibitions against Judaism were standard Roman procedure towards a conquered enemy who had rebelled, and were not actions directed against Jews just because they were Jews. Because AT Esther is not the same type of literature as the apocalyptic works written in Judea in the late first century BCE and early first century CE, and the Judean War was started by the Jews and was a response to an attempted annihilation of the Jews, it does not seem likely that AT Esther was written to address this particular historical context. Furthermore, the polemics of AT Esther argue in favor of the Jews' right to live by their own laws, and prior to 66 CE, this was not the issue it became after 70 CE. Therefore, it seems unlikely that AT Esther was written in Judea before 66 CE.

Since it seems unreasonable to suggest that AT Esther was written in response to events in Judea in the late second or early first century BCE when the Hasmoneans were in control and Jews were not threatened with annihilation by the Greeks, and it is not likely it was written in late first century BCE or first century CE Judea either, it is logical to look next at historical events in Alexandria for a possible historical context for the composition of AT Esther. Because OG Esther was taken to Alexandria in response to a particular time of crisis for the Jews of Alexandria during the reign of Ptolemy VIII Physcon (145–116 BCE), it is possible that AT Esther was written in response to another time of crisis for Alexandrian Jews, especially in light of the AT's dependence on the Old Greek.

Following the events that occurred early in the reign of Ptolemy VIII and the arrival of OG Esther in Alexandria in 142 BCE, there is no other record of persecution of Jews throughout the remaining period of Ptolemaic rule. In fact, "The Jews in Diaspora Egypt appear . . . to have enjoyed good relations with their Ptolemaic overlords. The one notable exception appears to be a short period of persecution under Ptolemy VIII."[1] The only other disturbance in Ptolemaic Alexandria that had any relationship to anti-Semitism besides the persecution in the time

---

1. David A. deSilva, *Introducing the Apocrypha: Message, Context and Significance* (Grand Rapids, MI: Baker Academic, 2002), 59.

of Ptolemy VIII was the riots of 88–87 BCE. The riots were related to anti-Jewish sentiment in that the Alexandrians were incensed with Ptolemy X's friendliness towards the Jews. However, the ultimate purpose of the riots was the removal of Ptolemy X from the throne, and there is no literary record of direct actions against the Jews. All in all, the period of Ptolemaic rule over Egypt was a time of cooperation between the Ptolemies and the Jews, in which the Jews were given the right of residence in Alexandria and one of the five districts of the city, where they were allowed to live by their own laws.[1] The privileges the Ptolemies gave the Jews included the recognition of the Sabbath, the ability to obtain ritually pure oil, and their own civil government.[2] In addition, "Jews throughout Egypt were included among the Hellene immigrant and upper class."[3] Jews demonstrated their loyalty to their rulers without compromising their beliefs, Jewish places of worship were declared inviolate, and Jews served in the army, the police force, and as civil servants throughout the Ptolemaic period.[4]

When the Romans took over Alexandria from the Ptolemies, freedom for the Jews to practice their religion was maintained. According to both Philo and Josephus, all the Roman emperors protected the rights of Jews and the practice of Judaism until the time of Gaius Caligula (37–41 CE). "The privileges the Jews enjoyed were based on 'the principle, dear to the Romans, of the free exercise of national customs for all the people,' a principle that carried the force of law. . . . [T]he observance of those customs constituted not merely tolerance but a genuine right, and any violation of this right was thus illegal."[5] However, life for the Jews of Alexandria changed abruptly soon after 37 CE, when Gaius became emperor.

After becoming emperor, Gaius instituted his personal cult, in which he was to be worshipped as a full-fledged god. This created

1. For a summary of primary sources that document the positive interaction between the Jews and the Ptolemies, see Margaret Williams, *The Jews among the Greeks and Romans: A Diasporan Sourcebook* (Baltimore, MD: Johns Hopkins University Press, 1998), 87–91.

2. Leo Duprée Sandgren, *Vines Intertwined: A History of Jews and Christians from the Babylonian Exile to the Advent of Islam* (Peabody, MA: Hendrickson Publishers, 2010), 218.

3. *ibid.*, 217.

4. Williams, *The Jews among the Greeks and Romans*, 88.

5. Hadas-Lebel, *Jerusalem Against Rome*, 47.

severe difficulties for the Jews, as they could not participate in emperor worship. There were also other consequences of Gaius' ascension that affected life for Alexandrian Jews. Flaccus, the Roman governor of Alexandria, was suddenly in a threatened position due to his relationship with the previous emperor, Tiberius. As a result of his fear and insecurity over his position, he became vulnerable to Greek nationalists, who offered to protect him against Gaius if he would rule against the Jews in their aspirations for Greek citizenship.[1] In order to keep his end of the bargain, Flaccus began to rule against the Jews in lawsuits, and undermined their civil position by issuing a proclamation that designated them "aliens and foreigners."

Already existing tensions between Jews and Greeks in Alexandria reached a climax in August 38 CE as a result of the arrival in Alexandria of the Jewish king Agrippa. While the details of the persecution and violence that followed have been summarized previously in the discussion as to why Philo wrote *On the Embassy to Gaius* and *Flaccus*, it is worth noting that the accompanying violation of the Jews' religious freedom in Alexandria in 38–39 CE actually broke Roman law.[2] As part of the overall violence against the Jewish community as a whole, many synagogues were destroyed. Synagogues that were not destroyed were desecrated and made unfit for use through the installation of images of Gaius. As a result, it became impossible for the Jews to observe their customs, which, until 38 CE, had been protected under Roman law.

---

1. E. Mary Smallwood, *The Jews Under Roman Rule: From Pompey to Diocletian* (Leiden: Brill, 1976), 237.
2. For more details concerning the events of 38-40 CE and of Flaccus' involvement in the prevention of Alexandrian Jews from observing the Sabbath, the allowance of images of the emperor in the synagogues, the decree against Jewish rights of citizenship, the establishment of the first known Jewish ghetto, and the killing of Jews and the plundering of their abandoned homes and businesses, see Sandra Gambetti, *The Alexandrian Riots of 38 CE and the Persecution of the Jews: A Historical Reconstruction* (Leiden: Brill, 2009), 137-93; Smallwood, *The Jews under Roman Rule*, 235-42; John J. Collins, *Jewish Cult and Hellenistic Culture: Essays on the Jewish Encounter with Hellenism and Roman Rule* (Leiden: Brill, 2005), 181-91; Schäfer, *Judeophobia*, 136-140; John M.G. Barclay, *Jews in the Mediterranean Diaspora: From Alexander to Trajan (323 BCE-117 CE)* (Berkeley, CA: University of California Press, 1996), 51-55; and Josephus, *Jewish Antiquities*, Books 18-20.

At this point, it is necessary to refer back to the previous discussion of Philo, who lived through these events and took an active role in response to these events. In light of the history of religious freedom the Jews of Alexandria had enjoyed under the Ptolemies and the Romans until the reign of Gaius Caligula, Philo's reasons for writing *On the Embassy to Gaius* and *Flaccus* are even more understandable. Not only were the historical circumstances of the Jewish community in Alexandria in the years 38–40 CE in sharp contrast to their preceding experiences, but because of their previous freedoms, Philo and the Jews of Alexandria obviously felt they had a right to appeal to the emperor for a reinstatement of the rights of the Jews to live by their own laws, as this was consistent with Roman law.

As a result of the preceding discussions, it is now possible to conclude that the persecution of the Jews of Alexandria in 38–39 CE and the resultant embassy to Gaius in Rome in 39–40 CE is the only probable historical context for the composition of AT Esther in the time period between the composition of OG Esther and the writings of Josephus.[1] In contrast to the other possible historical contexts that have been surveyed in this time period, the events that took place in Alexandria and Rome are unique in terms of their similarity to the issues addressed by AT Esther. In agreement with this conclusion, Kristin De Troyer states that, based on characteristic features found in the text itself, the changes made in the details of the story reflect this difficult period of time for the Jews of Alexandria.[2]

The type of statements found in AT Addition E: 26-29 would be especially pertinent to the case Philo attempted to present to Gaius. The king's reference to Mordecai as the "savior" of the kingdom, to Esther as his "blameless partner," and to the Jews as those governed by "most righteous laws" makes the case that the Jews are loyal subjects to a foreign king. Furthermore, the king declares that the Jews are not evildoers, and are sons of the only true God. Because of their loyalty to the king and their righteous laws, he argues, the Jews should be allowed to live by their own laws and should be allowed to defend themselves in

---

1. For an in-depth discussion of the dating of the embassy to Gaius, see Smallwood, *The Jews Under Roman Rule*, 242-5.

2. Kristin De Troyer, *The End of the Alpha Text of Esther: Translation and Narrative Technique in MT 8:1-17, LXX 8:1-17, and AT 7:14-41* (Atlanta, GA: Society of Biblical Literature, 2000), 400-402.

the face of attempted genocide. Indeed, these kinds of arguments are certainly of the type that Philo would have had to make to the emperor as he argued for the rights of the Jews in the context of current events in Alexandria.

The Date of Composition and the Author's Identity

Now that the historical setting of the composition of AT Esther has been identified as the events of 38–40 CE, it is possible to propose the author's identity, as well as the setting and date of composition. Since the events of 38–40 took place in both Alexandria and Rome, it is reasonable to suggest that AT Esther could have been written in either city at some point in this two-to-three-year time period. According to De Troyer, specific indicators for a date of composition include internal evidence that points to a Jewish author, who was familiar with OG Esther and rewrote elements of that version in Rome for the benefit of a Gentile audience.[1] Furthermore, she suggests the possibility that Philo may have been that author when she writes, "It is possible that the AT of Esther was in fact one of the five books of Philo which dealt with the Jewish question [during the time of Gaius], of which only the *Legatio ad Gaium* and *In Flaccum* have survived."[2]

Although it is not possible to establish the identity of the author of the AT with certainty, this is not an unreasonable hypothesis for several reasons. First of all, Philo was an Alexandrian Jew, who would have certainly been familiar with OG Esther, as OG Esther was taken to Alexandria in 142 BCE. Second, Philo was a prolific author who is known to have written five books that dealt with Jewish issues. As De Troyer mentioned, only two of them are known to have survived. Therefore, it is possible that AT Esther may be one of the other three books by Philo. Third, based on his own account, as well as that of Josephus, Philo is known to have been in Rome to see Gaius between 39 and 40 CE.[3] Not only did Philo have plenty of time to write in the months that the delegation was kept waiting to see the emperor, but Rome would be the most logical city in which to write a work that would have been written for the purpose of influencing Gaius. And finally, we

---

1. *ibid.*, 402.
2. *ibid.*, 402.
3. For a detailed discussion of the dating of Philo's embassy to Gaius, see Smallwood, *The Jews under Roman Rule*, 242-5.

know from his two surviving works and the fact that he went to Rome to intercede with the emperor just how concerned Philo was about the events in Alexandria. Philo's concern is corroborated by Josephus, who wrote that Philo's purpose in going to Rome was to make a defense against the accusations of Apion and the Greeks of Alexandria.[1] The combination of the fact that Philo would have been familiar with OG Esther in Alexandria, the fact that he had motive to rewrite elements of that version for a Gentile audience, and the fact that he had opportunity to write in Rome while he waited to see Gaius indicates that what is now known as the Alpha Text of Esther could have been one of the books Philo wrote concerning Jewish issues in the time of Gaius Caligula.

Whether or not Philo was the author of the AT, we know that his efforts to persuade Gaius concerning the rights of the Jews of Alexandria were not successful.[2] We also know from Josephus that the next emperor, Claudius, issued an edict that restored the rights of the Alexandrian Jews following a Jewish insurrection after the death of Gaius in January 41 CE.[3] This uprising was the result of the fact that "the nation of the Jews, which had been very much mortified under the reign of Gaius and reduced to very great distress by the people of Alexandria, recovered itself, and immediately took up their arms to fight for themselves."[4] It was in order to "quiet that disturbance" that Claudius sent the first of two edicts giving Jews the right to live by their own laws.[5]

The first edict, which specifically addressed the situation in Alexandria, re-established "all the rights, religious and political, held by the Jews before August 38," which included safeguarding the "sanctity of the synagogues."[6] This edict was followed by a second, granting the same rights to all Jews in the empire. The fact that a second edict "confirming for all Jews throughout the empire the same privileges as the Jews in Alexandria enjoyed" was deemed necessary is evidence of the existence of anti-Semitism beyond the confines of the city of Alexandria.[7] Further evidence of violent anti-Semitism is demonstrated by the persistence of

---

1. Josephus, *Jewish Antiquities*, 18.257-9.
2. Philo, *On the Embassy to Gaius*, 366-73.
3. Josephus, *Jewish Antiquities*, 19.278.
4. *ibid.*, 19.278.
5. *ibid.*, 19.279.
6. *ibid.*, 19.287-91.
7. *ibid.*, 19.287-291.

tensions that prompted a letter to Alexandria from Claudius in November 41, in which he addressed "the violence and rioting, or rather, to describe it accurately, the war against the Jews."[1] This letter confirmed again that "as long-established residents in Alexandria, the Jews are to be allowed to retain the religious liberty which Augustus had granted to them and which his own edict has restored."[2]

Conclusions

In light of the content of AT Esther, it is entirely possible this text may have influenced the emperor Claudius to issue the two edicts that protected the rights of Jews. It is also conceivable that this version of Esther encouraged the insurrection in Alexandria that preceded those edicts. These suggestions are not improbable due to previous conclusions concerning when and why this second Greek interpretation of the story of Esther was written.

It has been determined that the persecution of the Jews of Alexandria in 38–39 CE and the resultant embassy to Gaius in Rome in 39–40 CE is the only probable historical context for the composition of AT Esther. It is obvious in consideration of the events discussed above that it must have been written before Claudius issued his edict restoring the rights of Alexandrian Jews early in 41 CE, as there would have been no need to write a book that argued in favor of those rights after they had been restored. Therefore, it seems reasonable to conclude that AT Esther was written between 38 and 40 CE for the purpose of advocating for the restoration of the rights of the Jews of Alexandria, and to encourage them to defend themselves against violent pogroms.

The fact that the apologetics and polemics of AT Esther are so similar to those of OG Esther, combined with the fact that the apologetics and polemics of Philo and Josephus are so similar to those in the books of the Maccabees, demonstrates that Greek perceptions of Jews and Judaism – which in turn reflect their anti-Jewish Egyptian sources – continued to influence subsequent Roman authors. However, as history makes abundantly clear, anti-Judaism and anti-Semitism did not end with the Romans.

---

1. Smallwood, *The Jews under Roman Rule*, 246-9.
2. *ibid*. For further discussion of Claudius' letter to Alexandria, see Gambetti, *The Alexandrian Riots of 38 CE*, 220-27.

Rather, these forces have continued to thrive from antiquity until the present, and, ironically enough, have been fed in part by the additional content found in AT and OG Esther.

In short, the apologetic and polemic motivation behind the changes and additions to the Hebrew version has resulted in what were certainly unintended consequences. The content of both Greek interpretations of Esther encourage anti-Semitic critique of the story and negative perceptions of Jews. The fact that these perceptions are so similar to beliefs that feed current Christian anti-Zionism is of particular concern at a time when Jewish lives, as well as their way of life, are once again threatened with annihilation.

CHAPTER FOUR

The Greek Versions:
Historic Use and Literary Comparisons

This chapter will begin by looking at the use of Old Greek and Alpha Text Esther since the time of their composition. A knowledge of *which* version of the story was being read *when, where,* and *by whom* is foundational for understanding how historic understandings of Esther have contributed to anti-Semitic interpretations of the story. Following a discussion of the use of the two Greek versions of Esther throughout history, literary comparisons of particular elements in the Old Greek version with those in the Hebrew will demonstrate that the changes made in the Greek versions are the source of traditional interpretations and present-day beliefs concerning Jews.

It is noteworthy that it is the Greek versions – and in particular OG Esther – that are the source of anti-Semitic critique of the story and negative perceptions of Jews because OG Esther is the version included in the Septuagint. The Septuagint is read by a significant part of the Church today, which means it is the Old Greek version of Esther that is familiar to those readers. As a result, the Old Greek version continues to feed Christian anti-Semitic interpretation of the story of Esther.

Because Old Greek Esther is included in the Septuagint, insight into *who* was reading this version of Esther and *when* they were reading it can be gained by surveying the history of the translation of the Septuagint, its subsequent use by Jews and Christians compared with the use of the Hebrew Bible, and the authority attributed to the Septuagint by the Early Church. This survey will provide an important background for subsequent discussions of how historic anti-Semitic interpretations of the story contribute to a perception of Jews that is nearly identical to the one that directly, or indirectly, influences Christian anti-Zionism.

The History of the Translation of the Septuagint

The books of the Hebrew Bible that became part of the Septuagint were originally translated by Jews for Jews who could no longer read Hebrew during the Hellenistic period, and specifically for the concentration of Jews located in Alexandria, Egypt.[1] In fact, "the Septuagint is in its original form a typically Jewish translation."[2] The formation of the Septuagint in general, and the composition of Old Greek Esther in particular, reflect the tension of maintaining a Jewish identity at the same time as being Hellenized. More specifically, the composition of OG Esther demonstrates an effort to preserve the story of Esther, while at the same time making changes and adding features for the purpose of making that story more acceptable in Greek culture. However, "Hellenistic Judaism was by no means a capitulation to Hellenism. . . . [I]t was a highly creative effort to protect Jewish religious identity."[3] In order to maintain this identity, the Hebrew Bible was translated into Greek and the Septuagint "was accorded the status of an inspired text in the Hellenistic synagogue."[4] Having a Greek translation of the Bible while living immersed in Greek culture enabled Jews to maintain their Jewish identity, and gave them the means with which to present "Judaism in terms which a Greek could understand and appreciate."[5] In the case of the Greek version of Esther, the addition of the presence of God and the piety of Esther that is absent in the Hebrew version seems to reflect the

1. For a summary of the history of Jews in Hellenistic Egypt and the importance of the translation of the Bible into Greek, see Abraham Wasserstein and David J. Wasserstein, *The Legend of the Septuagint from Classical Antiquity to Today* (Cambridge: Cambridge University Press, 2006), 6-18; John M.G. Barclay, *Jews in the Mediterranean Diaspora: From Alexander to Trajan (323 BCE–117 CE)* (Berkeley, CA: University of California Press, 1996), 27-47; and John J. Collins, *Between Athens and Jerusalem: Jewish Identity in the Hellenistic Diaspora* (Grand Rapids, MI: Eerdmans, 2000), 64-9.
2. Henning Graf Reventlow, *History of Biblical Interpretation, Volume I: From the Old Testament to Origen* (trans. Leo G. Perdue; Atlanta, GA: Society of Biblical Literature, 2009), 21.
3. Rosemary Radford Ruether, *Faith and Fratricide: The Theological Roots of Anti-Semitism* (Eugene, OR: Wipf and Stock, 1997), 31.
4. *ibid.*
5. Collins, *Between Athens and Jerusalem*, 16.

intent to protect Jewish identity while simultaneously making the story more relevant to the religious environment of the Hellenistic period.

The first books to be translated into Greek were those of the Torah, and the earliest and best known source for the story of that translation is the *Letter of Aristeas*, written in Greek by a Jewish writer.[1] The tension of maintaining a Jewish identity whilst being Hellenized is evidenced by the author of the *Letter*, who was obviously a defender of Judaism, while at the same time exhibiting significant Hellenistic influence. "There is no doubt that the Hellenistic influence on the author was very strong. The language, the literary form and the philosophical ideas of the Letter – all testify to this."[2] However, the way the author concentrates on describing Judaism, and particularly the Temple in Jerusalem, represents a defense of Judaism that "is obviously in the tradition of 'apologetic' Alexandrian Jewish writings whose general aim was to demonstrate the high antiquity and respectability of Judaism."[3] As a result, the content of the *Letter* "demonstrates both the extent of his acculturation and the limits of his assimilation."[4]

The *Letter* is a lengthy document full of Jewish apologetics and polemics which also includes an account of how Ptolemy II Philadelphus (282–246 BCE) commissioned a translation of the Hebrew Torah into Greek for the purpose of augmenting his library in Alexandria. According to the *Letter*, Ptolemy wrote to the High Priest, Eleazar, in Jerusalem, and asked for six translators from each of the twelve tribes of Israel.[5] The seventy-two (or seventy, according to later versions of the story) translators were sent to Egypt, where they translated the Torah in seventy-two days.[6] In spite of serious doubts concerning the accuracy of the details concerning the number of translators and the time taken

---

1. For a concise summary of the significance and historical use of the *Letter*, see Wasserstein and Wasserstein, *The Legend of the Septuagint*, 19-26.
2. Victor Tcherikover, "The Ideology of the Letter of Aristeas," *The Harvard Theological Review* L1 (1958): 59-85.
3. Moses Hadas, ed., *Aristeas to Philocrates (Letter of Aristeas)* (New York: Harper and Brothers, 1951), 60.
4. Barclay, *Jews in the Mediterranean Diaspora*, 149.
5. Hadas, *Aristeas to Philocrates*, 32-39.
6. *ibid.*, 46-50, 307.

to complete this work, it is commonly agreed upon by scholars that the translation of the Torah from Hebrew into Greek did occur during the reign of Ptolemy II of Egypt.[1]

The author of the *Letter* claimed to be a courtier of Ptolemy II.[2] However, the consensus of current scholarship is that the *Letter* was not actually written by someone in the time of Ptolemy II, but was written in the mid-second century BCE, during the Hasmonean period.[3] A composition date in the middle of the second century is further indicated by the fact that the *Letter* demonstrates the same Maccabean beliefs, apologetics, and polemics found in other Jewish literature from the Hasmonean period, such as the books of I, II, and III Maccabees and OG Esther. As in other Hasmonean literature, the author of the *Letter* emphasizes Jewish law, glorifies Judaism, and writes enthusiastic descriptions of Jerusalem, the Temple, and the High Priest. The apologetics and polemics throughout the *Letter of Aristeas* demonstrate the author's intent "to preserve Judaism against any alien attack."[4] While Tcherikover concludes that the *Letter* "was composed not for propaganda among the Greeks, but for the needs of the Jewish reader,"[5] Thackeray believes the author's intent was "to magnify the Jewish nation in the eyes of the Greek world by narrating the honour bestowed upon it by a Greek monarch."[6] Whether the intended audience was Jewish, Greek, or possibly even both, the author of the *Letter* produced a document using Hasmonean-style apologetics and polemics that was written for the purpose of protecting and maintaining Jewish religious identity. As part of that purpose, the author provided an account of the translation of the Torah that demonstrated

---

1. Barclay, *Jews in the Mediterranean Diaspora*, 31; Martin Hengel, "The Septuagint as a Collection of Writings Claimed by Christians: Justin and the Church Fathers before Origen," in *Jews and Christians: The Parting of the Ways, A.D. 70 to 135* (ed. James D.G. Dunn; Grand Rapids, MI: Eerdmans Publishing Company, 1999), 39-83.
2. See the text of the letter in Hadas, *Aristeas to Philocrates*, 115-17.
3. *ibid.*, 5-18; Wasserstein and Wasserstein, *The Legend of the Septuagint*, 20; George W.E. Nickelsburg, *Jewish Literature between the Bible and the Mishnah* (Minneapolis, MN: Fortress Press, 2005), 198; Tcherikover, "The Ideology of the Letter of Aristeas," 60; H. St. J. Thackeray, *The Letter of Aristeas* (London: Macmillan and Co., 1904), 3-4.
4. Tcherikover, "The Ideology of the Letter of Aristeas," 70.
5. *ibid.*, 62-3.
6. Thackeray, *The Letter of Aristeas*, 2.

Jewish "preference for the text of the Septuagint over that of the original Hebrew,"[1] thereby supporting the use of the Septuagint as an inspired text in the Hellenistic synagogue.

The *Letter of Aristeas* is referred to by the two well-known early Jewish writers introduced previously: Philo (c. 25 BCE–c. 50 CE) and Josephus (37/8 CE–c. 100 CE). Philo, the philosopher from Alexandria, left a significant corpus of writings, including his *De Vita Mosis*. In *De Vita Mosis II*, V-VII,[2] he included a detailed account of the translation of the Hebrew into Greek in which he demonstrated dependence on the *Letter*.[3] However, Philo added to the *Letter*'s account that Ptolemy II had commissioned the translation of the Torah by ascribing divine inspiration to the translators, referring to the translators as prophets and priests.[4] In so doing, he was the first of many authors to introduce elements into the story of the translation of the Septuagint that suggest miraculous intervention. In addition, Philo believed the Septuagint to be completely reliable, arguing in favor of an exact equivalence between the Hebrew and the Greek.[5] These beliefs paved the way for the acceptance of the authority of the Septuagint and Old Greek Esther by the Church, an acceptance that has contributed historically to anti-Semitic interpretations of the story based on OG Esther.

Josephus was born into a prominent priestly family in Jerusalem in 37–38 CE and finished his history of the Jewish people, *Jewish Antiquities*, in 93–94 CE. He is the only other known Jewish writer besides Philo who wrote in Greek and also referred to the translation account of the Septuagint. In his *Antiquities*, Josephus was clearly dependent on the *Letter* for his knowledge of the story, as he paraphrased most of the *Letter* in his writings.[6] In contrast to Philo, Josephus made no mention of the elements of divine inspiration or miraculous intervention in the translation of

1. Tcherikover, "The Ideology of the Letter of Aristeas," 75.
2. Philo, *On the Life of Moses II*, V-VII in *The Works of Philo: Complete and Unabridged, New Updated Version* (trans. C.D. Yonge; Peabody, MA: Hendrickson Publishers, 1993), 493-4.
3. Wasserstein and Wasserstein, *The Legend of the Septuagint*, 37.
4. Philo, *On the Life of Moses II*, VII:40.
5. Barclay, *Jews in the Mediterranean Diaspora*, 166.
6. Josephus, *Jewish Antiquities*, Book 12, Chapter 2:1-15 in *The New Complete Works of Josephus* (trans. William Whiston; Grand Rapids, MI: Kregel Publications, 1999), 388-94; and Wasserstein and Wasserstein, *The Legend of the Septuagint*, 46.

the Septuagint. However, these elements would be emphasized by Jewish and Christian writers alike as they justified their use of the Septuagint in the centuries after its creation.

Early Use of the Septuagint by Jews and Christians

After the beginning of the Christian era, the Septuagint became of equal importance and usefulness for Christians, especially as Christianity spread among Greek-speaking Gentiles. As a result, "well into the Christian period, the Septuagint was read by Jews and Christians" and was used in both synagogue and church.[1] Jews and Christians not only benefited from the mutual use of the Septuagint, but also shared the common goal of legitimizing it by establishing its authority and divine inspiration. For the purpose of establishing its authority, various additions were made to the *Letter of Aristeas* – first by rabbis and then by Early Church Fathers – that transformed the original story of translation into an account of supernatural intervention and miracles.[2] The development of the miraculous version of the translation story began in the first century CE with the writings of Philo and the rabbis, but in light of their common goal, "it is not at all surprising that Christian writers should have taken the miracle story from rabbinic sources."[3] However, early Christian writers didn't just use the story developed by the rabbis; they added interpretations of their own. As a result, the transformed story of translation, which initially appeared to be "an exercise in Hellenistic Jewish apologetics . . . became the seedbed, the nursery and the forcing-house for the production of literary artifices that . . . became the underpinning of some Christian theological positions."[4]

The use of the *Letter*'s emphasis on the superiority of the Greek Bible to support distinctly Christian theological positions in the growing debate with Jews over the significance of particular differences between the Septuagint and the original Hebrew

---

1. Wasserstein and Wasserstein, *The Legend of the Septuagint*, 15.
2. For a detailed documentation of the development of the miraculous story of the translation within rabbinic circles from the time period between the destruction of the Temple in 70 CE and the writing of the Babylonian Talmud in the fifth century CE, see *ibid.*, 51-83.
3. *ibid.*, 69.
4. *ibid.*, x.

text caused rabbis to begin to regard the miraculous story of the translation of the Septuagint as a serious disaster. Evidence of early negative rabbinic perspective on the translation is found in the *Massakhet Soferim* I. 7-10, which refers to the day of the translation as "a hard day for Israel, like the day on which Israel made the [golden] calf."[1] As a result, a dramatic shift in rabbinic thought concerning the origins and authority of the Septuagint is evident from the time of the Palestinian and Babylonian Talmuds in the fourth and fifth centuries CE through the thirteenth century CE.[2] This complete change in rabbinic perspective concerning the authority of the Septuagint was accompanied by a rejection of its use within Judaism, in spite of the fact that both the Septuagint and the story concerning its origins had been written by Jews for Jewish purposes. In contrast, the *Letter of Aristeas* and the miraculous story of the translation of the Septuagint continued to be used by the Church to establish the authority of the Septuagint, which is still authoritative in the Roman Catholic and Eastern Orthodox parts of the Church to this day. The importance of the *Letter* in the validation of the Septuagint is demonstrated by the fact that the twenty-plus extant manuscripts of the *Letter* have all been preserved by various elements of the Church, while none were preserved by the Jews.[3]

The Authority Attributed to the Septuagint by the Early Church

The acceptance of the authority of the Septuagint by the Early Church is evidenced by the use of the text by the first Christian canonical and non-canonical writers, and by the Christian retellings of the story of its translation into Greek. While specific examples of the use of the Septuagint by early Christian writers to support distinct theological positions is beyond the scope of this discussion, a survey of the history of Christian use of the translation story found in the *Letter of Aristeas* is necessary in order to understand the authority attributed to the Septuagint

1. Hadas, *Aristeas to Philocrates*, 80-81.
2. See the negative accounts of the translation found in rabbinic writings as late as the thirteenth century CE in Wasserstein and Wasserstein, *The Legend of the Septuagint*, 69-83.
3. *ibid.*, 19.

by Christians. This survey will in turn help explain why the use of the Septuagint had such a significant impact on subsequent interpretations that fueled anti-Semitic interpretations of the story and negative perceptions of Jews.

Justin Martyr, Irenaeus, and Clement of Alexandria

Christian retellings of the story of the translation of the Septuagint included the elements of miraculous inspiration first introduced by Jewish writers, but expanded the story even further. Justin Martyr's *Dialogue with Trypho*, Irenaeus' *Against Heresies*, and Clement of Alexandria's *The Stromata* all recount the translation story found in the *Letter*, with various additions, including the miraculous translation of the entire Hebrew Bible, the claim that the text should be exclusively Christian, the claim that the Septuagint was superior to the Hebrew, and the claim that the translation had been made for the purpose of reaching Greek ears.

Justin Martyr (mid-second century CE) was the first Christian author to use the expression "the seventy" as "a designation for a 'holy text,'"[1] and he made reference to the translation done by "the seventy" or "the seventy elders at the court of Ptolemy" in his *Dialogue with Trypho*.[2] Ptolemy is mentioned in connection with the "translation of the seventy elders" in Justin's first *Apology*. Furthermore, Philo and Josephus are called "wise and esteemed men who have written of these things" in the pseudo-Justinian *Hortatory Address to the Greeks*.[3] However, in contrast to Josephus, who only referred to the translation of the law of Moses as the work that was ordered by Ptolemy II, Justin expanded the work of "the seventy" to include all of the Hebrew Bible, as evidenced by his extensive quotes of the prophets and the psalms from the Greek.[4] He was

---

1. Hengel, "The Septuagint as a Collection of Writings Claimed by Christians," 41.
2. Justin Martyr, *Dialogue with Trypho*, 68.7, 71.1, 84.3, 120.4, 124.3, 131.1, and 137.3 in *Ante-Nicene Fathers, Volume 1: The Apostolic Fathers, Justin Martyr, Irenaeus* (ed. Alexander Roberts, DD, and James Donaldson, LLD; Hendrickson Publishers, 1994).
3. Justin Martyr, *Apology*, I.31.2 and *Justin's Hortatory Address to the Greeks*, XIII in *Ante-Nicene Fathers, Vol. 1*.
4. Hengel, "The Septuagint as a Collection of Writings Claimed by Christians," 43.

in agreement with Philo that the translation was miraculously inspired, and he made a strong case in favor of the Septuagint as an exclusively Christian text.[1]

Irenaeus was a bishop in Gaul in the later part of the second century CE. Irenaeus, like Justin before him, not only gave complete credibility to the translation account given in the *Letter of Aristeas*, but, in agreement with Justin, expanded that account to include the translation of the entire Hebrew Bible. He also credited the Septuagint translation as having been "interpreted by the inspiration of God."[2] In addition, the separation of the translators while they worked, combined with the complete uniformity of the resulting translations according to the account in the *Letter*, not only demonstrated the inspired condition of the translators, but made "the entire work sacrosanct and excludes any and all criticism of its original text."[3] Consequently, the Septuagint was believed to be superior to the Hebrew original since it contained the inspired interpretation of the Hebrew. Even where the Greek text obviously deviates from the Hebrew, Irenaeus believed that this too was "willed by God."[4] This belief in the superiority of the Greek translation, even when it deviated from the Hebrew, was echoed by Clement of Alexandria (c. 150–211/216 CE), one of the most distinguished teachers of the church in Alexandria, when he stated that the translation had been made "for the benefit of Grecian ears."[5]

As can be seen, the *Letter of Aristeas*, with various additions, was adopted by the Early Church for the purpose of validating the authority attributed to the Septuagint. Because the *Letter* was used to support distinctly Christian theological positions in the growing debate with Jews over the significance of particular differences between the Greek and Hebrew texts, the use of the Septuagint declined within Judaism. However, Hellenistic Jews

---

1. *ibid.*, 68.
2. Irenaeus, *Against Heresies*, XXI:2 in *Ante-Nicene Fathers, Volume 1: The Apostolic Fathers, Justin Martyr, Irenaeus* (ed. Alexander Roberts, DD, and James Donaldson, LLD; Hendrickson Publishers, 1994).
3. Hengel, "The Septuagint as a Collection of Writings Claimed by Christians," 76.
4. *ibid.*
5. Clement of Alexandria, *The Stromata*, XXII in *Ante-Nicene Fathers, Volume 2: Fathers of the Second Century: Hermas, Tatian, Athenagoras, Theophilus, and Clement of Alexandria* (ed. Alexander Roberts, DD, and James Donaldson, LLD; Hendrickson Publishers, 1994).

still needed a Greek translation of their Bible. Consequently, in the second century CE, three other Greek translations of the Hebrew Bible were made by Jews for use by Jews. These translations are known as the work of Aquila (128 CE), Symmachus (late second century CE), and Theodotian (second century CE).

Origen and Jerome

Because of the multiple versions of the Bible in circulation by his time, Origen (184/5–254/5 CE), another early Church Father, sought to reconstruct the original text of the Septuagint through a comparison of the textual differences between these versions. In order to compare these differences, he created a chart containing six columns. In the first column, he put the Hebrew text; in the second column, he put a Greek transliteration of the Hebrew; in the third, he put Aquila's Greek translation; in the fourth, he put Symmachus' Greek translation; in the fifth, he put his own revised Greek text; and in the sixth, he put Theodotian's Greek translation. The resultant work was called the *Hexapla* and was probably compiled between 230 and 240 CE in Caesarea. The translations of Aquila, Symmachus, and Theodotian have not survived, but all surviving Greek biblical manuscripts demonstrate the influence of Origen's *Hexapla*.

Origen's revised version of the Greek text found in the fifth column of the *Hexapla* became the first "standardized text" of the Christian Church. It then became the authoritative text for the Eastern Church, while the Western Church was using a collection of Latin texts known as the Vetus Latina that had been translated from the Septuagint beginning in the second century. Vetus Latina is the collective title for a large and diverse collection of Latin biblical texts used by Christian communities beginning in the second century, when it became necessary to translate the Septuagint into Latin for those in the Roman Empire who did not read Greek.

Because there was no "standardized" Latin text, the Western Church commissioned Jerome (c. 347–420 CE) to produce a new translation in Latin that would be known as "the Vulgate." Jerome had Origen's redaction of the Septuagint available to him, but he decided to use the Hebrew text as his source based on the use New Testament authors made of the Hebrew Bible rather than the Septuagint on some occasions. However, in spite of his claim that his Latin version was a translation from the Hebrew, "Jerome did not always succeed in freeing himself entirely from the shackles of the Septuagint background of the Vetus Latina," partly because "the tradition of the Church had, by the time of Jerome, already sanctified some parts of the Latin text of the Vetus Latina to such an extent that Jerome's 'Hebraized' version simply could not replace it."[1] In particular, there is distinct evidence that Jerome was influenced by the OG in his work on Esther, because of his inclusion of the Greek additions to the story. But rather than simply include them, he removed all but the last addition to the Hebrew book of Esther and grouped them together at the end of the canonical book, thereby demonstrating that he was indeed looking at OG Esther as he did his translation.[2]

Jerome's new Latin Vulgate translation, which reflected OG Esther, was then used by the expanding Western Church. As a result, the Greek interpretation of Esther's character and actions was spread wherever the Vulgate was used. In spite of the production of the new Latin translation, the Western Church, along with the Eastern Church, continued to view Origen's revised Septuagint as authoritative as well. Evidence of the continued use and importance of the Greek Bible is demonstrated in the oldest, extant, relatively complete manuscripts of the Septuagint, known as *Codex Vaticanus* (fourth century CE), *Codex Sinaiticus* (fourth century CE), and *Codex Alexandrinus* (fifth century CE).

John Chrysostom and Augustine

In the same time period that *Codex Vaticanus* and *Codex Sinaiticus* were being written, two extremely influential Church Fathers, John Chrysostom and Augustine, were preaching and writing on the authority and superiority of the Septuagint. John Chrysostom (347–407 CE), the archbishop of Constantinople and a representative of the Eastern Church, said of the Septuagint, "He [the Holy Spirit] arranged that they [the Scriptures] should be translated by the Seventy. They did translate them . . . and the Apostles disperse[d] them among men."[3] Not only did

---

1. Wasserstein and Wasserstein, *The Legend of the Septuagint*, 14.
2. Nickelsburg, *Jewish Literature between the Bible and the Mishnah*, 202.
3. Chrysostom, *Homily VIII: Chapter 9* in *Nicene and Post-Nicene Fathers: Volume 14; Chrysostom: Homilies on the Gospel of Saint John and the Epistle to the Hebrews* (ed. Philip Schaff, DD, LLD; Hendrickson Publishers, 1994).

Chrysostom believe that the Septuagint was the result of the inspiration of the Holy Spirit, but he believed that the translation of "the seventy" was superior to all other translations, particularly those done by later translators such as Aquila, Symmachus, and Theodotian. He said:

> [T]he Seventy were justly entitled to confidence above all the others. For these [referring to later translators such as Aquila, Symmachus, and Theodotian] made their translation after Christ's coming, continuing to be Jews, and may justly be suspected as having spoken rather in enmity, and as darkening the prophecies on purpose; but the Seventy, as having entered upon this work an hundred years or more before the coming of Christ, stand clear from all such suspicion, and on account of the date, and of their number, and of their agreement, would have a better right to be trusted.[1]

This quote from Chrysostom not only reinforces and perpetrates the Christian claim for the superiority and authority of the Septuagint based on Aristeas' account of its translation, but it testifies to the ongoing debate between Christians and Jews concerning the authority of the Septuagint versus the authority of the later Jewish translations of the Hebrew text. Jews and Christians engaged in a war of words and accusations concerning each other's motives for accepting their respective Greek translations. Jews accused Christians of tampering with the text of the Septuagint for the purpose of interpreting the prophets in the light of Jesus Christ, while Christians accused Jews of making new translations with the motive of "darkening" those same prophecies. As a result, the Christian belief in the authority and superiority of the Septuagint was a significant factor in the development of anti-Judaism/ Semitism in the Early Church. The belief in the Septuagint also contributed to the priority of OG Esther within the Church, which paved the way for anti-Semitic interpretations of the story based on the changes and additions found in the Greek text.

In agreement with Chrysostom and all the previous Church Fathers, Augustine (354–430 CE), the bishop of Hippo and one of the most important figures in the development of Western Christianity, said:

---

1. Chrysostom, *Homily V: Chapter 4* in *Nicene and Post-Nicene Fathers: Volume 10; Chrysostom: Homilies on the Gospel of Saint Matthew* (ed. Philip Schaff, DD, LLD; Hendrickson Publishers, 1994).

For while there were other interpreters who translated these sacred oracles out of the Hebrew tongue into Greek, as Aquila, Symmachus, and Theodotian . . . the Church has received this Septuagint translation just as if it were the only one; and it has been used by the Greek Christian people. . . . [T]he churches of Christ judge that no one should be preferred to the authority of so many men, chosen for this very great work by Eleazar, who was then high priest. . . . For the same Spirit who was in the prophets when they spoke these things was also in the seventy men when they translated them.[1]

This quote from Augustine acknowledges the translations of Aquila, Symmachus, and Theodotian, but maintains the claim that the Septuagint was superior, as it was the translation that was inspired by the "same Spirit" who inspired the prophets when they spoke.

The authority attributed to the Septuagint by the Early Church, as demonstrated through the use of the story of its translation, was firmly established by the time of John Chrysostom of the Eastern Church and Augustine of the Western Church. The continued belief in the divine inspiration and superiority of the Septuagint in both parts of the Church is evidenced by the fact that wherever Christianity spread, translations of the books found in the Hebrew Bible were based on the Greek rather than the Hebrew text. The Greek Bible was the source of translations into Old Latin, Arabic, Ethiopic, Armenian, Coptic, Georgian, and Old Church Slavonic. As a result, all of these translations reflect the changes and additions found in the OG version of Esther as well.

The continuous use of books found in the Septuagint throughout the Middle Ages is indicated by their presence in extant medieval manuscripts that date from the eighth to the thirteenth century.[2] The inclusion of OG Esther in manuscripts

---

1. Augustine, *City of God*, Book 18, chapter 43 in *Nicene and Post-Nicene Fathers, Volume 2: Augustine: City of God, Christian Doctrine* (ed. Philip Schaff, DD, LLD; Hendrickson Publishers, 1994).
2. Manuscripts containing Old Greek Esther in the context of canonical books include the *Biblioteca Apostolica Vaticana (BAV) 2106* from the eighth century; *British Library London Royal ID 2* (Rahlfs 93) from the thirteenth century; *BAV Vat. Gr. 330* (Rahlfs 108) from the thirteenth century; and the *Florence San Marco 700* from the thirteenth century.

that date from these centuries and primarily contain canonical books indicates that this version of Esther was considered authoritative in the Middle Ages. This is confirmed by the fact that the Roman Catholic counter-Reformation Council of Trent in 1546 decreed the apocryphal books of the Septuagint, including Old Greek Esther, canonical, and therefore authoritative. By way of contrast, following the Protestant Reformation, which began in 1517, Protestant Bibles were translated from the Hebrew text and no longer included the Apocrypha. Furthermore, the books found in the Apocrypha were classified as "writings which do not defile the hands" within Judaism. This term means that such writings are not considered Scripture, and therefore the apocryphal books are not included in the Jewish canon. All surviving manuscripts of the Septuagint, including the Sinaiticus, Alexandrinus, and Vaticanus codices from the and fifth centuries, were preserved by the Roman Catholic Church and not by the Protestants or the Jews. Centuries of use of the Septuagint in both the Roman Catholic and Eastern Orthodox parts of the Church would inevitably solidify the Old Greek version's portrayal of the character and actions of Esther in the minds of interpreters to this day.

Historical Use of the Alpha Text of Esther

Old Greek Esther was not the only Greek version to have a dramatic influence on the interpretation of the story of Esther, as evidenced by the fact that the Alpha Text (AT) was read from the first century CE to at least the thirteenth century. Use of the AT is first demonstrated by Josephus, who exhibits a dependency on it in his version of Esther in *Antiquities*, written in 90 CE. The second century Vetus Latina (VL) also includes variants that are in common with the AT, showing that "the 'author' of the Vetus Latina did know the AT of Esther."[1] The dependency of the VL on the AT means that interpretations of Esther in Christian communities throughout the Roman Empire would have been influenced by the AT beginning in the second century CE. In his work on Esther in his third century *Hexapla*, Origen made corrections "similar to the AT," indicating that he "knew and

---

1. Kristin De Troyer, *Rewriting the Sacred Text: What the Old Greek Texts Tell Us About the Literary Growth of the Bible* (Atlanta, GA: Society of Biblical Literature, 2003), 66.

used the AT."[1] In the fourth century, John Chrysostom quoted from AT 6:2-11 in his Homily XXXVIII on Acts 17:16-17. However, Chrysostom did not provide the source of this quote, indicating that the AT was familiar enough to his audiences that there was no need to give the source in the context of the sermon.[2] Therefore, by the fourth century, it is evident that interpretations of the character and actions of Esther were not only dependent on Greek and Latin versions of the story, but on the use of those texts in sermons as well.

The use and influence of the Alpha Text of Esther continued beyond the fourth century, as demonstrated by its preservation in five extant Greek manuscripts from the Middle Ages, which are identified by Rahlfs numbers 19, 93, 108, 319, and 392. While the first four of these manuscripts provide consistent witnesses to the AT text, manuscript 392 mixes the OG text with that of the AT.[3] Manuscript 392 provides evidence of the simultaneous use of OG and AT Esther by mixing them, but manuscripts 19, 93, and 108 provide evidence of the simultaneous use of both Greek texts in other ways. Rahlfs 19, or *BAV Chigi*, is from the twelfth century, and includes the colophon at the end of the text; a feature that demonstrates dependency of the AT on the OG as the colophon is otherwise only found in manuscripts of OG Esther. Rahlfs 93, or *British Library London Royal ID 2*, is from the thirteenth century and contains both AT Esther and OG Esther. It is interesting to note that in this manuscript, AT Esther precedes OG Esther.[4] In addition to the fact that Rahlfs 93 contains both Greek versions of Esther, the text of AT Esther contains nine corrections, six of which are filled in by a second hand with text from OG Esther. This demonstrates that manuscripts of AT Esther were corrected using manuscripts of OG Esther.[5] And finally, Rahlfs 108, or *BAV*

---

1. *ibid.*, 74. For a detailed discussion of how Origen's correction towards the Hebrew demonstrates knowledge of the AT, see Robert Hanhart, ed., *Esther: Septuaginta* (Göttingen: Vandenhoeck and Ruprecht, 1983), 69-77.
2. Hanhart, *Esther*, 93.
3. For a further discussion of how manuscript 392 mixes the OG text with the AT, see Hanhart, *Esther*, 15-16.
4. Rahlfs 93 contains the following books in this order: Ruth, 1-4 Kings, 1-2 Chronicles, 2 Esdras, AT Esther, 1-3 Maccabees, OG Esther, Isaiah.
5. Karen H. Jobes, *The Alpha Text of Esther: Its Character and Relationship to the Masoretic Text* (Atlanta, GA: Scholars Press, 1996), Appendix 2: The Manuscripts.

Vat. Gr. 330, is from the thirteenth century and also contains both AT and OG Esther. And just as in Rahlfs 93, AT Esther appears before OG Esther.[1]

Manuscripts 19, 93, 108, 319, and 392 provide overwhelming evidence of the simultaneous use of AT and OG Esther through the Middle Ages, and evidence of the dependency of the AT on the OG as well. All these witnesses to the AT include the additions found in the OG: manuscript 19 includes the colophon found in the OG; manuscript 93 uses text from the OG to correct the AT; and manuscripts 93 and 108 contain both AT and OG Esther, with AT Esther preceding OG Esther. Further evidence of dependency on the OG is evidenced by the obvious influence of the Septuagint on the order of the books in these manuscripts. The order of the canonical books is the same as that found in the Septuagint (in contrast to that found in the Hebrew Bible), and the non-canonical books are representative of those found in the Apocrypha of the Septuagint. The fact that AT Esther was included in medieval manuscripts containing canonical and apocryphal books indicates that it was treated as authoritative at least through the thirteenth century, and, as a result, would have influenced interpretations of Esther for a minimum of 1,200 years, if not more.

Preliminary Conclusions

The historical use of the AT from the first through the thirteenth centuries CE has been confirmed by Josephus' knowledge of it by 90 CE, the use of the text in early Christian communities as indicated by the dependency of the Vetus Latina on it, its use by Chrysostom, and its inclusion in five medieval manuscripts – Rahlfs 19, 93, 108, 319, and 392 – that contain canonical and apocryphal books. These manuscripts also provide additional evidence of the dependency of the AT on the OG, as well as the influence of the Septuagint on the order of the canonical books in those manuscripts, thereby offering significant testimony concerning the importance of the Septuagint and OG Esther in the Church.

---

1. Rahlfs 108 contains the following books in this order: The Octateuch, 1-4 Kings, 1-2 Chronicles, 1-2 Esdras, Judith, AT Esther, OG Esther, Tobit.

The historical use of OG Esther as part of the Septuagint has been demonstrated through discussions on the authority attributed to the Septuagint by the Early Church, and the continuous use of OG Esther throughout the Middle Ages as evidenced by its inclusion in extant manuscripts such as the *Biblioteca Apostolica Vaticana (BAV) 2106* from the eighth century, *British Library London Royal ID 2* (Rahlfs 93) from the thirteenth century, *BAV Vat. Gr. 330* (Rahlfs 108) from the thirteenth century, and the *Florence San Marco 700* from the thirteenth century. This evidence, combined with the decree by the Roman Catholic counter-Reformation Council of Trent in 1546, and the fact that OG Esther is still included in the apocryphal books of the Bible, proves that this version of Esther has been authoritative in the parts of the Church that consider the Apocrypha canonical, or "deutero-canonical," for the last 2,000 years. Because OG Esther has been read continuously throughout Church history wherever the Apocrypha is considered canonical, its portrayal of the character of Esther and the role of the Jews in the story have become entrenched in the minds of interpreters to this day. As a result, it is the changes made in this Greek version that are the primary source of traditional interpretations and present-day beliefs concerning Jews.

Interpretations of the Story
and the Character of Esther

The preceding discussion of the historical use of AT Esther concluded that it was treated as authoritative at least through the thirteenth century. Because it was preserved by the Church, it would have influenced Christian interpretations of Esther for a minimum of 1,200 years, if not more. The Excursus established the dependency of the AT on the OG version, which in turn testifies to the importance of OG Esther in the Church. The authors of both Greek versions rewrote pertinent details in the story, which resulted in transformative changes to the character of Esther and to the role she and the Jews of Persia played in the events in which they were involved. Because AT Esther is dependent on the Old Greek, and the modifications made by the author of the AT essentially enhance those made by the author of the OG, this section will not analyze the differences between the AT and the other two versions. Instead, this discussion will focus on how differences between the character of OG Esther and Hebrew Esther have affected interpretations of the story.

In particular, the following literary comparisons will demonstrate how the changes made by the author of Old Greek Esther fuel anti-Semitic interpretations of the story and the character of Esther that are so similar to the negative perceptions of Jews that feed Christian anti-Zionism. This analysis will include features in the text that specifically invite feminist critique of the person and actions of Esther. Feminist critique is relevant to this discussion because there is an inherent relationship between feminist and anti-Semitic interpretation due to their roots in feminist and Christian theology, both of which incorporate anti-Judaism. Therefore, before beginning the literary comparisons of Hebrew and Greek Esther, a brief discussion of the relationship between feminist and Christian theology is necessary.

Feminist and Christian Theology

Feminist critique of the character and actions of Esther contributes to anti-Semitic interpretation because "the anti-Jewish myth . . . manifests itself in feminist theological writings."[1] To some extent, feminist theology is inherently anti-Jewish, because it credits Judaism with being the source of sexism and patriarchy.[2] Judaism is seen as a religion that marginalizes women, and "the critical principle which guides the feminist critique of, and search for, truth in religion is that whatever denies, diminishes, or distorts the full humanity of women is . . . appraised as not redemptive."[3] Where anti-Judaism is manifested in feminist theological writings, those writings either purposefully or inadvertently contribute to anti-Semitism because, as the previous discussions on what Greek and Latin authors wrote about Jews and Judaism demonstrated, anti-Judaism always contributes to anti-Semitism. In the case of Esther, when her character is viewed

---

1. Katharina von Kellenbach, *Anti-Judaism in Feminist Religious Writings* (Atlanta, GA: Scholars Press, 1994), ix.
2. For an insightful discussion of the feminist perception of sexism and patriarchy in Judaism, see *ibid.*, 15-19.
3. Rosemary Radford Ruether, *Sexism and God-Talk: Toward a Feminist Theology* (Boston, MA: Beacon Press, 1983), 18.

as diminished or distorted due to sexism and/or patriarchy, feminist anti-Judaism – which is defined as the incorporation of the "anti-Jewish myth" into feminist theological writings – results in anti-Semitic interpretation of her actions and her story.

The "anti-Jewish myth" is also manifest in feminist theology as a result of the relationship between feminist anti-Judaism and Christian anti-Judaism, which is based on theological differences that act as identifying features of Christianity. In fact, anti-Judaism is "a pervasive aspect of Christianity," and as such, "it has been adopted consciously or sub-consciously, willingly or unwillingly, by feminist theologians."[1] The relationship between feminist and Christian theology, and their relationship to anti-Judaism and the historical interpretation of Esther, will be further demonstrated through a literary comparison of Hebrew Esther and Old Greek Esther. But before beginning the literary comparisons, a look at the relationship between anti-feminism and anti-Judaism in the Hebrew version of Esther and in twentieth-century German theology will illustrate the connection between feminist and Christian anti-Judaism.

Anti-Feminism and Anti-Judaism in Hebrew Esther and Twentieth-Century German Theology

Anti-feminism and anti-Judaism in the Hebrew version of Esther are inextricably linked through the actions of Vashti and Esther, and through the similarities in the two decrees that addressed the issues of wives and Jews in the Persian Empire. Vashti's resistance to the demands of the king in chapter 1 was viewed by the king and his advisors as a threat to the stability of the entire kingdom. Likewise, Haman was able to convince the king that the Jews were a threat to the security of his kingdom. In both cases, a decree had to be sent to the entire kingdom to deal with these perceived threats. The first decree (1:19-22) ordered the submission of all wives to their husbands, and the second decree (3:12-15) ordered the annihilation of all the Jews. Through these two decrees, a state-sanctioned persecution was directed against all women and against all Jews. The similarity in the way in which the danger of women and Jews is presented, combined with the similarity in the decrees deemed necessary to

---

1. von Kellenbach, *Anti-Judaism in Feminist Religious Writings*, 13.

deal with these supposed threats, demonstrates the connection
between anti-feminism and anti-Judaism in Esther, and "links
the solution of the question of women's rights inseparably to
the deliverance of the Jewish people."[1] Vashti's resistance to
anti-feminism and Esther's resistance to anti-Judaism illustrate
how "the rise of women against supremacy and oppression is
essential," as well as "how the fight against sexist power and
for the liberation of Jewish people from anti-Semitic threat are
linked together."[2]

The relationship between anti-feminism and anti-Judaism is
not limited to the book of Esther, but is apparent in twentieth
century German theology as well. In her article entitled, "Images
of Women and Jews in Nineteenth and Twentieth Century
German Theology," Briggs summarizes the development of
German theological ethics from 1815 to the Third Reich and
concludes that "the roles of women and Jews were differently
defined but . . . interlinked."[3] By the mid-nineteenth century,
Richard Rothe had identified "un-Christianized Jews" and
"unfeminine women" – who were defined as unmarried and/
or as women who worked outside the home – as "signs of the
incompleteness of the moral process of society."[4] In the same
century, Hans Lassen Martensen favored the subordination
of women and Jews "because of their essential characters,"[5]
claiming that the individuality of female and Jewish character
was a "perversion when it encroached on the public sphere of
male Christians."[6] Then, in 1921, Reinhold Seeberg "associated
the formulations of female character by nineteenth-century
theologians with Jewish character," thereby making "explicit
the link between Judaism and femininity, Judaism and

---

1. Klara Butting, "Esther: A New Interpretation of the Joseph Story in
   the Fight Against Anti-Semitism and Sexism," in *Ruth and Esther:
   A Feminist Companion to the Bible* (ed. Athalya Brenner; Sheffield:
   Sheffield Academic Press, 1999), 239-48.
2. *ibid.*, 245.
3. Sheila Briggs, "Images of Women and Jews in Nineteenth and
   Twentieth Century German Theology," in *Immaculate and Powerful:
   The Female in Sacred Image and Social Reality* (ed. Clarissa W. Atkinson,
   Constance H. Buchanan, and Margaret R. Miles; Boston, MA: Beacon
   Press, 1985), 226-59.
4. *ibid.*, 233.
5. *ibid.*, 235.
6. *ibid.*, 236.

individualism."[1] The identification of feminism and Judaism as threats to the ideal male Christian world by German theologians is no different than the perception that women and Jews posed a threat to the stability and security of the Persian Empire. The timelessness of the perceived threat of feminism and Judaism revealed through the relationship between anti-feminism and anti-Judaism in Hebrew Esther and twentieth-century German theology illuminates the significant connection between feminist and Christian anti-Judaism.

Literary Comparisons of Hebrew and Old Greek Esther

As previous chapters have demonstrated, the two Greek versions of Esther were written, in part, to address the dangers that confronted Jews as a result of anti-Judaism/Semitism. It is therefore ironic that the story of Esther is the object of such a long history of anti-Semitic critique. However, this history can be better understood as a result of looking at some of the particular changes that were made to the original Hebrew version of the text. The authors of both Greek versions made changes to pertinent details in the events, and the additions include elements of Greek drama. As a result, transformative changes are made to the character of Esther and to the role she and the Jews of Persia played in the events in which they were involved. The following literary comparisons will demonstrate the source of anti-Semitic interpretation of the story and present-day beliefs concerning Jews by focusing on specific aspects that fuel a significant misunderstanding of the story.

Literary comparisons of relevant elements from Hebrew and Old Greek Esther will demonstrate that it is in fact OG Esther that invites feminist critique of the character and actions of Esther and fuels anti-Semitic interpretations of the book as a whole. As will be seen, feminist and anti-Semitic critique cannot be supported by a reading of the Hebrew text alone. In order to compare and contrast Hebrew and OG Esther, the Hebrew version's account of the development of Esther's character and her role in the events in which she was involved will be presented first, followed by an analysis of how relevant elements were changed by the author of the Greek version.

---

1. *ibid.*, 250-55.

The Character and Actions of Hebrew Esther

Esther is introduced in the Hebrew 2:7 as an orphan, the cousin and adopted daughter of Mordecai, and as a "girl" or "young woman" who was marriageable.[1] She is described as a young woman who was "beautiful in form and appearance." Her introduction immediately follows the account of the deposition of Vashti and the king's decision to appoint commissioners to gather "all the beautiful young virgins" for the purpose of seeking a replacement for Vashti. Literarily, Esther is introduced as the kind of young woman the king's men will be looking for, except for the fact that the term "virgin" is not included in the description of Esther. While the description of Esther's age and beauty matches the description of the women being sought to replace Vashti, the text does not identify Esther as a virgin. In other words, at the time she was introduced, she was a woman of marriageable age, but not necessarily a virgin. While it is often assumed that Esther was a virgin based on the fact that 2:2-3 states the king's intent to gather all the "young virgins," the women gathered for the king are only described as "young women" in 2:8. This suggests that young women who were not virgins may also have been gathered. Furthermore, 2:17 says that the king loved Esther more than all "the women," as well as all "the virgins." The significance of the possibility that Esther could have been collected for the king on the basis of being one of the young women but not a virgin will be discussed in detail in the following analysis of the changes made to the character of Esther in the Old Greek version. For the purposes of this current discussion, it is sufficient to point out that, except for not being described as a virgin, Esther is introduced as one of the young women who would be taken to the king.

Following Esther's introduction in 2:7, verse 8 reports that Esther was "taken" along with many other young women and they were all "gathered" in Susa. It is significant to point out here that both "taken" and "gathered" are passive verbs, indicating that these young women were the objects of the action and that none of those who were gathered had a choice concerning what was happening to them.[2]

---

1. The definition for the Hebrew word for "girl" or "young woman" is taken from Francis Brown, S.R. Driver, and Charles A. Briggs, *The BDB Hebrew and English Lexicon* (Peabody, MA: Hendrickson, 2000), 655.
2. As Michael Fox says, "Esther's induction into the harem was beyond

After Esther was "taken" to the king's house, she was put in the custody of Hegai, who gave her everything she needed to prepare herself to be "taken" to the king. According to 2:12, the preparation for being taken to the king involved a twelve-month-long beauty treatment, a ritual that was prescribed for women to fulfill the desire of the king. As in 2:8, Esther is still the object of the action. Furthermore, "all the active roles clearly belong to the men. . . . [W]hat it amounts to is that a man knows what a woman needs. . . . [W]hat the man thinks that the woman needs, she needs. . . . [T]here is no room for what the woman thinks."[1] After Esther completes her beauty treatment, a passive verb is used again in 2:16 to describe how Esther was "taken" to the king, and in 2:17, she remains the object of the action when the king put the royal crown on her head and "caused her to be queen". So far, Esther is playing "the typical feminine role," which is one of being "passive, obedient, dependent and silent."[2] This "typical feminine role" is an obvious source of fuel for feminist critique of the character of Esther, because it raises the question of why she didn't take action and resist what was being done to her. However, Berman argues that Esther's apparent compliance with the events in her life "reflects an adaptation strategy fitted to the realities of her situatedness," a strategy that enabled her to survive and ultimately succeed in the context in which she found herself.[3]

In 4:4, Esther is, for the first time, the subject of an action in which she is involved. Even though she was responding to the report of Mordecai's mourning in 4:1, her action was finally one that she initiated. Upon hearing from her young women and eunuchs concerning Mordecai's condition, Esther "writhed

---

her and Mordecai's decision" and the absence of any hint from the author as to how Esther felt about what was happening to her is due to the author's intent "to convey the insignificance of her will and mind *at this stage.*" Michael V. Fox, *Character and Ideology in the Book of Esther* (Columbia, SC: University of South Carolina, 1991), 197.

1. Kristin De Troyer, "An Oriental Beauty Parlor: An Analysis of Esther 2.8-18 in the Hebrew, the Septuagint and the Second Greek Text," in *A Feminist Companion to Esther, Judith and Susanna* (ed. Athalya Brenner; Sheffield: Sheffield Academic Press, 1995), 47-70.
2. Rivkah Lubitch, "A Feminist's Look at Esther," *Judaism: A Quarterly Journal of Jewish Life and Thought* 42.4 (Fall 1993): 438-46.
3. Joshua A. Berman, "Hadassah Bat Abihail: The Evolution from Object to Subject in the Character of Esther," *JBL* 120/4 (2001): 647-69.

in anxiety" at the news of the mourning of the Jews and sent garments to clothe Mordecai. When Mordecai refused to wear the clothes she sent, Esther called for Hathach in 4:5 and sent him to Mordecai to find out what was happening. Not only did Esther exhibit a visible reaction to an event for the first time, but she took the initiative to try to clothe Mordecai and to find out the source of his grief.

4:6-17 gives the account of the dialog between Mordecai and Esther through the intermediary Hathach concerning the need for Esther to intercede with the king on the behalf of her people. It is at this point in the story that the character of Esther undergoes a profound change, and Esther begins to assume the role of a leader. After telling Mordecai that she can't do what he was asking her to do in verses 8-11 because she hasn't been called by the king for thirty days, Esther has a change of heart. In 4:16, she "commanded" Mordecai to assemble the Jews for the purpose of fasting for her and declared that she too would fast for three days and nights in preparation for going to the king. As Berman says, "Esther's call for a fast in the face of doom is in line with a well-established biblical tradition of intercessory fasts in circumstances of crisis."[1] However, Berman fails to note that in the "well-established biblical tradition of intercessory fasts," it is always men who call the fasts. Esther is unique in the biblical text as a woman who calls a fast. It is also unique that in response to Esther's call, Mordecai "did all that Esther commanded him" (4:17).

Until this development in the story, Esther was the one who "was taken," and "caused to be queen," and she waited to be called by the king. By the end of chapter 4, however, she was not only obeyed by Mordecai as she assumed a leadership role and became the only woman in the biblical text to call a fast, but she made the decision to approach the king uninvited. From this point on, "Esther is not a passive character."[2] To the contrary, Esther becomes active, assertive, and independent, and from chapter 4 on, she is the only subject in the book who clearly plays a decisive role as she initiates plans that determine the rest of the action. Not only does the character of Esther undergo

---

1. Berman, "Hadassah Bat Abihail," 655.
2. Sidnie Ann White, "Esther: A Feminine Model for Jewish Diaspora," in *Gender and Difference in Ancient Israel* (ed. Peggy L. Day; Minneapolis, MN: Fortress Press, 1989), 161-77.

a profound change in this chapter, but "the events of chapter 4 constitute only the initial stages of her evolution . . . that extends all the way through the scroll's final verses."[1]

Instead of waiting to be called by the king, Esther did the calling by inviting Ahashverosh and Haman to a banquet. "The Scroll presents Esther's encounter with the king as a product of her own initiative"[2] and the venue of a banquet is "a space defined by Esther's will rather than Ahasuerus' authority."[3] The ensuing plot reveals that Esther has devised a creative agenda that the men in the story – Mordecai, Ahashverosh, and Haman – all follow. When she went before the king in 5:1-5, she did not tell the king her reason for inviting him and Haman to a banquet. Even when the king asked her what her request was in 5:6, she answered by inviting the two men to a second banquet without revealing her reasons for initiating either banquet. As Fox says, "the best explanation for Esther's delaying her request until the second banquet is that she is unfolding a premeditated strategy."[4] This strategy of not answering immediately is evidence of tact and wisdom on the part of Esther. If she had revealed what the problem was prematurely, she would have risked implicating the king in the scheme (since he had agreed to Haman's plan), thereby putting him on the defensive. Instead, she apparently decided a second banquet would be necessary in order to put the king in a receptive frame of mind, and in the context of that banquet, she revealed Haman's plan to have her and her people destroyed. The position of power that Esther held by this point in the story is testified to by the actions of Haman, as he pleaded with the queen for his life.

In 8:1, we learn that on the same day that Haman was hung, the king gave the house of Haman to Esther. In addition, Mordecai was able to go before the king because Esther told the king "what he was to her." In contrast to 2:7, in which Esther is introduced in terms of her relationship to Mordecai, now Mordecai is introduced to the king in terms of who he is to Esther. At this point, the reversal of authority in the relationship between Esther and Mordecai is complete. In 4:8, Mordecai had commanded

1. Berman, "Hadassah Bat Abihail," 647.
2. Leila L. Bronner, "Reclaiming Esther: From Sex Object to Sage," *Jewish Bible Quarterly* 26/1 (1998): 7.
3. Berman, "Hadassah Bat Abihail," 659.
4. Fox, *Character and Ideology in the Book of Esther*, 201.

Esther through Hathach to go to the king to plead for her people, but by chapter eight, Mordecai has not only done everything Esther has commanded him to do, but she is responsible for everything that happens to him throughout the rest of the story. As a result of Esther introducing Mordecai as a relative, he was put in a position of authority as symbolized by the gift of the king's ring in 8:2. In addition, Esther put Mordecai over the house of Haman. In other words, Mordecai was totally dependent on Esther for everything he received. If Esther had not put her life on the line for her people and exercised decisive influence on all the subsequent events of the story, Mordecai presumably would not have lived to obtain the honor, position, and wealth he had by the end of the story.

In 8:3-6, Esther spoke again with the king, asking that Haman's decree ordering the annihilation of the Jews be revoked. In 8:8, in lieu of revoking the decree, the king gave Esther, along with Mordecai, the authority to write a second decree that would counter the original one. As we have seen, the counter-decree of 8:11 allowed the Jews to assemble and stand for their lives, and to take the same actions against their attackers that Haman's decree had ordered to be taken against them. The fact that both Esther and Mordecai were involved in the writing of the counter-decree is demonstrated in 8:8 through the use of the plural personal pronoun in the Hebrew, as well as the plural imperative. Esther's involvement in the writing of a royal decree is often ignored by those who minimize her role in the events of the story. However, her involvement in writing the decree, along with the part she played in determining all the events of the story beginning in chapter 4, is an obvious contradiction of feminist critique of her character.

According to 9:13, after one day of fighting, Esther requested that the Jews of Susa be allowed "to do according to the law" a second day, as all the enemies of the Jews had not yet been defeated. It is significant to note here that Esther's request was in response to the king asking her if there was anything else that needed to be done. Esther did not initiate the request. And yet, in spite of the fact that the king initiated the question, and in spite of the fact that he was the ultimate authority and made the final decision in favor of an additional day of fighting, this verse and those following it have been used to support accusations of vindictiveness and blood-thirstiness on the part of Esther and the Jews of Susa.[1] Indeed, in early twentieth-century German scholarship, Esther's request and the subsequent actions of the Jews of Persia provoked such remarks as, "All the worst and most unpleasing features of Judaism are here displayed without disguise;"[2] and "[the book ascribes] rabid hatred against all gentiles."[3] Fox references the work of Wolfram Hermann (1986) for "a survey of the spite heaped on the book of Esther for its supposedly spitefulness" and the work of Elias Bickerman (1967), who "describes how and why the theologians of the German Enlightenment taught that Esther is a document of Jewish intolerance and hatred toward the human race."[4]

Esther's request in response to the king's question simply demonstrates that she was aware that all the enemies of the Jews had not yet been defeated and that the Jews needed one more day to defend themselves according to the law. The study in Chapter One concluded that, rather than being motivated by vindictiveness or a blood-thirsty desire to kill, the Jews simply took actions that were necessary for self-defense due to a decree that called for their annihilation. As such, Esther's action is "precautionary, eliminating opponents who might cause problems in the future."[5] After all, a second day of fighting in Susa would not have been necessary if there had been no more enemies still willing to attack.

Following their successful resistance against those who intended to annihilate them, the Jews rested and celebrated with feasting and rejoicing. According to 9:20-23, Mordecai wrote to the Jews instructing them to observe these days of feasting and rejoicing every year. However, Mordecai's instructions to observe the days of Purim apparently needed to be confirmed by a second letter written by Esther, because it was this second letter, referred to in 9:29, "issued on her authority as queen that establishes the festival for all time."[6] When Esther writes the second letter, "the

---

1. For example, see Lewis Bayles Paton, *The International Critical Commentary: A Critical and Exegetical Commentary on the Book of Esther* (Edinburgh: T and T Clark, 1908), 287; and Carey A. Moore, *The Anchor Bible: Esther* (New York: Doubleday, 1971), 88.
2. Carl Cornill, *Introduction to the Canonical Books of the Old Testament* (trans. G.H. Box; New York: G.P. Putnam's Sons, 1907), 257.
3. Karl Budde, *Geschichte der althebräischen Literatur* (Leipzig: 1906), 237.
4. Fox, *Character and Ideology in the Book of Esther*, 217.
5. *ibid.*, 112.
6. Bronner, "Reclaiming Esther," 8.

codification of the festival is complete,"[1] and chapter 9 concludes with the statement that this saying of Esther was written in a book. These events are particularly significant in light of feminist critique of Esther because not only was Esther's letter necessary for the establishment of Purim, but it was recorded as part of written tradition. In no other biblical text does a woman establish the observance of a festival, and "in no other biblical context do we find a woman serving as the catalyst for the writing down of an oral tradition."[2]

In Hebrew Esther, the character of Esther developed from that of a young woman who was the object of all the action to that of a leader who, beginning in chapter 4, is the only subject who clearly plays a decisive role in determining the rest of the events in the story. In chapters 4-9, she is portrayed as a woman who matured to the point of taking responsibility for the lives of her people and demonstrated that maturity by initiating the rest of the action. The Hebrew Esther is a woman who not only saved her people from annihilation, but is credited with establishing the observance of Purim. In her response to the challenge of 4:14, this Esther "shows how an ordinary person, one with little initial promise, can rise to a crisis and grow to meet its demands. . . . [T]hrough the person of Esther, the author links the issue of national salvation to individual character."[3] However, this description of Esther and her role in the events in which she was involved only applies to the Esther found in the Hebrew version. The Old Greek version presents a very different interpretation of her character, as well as her actions, from chapter 4 to the end of the book.

The Character and Actions of OG Esther

Now that the character and actions of Hebrew Esther have been determined, it is possible to compare and contrast how Esther is portrayed in the Old Greek version. The following

---

1. Leila Leah Bronner, "Esther Revisited: An Aggadic Approach," in *A Feminist Companion to Esther, Judith and Susanna* (ed. Athalya Brenner; Sheffield: Sheffield Academic Press, 1995), 176-97.

2. *ibid.*, 196.

3. Michael V. Fox, "Three Esthers," in *The Book of Esther in Modern Research* (ed. Sidnie White Crawford and Leonard J. Greenspoon; London: T and T Clark, 2003), 54.

analysis of specific passages will show how feminist critique of the character of Esther and its associated anti-Judaism are dependent on the Old Greek version of the story, as feminist charges and anti-Semitic diatribes cannot be supported by a reading of the Hebrew text alone. As will be seen, almost all of the changes and additions in Old Greek Esther affect the character of Esther. As a result, most of the discussion in this section will address feminist critique and its subsequent contribution to anti-Semitic interpretation of the story in light of the previous discussion of the relationship between feminist religious writings and anti-Judaism. However, in addition to the changes to Esther's character that specifically fuel feminist critique, there is a significant change made to the counter-decree in 8:11 that directly results in anti-Semitic diatribes against the book of Esther. Therefore, before beginning the more lengthy analysis of the changes to the character of Esther, there will be a brief comparison of the differences between the Hebrew and Old Greek versions of 8:11.

In Chapter One, a detailed study of the verbs used in the counter-decree of Hebrew 8:11 and the verbs used in the original decree of Hebrew 3:13, as well as other pertinent elements in the following story, demonstrated that the same verbs were used in both decrees in the Hebrew. This study concluded that the actions of the Jews of Persia, when faced with attempted annihilation, were those of self-defense. The counter-decree of Hebrew 8:11 gave the Jews the right to assemble for the purpose of standing for their lives and to take the same actions against their attackers that Haman's decree had ordered to be taken against them. It allowed the Jews to resist those who would attack them according to the original decree of 3:13, but did not give them the right to initiate an attack against anyone.

In contrast, OG 8:11 leaves out the repetition of all the verbs meaning "to destroy," "to kill," and "to exterminate" that are used in the Hebrew version, thereby losing the direct analogy that is found in Hebrew between the two decrees. Where the Hebrew version makes it clear through the exact repetition of verbs that the Jews are being allowed to defend themselves with identical means to those their attackers intend to use, the OG states that the king "ordered" the Jews to treat their enemies "as they wished." This is a significant change to Hebrew 8:11, in which the king only allowed the Jews to assemble for the purposes of self-defense. The rewriting of the decree in the OG creates a much more violent image of the actions of the Jews, resulting in subsequent anti-Semitic critique of those actions.

In addition to the rewriting of 8:11, numerous changes are made to the character and actions of Esther that encourage feminist critique and its associated anti-Judaism, which in turn further fuels anti-Semitic interpretation of the story. The first change made to OG Esther's character in contrast to Hebrew Esther has to do with her relationship to Mordecai. Esther is introduced in OG 2:7 as the orphaned daughter of the brother of Mordecai's father, who was being brought up by Mordecai. However, in contrast to the Hebrew, which says that "Mordecai took her to himself as a daughter," the OG says "he brought her up for himself as a wife." This change in Esther's identity from "daughter" in the Hebrew to "wife" in the OG may not initially appear to be particularly relevant to a discussion of feminist critique of Esther. However, the following analysis will demonstrate that this change in her relationship to Mordecai redefines her relationship to the king, and that Esther's relationship to the king is relevant to feminist critique of the story.

At the beginning of the preceding discussion on the character of Hebrew Esther, Esther was identified as a "girl" or "young woman" who was marriageable. It was noted that Esther fit the description of the kind of young woman the king's men would be gathering for the king, except for the fact that the term "virgin" is not included in the description of Esther. It was also observed that, while it is often assumed that Esther was a virgin, 2:8 only describes the women as "young women." The possibility that some of the young women were not virgins becomes a probability due to the fact that Esther was one of them, and the fact that in 2:7, she is described as a "young woman," but not as a "virgin." This conclusion is even more probable in light of Hebrew Esther 2:17, which says that the king loved Esther more than all "the women," as well as all "the virgins." According to the medieval Torah commentator Rashi (1040–1105 CE), the use of the term "the women" in addition to the term "the virgins" indicates that married women were gathered as well as virgins.[1] Rashi was

---

1. Barry D. Walfish, "Kosher Adultery? The Mordecai-Esther-Ahasuerus Triangle in Talmudic, Medieval and Sixteenth Exegesis," in *The Book of Esther in Modern Research* (ed. Sidnie White Crawford and Leonard J. Greenspoon; London: T and T Clark International, 2003), 111-36.

not alone in this interpretation. The Babylonian Esther Midrash[1] quotes Rabbi Rava (270–352 CE) as saying, "he [the king] wished to taste the taste of a virgin, and he tasted; the taste of a non-virgin, and he tasted."[2] According to Eliezer Segal, because both "women" and "virgins" are referred to in 2:17, "the two terms must designate separate categories" because "from a midrashic perspective it is unacceptable that Scripture should waste its words on mere synonyms."[3] Likewise, both Targums of Esther[4] maintain the use of the two terms, "women" and "virgins," in their translations of Hebrew 2:17.[5] In light of these various commentaries, and the fact that the text does not refer to Esther as a "virgin" but does include her among the "young women" as well as the "women" – a word that also means "wives" – it seems reasonable to suggest that a married relationship between Esther and Mordecai was possible. When additional features of the text and its historical setting are considered in addition to the textual evidence just presented, it is possible to conclude that the author of OG Esther made an intentional decision in the use of the word "wife" in 2:7, thereby making an intentional change to the identity of Esther.

One of the features of the text that would have influenced the author of OG Esther to use the word for "wife" in 2:7 is the use of the verb that means "to take" in the Hebrew text. This is a verb used elsewhere in the Hebrew Bible in relation to taking a wife. Because this verb is used to describe the action of Mordecai towards Esther, it is probable that the author of OG Esther interpreted this to mean that Mordecai had raised Esther for the purpose of taking her as a wife. In fact, the ancient Near Eastern practice of adoption-marriages, "in which a man would adopt a child with the intention of marrying her when she was old

1. A midrash is an exegetical interpretation of biblical texts. The Babylonian Esther Midrash is part of the Talmud, a central text of Rabbinic Judaism, written between 200 and 500 CE.
2. Eliezer Segal, *The Babylonian Esther Midrash: A Critical Commentary, Volume 2* (Atlanta, GA: Scholars Press, 1994), 65.
3. *ibid.*
4. Esther is the only book of the Bible that had two targums written about it. Targums are paraphrases and explanations of biblical books given by a rabbi.
5. Bernard Grossfeld, *The Two Targums of Esther: Edited, with Apparatus and Notes* (Collegeville, MN: The Liturgical Press, 1991), 46, 138.

enough," may have supported this interpretation.[1] Furthermore, even if Mordecai had "taken" Esther as a "daughter," "as cousins they could have married."[2] The relationship of Esther and Mordecai as cousins is evidenced by the identification of Esther in Hebrew 2:7 as the daughter of Mordecai's uncle and in OG 2:7 as the daughter of the brother of Mordecai's father. According to Semitic custom, the most suitable wife was a cousin on the father's side, which was the relation Esther was to Mordecai. The combination of the use of this verb and the historical evidence for this type of marriage supports the suggestion that Esther and Mordecai could have been married when Esther was taken to the king.

This possibility is further reinforced by the fact that the Babylonian Esther Midrash also states that Mordecai raised Esther to be his wife.[3] The interpretation found in the Midrash is evidence of an ancient exegetical position that, based on its appearance in OG 2:7, appears to date to the Hasmonean period. The Midrash makes "a play on 'daughter' and 'house,' the latter understood as an epithet for wife."[4] This play on words is possible due to the similarity in spelling of the two words, "daughter" and "house," in the Hebrew. As a result, the Hebrew word for "house" is used for "wife" in the Talmud, which is a rabbinic work like the Esther Midrash.[5] This play on words supports the understanding of Esther as Mordecai's wife through a discussion of 2 Samuel 12:3, in which Uriah's wife, Bathsheba, is compared to a lamb that would "lie in his bosom," and "was like a daughter to him." In spite of this comparison, it is clear in the text that the relationship between Uriah and Bathsheba was one of husband and wife. But, because of the use of "daughter" in relation to Bathsheba the wife, "so too in Esther we are justified in midrashically altering the meaning."[6] On the basis of the use of "house" for "wife" in rabbinic Hebrew, the use of "daughter" for "wife" in 2 Samuel 12:3, and "other

---

1. Fox, *Character and Ideology in the Book of Esther*, 276.
2. *ibid.*, 30.
3. Segal, *The Babylonian Esther Midrash*, 48-52.
4. Fox, *Character and Ideology in the Book of Esther*, 275.
5. Paul Haupt, "Critical Notes on Esther," in *Studies in the Book of Esther* (ed. Carey A. Moore; New York: KTAV Publishing House, 1982), 1-79.
6. Segal, *The Babylonian Esther Midrash*, 50.

biblical references in which the term 'daughter' signifies 'wife',"[1] the rabbis "assert that Hadassah and Mordecai are married."[2] The change of Esther's identity from daughter to wife in the OG, in combination with the early rabbinic interpretation of the relationship between Esther and Mordecai, indicates "that we are dealing with an ancient exegetical position;"[3] a position first demonstrated in Old Greek Esther.

Michael Fox suggests that the OG's interpretation of Esther's relationship to Mordecai as a wife, rather than a daughter, may also have been motivated by a "sense of propriety" to "obviate something of the impropriety of Mordecai taking an unmarried girl into his house."[4] However, a married relationship between Esther and Mordecai then creates another potential impropriety because Esther could then be viewed as committing adultery once she was taken to the king. To deal with this problematic interpretation, the rabbis explained the relationship between Esther and the king as a forced relationship, in which Esther was an unwilling participant. According to the Jewish legal interpretation, "she was engaged in an involuntary sexual relationship with the king, or, in other words, she was being raped regularly by him."[5] Therefore, "what went on between Esther and Ahasuerus was not adultery because it was non-consensual."[6] While feminist critique of Esther may not be particularly interested in the ancient exegetical position concerning a possible married relationship between Esther and Mordecai, Esther's identity as Mordecai's wife is relevant because this change in her identity redefines her relationship to the king, and it is Esther's initial passivity in her relationship to the king that is relevant to feminist critique. The rabbis' explanation that Esther was in an involuntary, forced relationship, combined with the use of passive verbs in the text in reference to everything that happened to Esther before 4:14, provides an answer for feminist

---

1. Another example of the use of the term "daughter" for a woman who would be a "wife" is found in Ruth 3:10-11. In the context of Ruth approaching Boaz for the purpose of asking him to perform his duty as kinsman-redeemer and marry her, Boaz addresses Ruth as "daughter."
2. Jo Carruthers, *Esther Through the Centuries* (Oxford: Blackwell Publishing, 2008), 103.
3. Segal, *The Babylonian Esther Midrash,* 51.
4. Fox, *Character and Ideology in the Book of Esther,* 275-6.
5. Walfish, "Kosher Adultery?" 118.
6. *ibid.,* 119.

criticism concerning that passivity. The text and subsequent commentary makes it quite clear that Esther was the object of the action being taken and her "induction into the harem was beyond her and Mordecai's decision."[7] As has been said previously, Esther's compliance with the events in her life "reflects an adaptation strategy fitted to the realities of her situatedness;"[8] a strategy that enabled her to survive and ultimately succeed in the context in which she found herself. And as the previous discussion on the character of Hebrew Esther demonstrated, she succeeded in assuming a role that "is good enough for any feminist."[9]

Following the introduction of Esther in 2:7, the overall plot of OG 2:8-17 is in agreement with Hebrew 2:8-17 in relation to the events that culminated in Esther being made queen. The OG's account of Esther's action of sending clothes to Mordecai in 4:4 and the calling of the fast in 4:16-17 is also quite similar literarily to that of the Hebrew text. It is what the author of the OG added after 4:17 that presents a very different view of the character of Esther. Following Hebrew 4:17, OG Addition C was inserted. Addition C contains two chapters, numbered 13 and 14 by Jerome (347–420 CE) when he removed all the Greek additions and put them together at the end of the Hebrew version in the process of producing his Latin Vulgate version of the Bible.[10] Chapter 13 of Addition C contains the contents of the prayer of Mordecai in

---

7. Fox, *Character and Ideology in the Book of Esther*, 197.

8. Berman, "Hadassah Bat Abihail," 649.

9. Lubitch, "A Feminist's Look at Esther," 1.

10. In Jerome's Vulgate, the Septuagint additions to Esther were removed from their logical position in the storyline, grouped together at the end of the Hebrew version, and given chapter numbers that followed the chapter numbers of the Hebrew version. When these additions were put back into their logical position in the story line of the Septuagint, Jerome's chapter numbers were retained. Thus, Septuagint Addition A, which precedes Hebrew chapter 1, is divided into Vulgate chapters 11 and 12; Septuagint Addition B, which is inserted between Hebrew 3:13 and 3:14, is Vulgate chapter 13; Septuagint Addition C, which follows Hebrew 4:17, is divided into Vulgate chapters 13 and 14; Septuagint Addition D, which follows Septuagint Addition C and precedes Hebrew 5:3 (Hebrew 5:1-2 is omitted from the Septuagint), is Vulgate chapter 15; Septuagint Addition E, which is inserted between Hebrew 8:12 and 8:13, is Vulgate chapter 16; and Septuagint Addition F, which follows Hebrew 10:3, begins with Septuagint 10:4 and ends with Septuagint 11:1.

response to the threat of annihilation, and chapter 14 contains narrative describing Esther's response to the impending genocide, as well as the contents of her subsequent prayer. OG 14:1 says that Esther was "seized with deadly anxiety" as she "fled to the Lord." She took off her queenly clothes, covered herself with ashes and dung, and prayed to the Lord God of Israel. 14:3-19 contains the contents of her prayer, which ends with a plea to be saved from her fear. This addition changes Esther's character in that, besides being portrayed as pious,[1] she is portrayed as fearful and seized with deadly anxiety at the thought of approaching the king. This is quite a contrast to Hebrew Esther, who, in 4:16, resolved rather matter-of-factly to go to the king at the risk of her life.

Following chapter 14 of Addition C, the OG added Addition D, or chapter 15 as it was numbered by Jerome. Addition D describes Esther's preparation for going before the king, as well as providing a detailed description of the encounter between her and the king. In OG 15:2-5, Esther took two servants with her as she went to see the king and had to lean on one of them because "her heart was frozen with fear." After arriving in the presence of the king in 15:6-7, Esther "faltered, turned pale and faint and collapsed" because the king looked at her in anger. However, according to 15:8-10, God changed the king's spirit to one of gentleness, causing the king to leave his throne, take Esther in his arms, and assure her that she would not die, because the law prohibiting anyone from approaching the throne uninvited applied only to their subjects (15:10). But in spite of these words and the fact that the king raised his scepter and touched Esther with it, she fainted again while in the process of speaking to the king (15:15).

Just as the content of chapter 14 in Addition C changes Esther's character, so too does the content of Addition D. The description of Esther's heart being "frozen with fear," combined with the dramatic account of her collapsing and fainting, not once but twice, "makes her into a fainthearted, delicate lady."[2] In fact, the physical reaction to her fear is evidence of "a certain degree of weakness, [a] character trait [that] is much more pronounced here."[3] In addition,

---

1. The addition of Esther's piety made the story more acceptable to the author of OG Esther in his Hasmonean setting, as well as to the Hellenistic Jews in Alexandria to whom it was sent.
2. Fox, "Three Esthers," 58.
3. Linda Day, *Three Faces of A Queen: Characterization in the Books of Esther* (Sheffield: Sheffield Academic Press, 1995), 197.

this entire scene "actually violates the logic of the narrative."[1] If the king's explanation in 15:10 that the law about approaching the king only applied to their subjects, then why did he look at her with such anger in 15:7 when she did approach him? Furthermore, why would Esther have been so deadly afraid of approaching him uninvited that she fainted twice?

Since Esther's behavior, as well as the behavior of the king, is not consistent with the king's explanation of the law in 15:10, there must be another motivation besides logic behind this literary addition. As has been noted, chapters 14 and 15 contain descriptions of Esther's piety, her thoughts and feelings, her emotions, her frailty, and accounts of her fainting. Unlike the Hebrew version, which doesn't include any of these elements, these features are "known from the Hellenistic romances" that consistently portray the heroine as pious and frail.[2] Since OG Esther was written for a Hellenistic Jewish audience, it would appear that the addition of these descriptive elements was for the purpose of making the character of Esther more attractive to that Hellenistic audience. Furthermore, the rewriting of Hebrew Esther, as well as the translation of the Hebrew Bible as a whole, "is perhaps the quintessential exemplar of how Judaism acculturated itself to the dominant society of the Hellenistic age without conceding the integrity of its tradition."[3] However, the Greek additions that portray Esther as frail and fearful do more than just add Hellenistic elements for the sake of acculturation. The change in the character of Esther from the self-assured Esther of the Hebrew version to the fearful Esther of the Old Greek illustrates the "progressive deterioration in the status of women in Hellenistic culture,"[4] whereby women were expected to be less self-confident and more frail. In light of the historical use of the Septuagint discussed earlier in this chapter, it is easy to see how this dramatic change in the character of Esther has contributed to feminist critique, as well as anti-Semitic critique, wherever OG Esther is read.

In contrast to the contribution that Additions C and D make to feminist critique of the character of Esther, the Babylonian Esther Midrash contains interpretations that demonstrate the

---

1. Fox, "Three Esthers," 58.

2. *ibid.*, 59.

3. Joshua Ezra Burns, "The Special Purim and the Reception of the Book of Esther in the Hellenistic and Early Roman Eras," *Journal for the Study of Judaism* XXXVII: 1 (2006): 1-34.

4. Fox, "Three Esthers," 59.

rabbis' approval of the actions of Esther following her decision to go to the king in 4:16. A significant example of this is found in the commentary on Hebrew 5:1 in 14b and 15a of the Midrash. Hebrew 5:1 says that on the third day of the fast called by Esther in 4:16, Esther "put on queenly attire" in preparation for approaching the king. It is important to note that this description of Esther's preparation differs greatly from the account in OG 15:1-2, and it is also significant that Hebrew 5:1-2 is omitted in the Old Greek. It seems the author of the OG did not think it was sufficient to rewrite the Hebrew description of Esther's preparation to go before the king. Rather, that description needed to be excluded entirely.

The Midrash interprets 5:1 as meaning that "Esther put on royalty" and according to R. Eleazar and R. Haninah, "this teaches that the Holy Spirit clothed her" or that "she put on the Holy Spirit."[1] "The rabbis' claim here is that she has been ordained from above and given approval for all the actions she will take in the future. . . . [W]ith her first assertive action the rabbis gave their approval."[2] The rabbis also demonstrate their approval of Esther by including her as one of the seven prophetesses in the list found in *Seder 'olam*. Esther's status as prophetess is based on the fact that her letter in 9:29 established the annual celebration of Purim. The rabbis concluded that "the authority for such an enactment – which included the acceptance of the Book of Esther into the canon – must have been divinely inspired; i.e., prophetic." [3] Rather than fueling feminist critique by weakening the character of Esther as OG Additions C and D do, the Babylonian Esther Midrash strengthens her character by demonstrating approval of her actions and by referencing her identity as a prophetess ordained by God. The rabbis have attributed courage and authority to Esther by portraying her "as an outstanding political figure and communal savior."[4]

Conclusions

The preceding analysis reveals that the overall role Old Greek Esther played in the events in which she was involved did not differ significantly from her role in the Hebrew text. Both versions

1. Segal, *The Babylonian Esther Midrash*, 266-7.
2. Lubitch, "A Feminist's Look at Esther," 438.
3. Segal, *The Babylonian Esther Midrash*, 214.
4. Lubitch, "A Feminist's Look at Esther," 446.

portray her as a woman who transitioned from being passive in chapter 2 to being the only subject who clearly played a decisive role in the action from 4:14 to the end of the book. Hebrew Esther assumed a leadership role by being the only woman in the biblical text to call a fast, by devising a creative agenda that the male characters in the story all followed, and by being involved in the writing of a royal decree. As a result, she was responsible for all the honor and wealth that Mordecai received, her letter established the observance of a festival, and the lives of the Jews of Persia were saved. Indeed, Hebrew Esther is distinct in her biblical and ancient Near Eastern context, and "there are few books from the ancient Near East that can stand up so well to an assessment by feminist standards."[1]

While the Old Greek version retains the account of the actions of Hebrew Esther, the significant changes made to her character by the descriptive, dramatic elements found in the additions illustrate the deterioration in the image and status of women in the Hellenistic period and contribute to an interpretation that supports feminist critique of the person of Esther. By failing to distinguish between the qualities demonstrated by OG Esther versus Hebrew Esther, feminist scholarship erroneously attributes the diminished character of Esther to Judaism, which it believes to be the source of sexism and patriarchy. This type of critique fans the fire of anti-Semitic interpretation of the story, as explained in the previous discussion of the relationship between feminist theology and anti-Semitism. By way of contrast, the rabbis' interpretations in the Babylonian Esther Midrash strengthen the character of Esther, and in so doing, refute the charge that Judaism is by definition anti-feminist. The combination of the rabbis' interpretations of Hebrew Esther and the literary comparison of relevant elements in these two versions of Esther demonstrates that feminist critique of the book of Esther, its associated anti-Judaism, and resulting anti-Semitic interpretation, is dependent on the Greek version of the story as these charges cannot be supported by a reading of the Hebrew text alone.

In light of the historical use of this Greek version of the story, it is easy to understand how the image of a fearful and powerless Esther, who was somehow vengeful, bloodthirsty, and greedy at the same time, has been the widespread, predominant image from the time this text was written until the present. As a result,

---

1. Fox, *Character and Ideology in the Book of Esther*, 211.

feminist and anti-Semitic critique of the story continues to abound in spite of the fact that Hebrew Esther gives an account of a woman's leading role in preventing the genocide of the Jews of Persia, and the fact that the Old Greek version was written, in part, to address the dangers that confronted Jews as a result of anti-Semitism. Furthermore, because of the preservation and use of the Greek version by the Church, the Hebrew version's emphasis on the right to self-defense when threatened with annihilation has been ignored or misunderstood by a significant part of the Christian world. As the next chapter will demonstrate, a negative perception of Jews – one that is remarkably similar to these historic anti-Semitic interpretations of the character of Esther and the actions of the Jews of Persia – continues to feed current beliefs concerning Jews and the State of Israel, that in turn, influence Christian anti-Zionism.

CHAPTER FIVE

From Historic Anti-Judaism to Current Anti-Zionism

This chapter will examine the connection between historic Christian anti-Judaism and current Christian anti-Zionism in relation to the contested legitimacy of the State of Israel in the context of the Arab-Israeli conflict. It is necessary to clarify this association before discussing specific examples that demonstrate how anti-Judaism informs anti-Zionism today. The first step in this analysis will be to summarize the development of Christian anti-Judaism, as revealed through replacement theology, and the role that erroneous Christian doctrine has played in historic anti-Semitism, even to the point of fueling and justifying the Holocaust. The second step will be to identify significant features of Christian anti-Judaism, which will not only provide a more complete definition of the term, but will illustrate how anti-Jewish theology is used to define Christian identity. And finally, an analysis of the statements and activities of particular organizations and individuals will expose the doctrine at the heart of current Christian anti-Zionism, a crusade that is justified through a customized form of anti-Jewish theology.

Definition of Terms

Before beginning the discussion of the history of Christian anti-Judaism, it will be helpful to define terms that will be used throughout this chapter. These terms are "anti-Judaism," "anti-Semitism," "anti-Zionism," and "replacement theology."

Theoretically, "anti-Judaism" refers specifically to the opposition to, and persecution of Jews based on their religion, or the denial of the right of Jews to exist in terms of their own self-understanding. "Anti-Semitism" is theoretically defined as opposition to Jews on the basis of ethnicity, which results from and includes delegitimizing, demonizing, and dehumanizing Jews as a people group. However, in spite of the fact that anti-Judaism is defined in religious terms and anti-Semitism in terms of race, there is essentially no difference between the two on the practical level. An underlying contempt towards Jews is the foundation for both, and opposition to Judaism almost always, if not always, results in opposition to Jews. As Perry and Schweitzer state, "One must avoid any kind of apologetic in the use of the term anti-Judaism that would separate the two phenomena as unconnected. Historically, one is the seedbed of the other."[1] As the analysis of the historical context of the composition of Old Greek Esther demonstrated, the persecution of Jews as a people during the Greco-Roman period was a direct consequence of opposition to the essential identifying features of Judaism, which are God, Torah, and the Land of Israel. Anti-Semitism was justified in the ancient world as the appropriate response to Jewish characteristics deemed "undesirable" that were attributed to features of the Jewish religion.

Unfortunately, this ancient phenomenon has not changed, but is alive and well in the modern world. It has simply manifested under a new name: "anti-Zionism." "Anti-Zionism" is defined as opposition to Zionism, which is a movement in support of the existence of a Jewish State in the ancient homeland of the Jewish people, the Land of Israel. Therefore, anti-Zionism can also be defined as a denial of the Jewish people's right to self-determination. Just as ancient anti-Semitism was justified as the appropriate response to undesirable characteristics of the Jewish religion, anti-Zionism is justified as the proper response to one of the identifying features of Judaism – the historic centrality of the Land of Israel. Anti-Zionism is synonymous with anti-Judaism in that the right of Jews to exist in terms of their own self-understanding – in this case, the right to have a Jewish State in their ancient homeland – is denied them. Anti-Zionism is also synonymous with anti-Semitism in that by opposing the existence of a Jewish State, Jews are opposed on the basis of ethnicity. In the context of the Arab-Israeli conflict, this opposition includes the demonization and delegitimization of Jewish Israelis as a people group. Just as anti-Judaism is the

---

1. Marvin Perry and Frederick M. Schweitzer, *Antisemitism: Myth and Hate from Antiquity to the Present* (New York: Palgrave Macmillan, 2002), 5.

seedbed of anti-Semitism, so too it and anti-Semitism provide the necessary fertile seedbed for anti-Zionism.

"Replacement theology" refers to a theological position held by parts of the Church that states that the Church has taken the place of, or replaced, Jews and Judaism in the purposes of God. The roots of this belief are found in the teaching of contempt towards Judaism and the theological anti-Judaism that originated with the *adversos Judaeos* teachings of the Early Church Fathers. This theological position is dependent upon the delegitimization and demonization of Jews and Judaism, and inevitably leads to overt anti-Semitism and anti-Zionism.[1]

History of Christian Anti-Judaism

Due to the fact that Christianity grew out of Judaism, both Judaism and anti-Judaism are relevant to Christian identity. The Jewish roots of Christianity were vital for the first Christian apologists, who were faced with "the necessity of having to defend Christianity against the Roman claim that it was a new and, therefore, an illegal religion."[2] So, for the sake of legitimacy at the beginning of the Christian era, the Church claimed an integral identity with Judaism. However, in the process, the Church started to identify itself as the true Israel, and Christianity as the scriptural fulfillment of Judaism. This was the beginning of the development of replacement theology, which, to this day, identifies Christians as the heirs of Jewish history and the Hebrew Bible. Because the Church is believed to have replaced the Jews in the purposes of God, this theology concludes that there is no further purpose for either Jews or Judaism. In fact, "the entirety of the religious conceptions of Judaism as proclaimed in the Old Testament was rejected as superseded by the Church."[3]

1. For an excellent detailed discussion of supercessionism and replacement theology, and their relationship to anti-Judaism and anti-Semitism from the time of the Early Church to the present, see Marvin R. Wilson, *Our Father Abraham: Jewish Roots of the Christian Faith* (Grand Rapids, MI: Eerdmans Publishing Company, 1989), 87-103.
2. Leonard V. Rutgers, *Making Myths: Jews in Early Christian Identity Formation* (Leuven: Peeters, 2009), 68.
3. James Parkes, *The Conflict of the Church and the Synagogue: A Study in the Origins of Antisemitism* (New York: Atheneum, 1969), 373.

Replacement Theology

The foundation of replacement theology is an allegorical interpretation of the Bible. Through this methodology, the terms "Israel" and "Jews" do not refer to the literal Land of Israel, or a literal people of Israel, known as "Jews" since biblical times. Instead, "Israel" and "Jews" are understood in spiritual terms. As a result, whenever believers in replacement theology come across these terms in the Bible, they immediately interpret them as a reference to the Church and Christians, who are the only "true" believers in God in this theological construct. Some Christian denominations that held this belief historically have since repudiated it, including Roman Catholics, the Netherlands Reformed Church, and several German Protestant churches. Unfortunately, some Evangelicals have begun to adopt it instead.

The Early Church's need to maintain its claim of identity with Judaism for the sake of legitimacy in the Roman Empire was soon replaced by its intent to establish an individual identity distinct from Judaism. As a result, early Christian leaders began to teach that Christianity was superior to Judaism, and had in fact replaced the Jews and their religion. However, the continued presence of Jews and the fact that Judaism continued to flourish in Late Antiquity represented a threat to the identity of early Christianity "on both a day-to-day basis as well as on a broader, ideological level," and "raised disconcerting questions that stuck at the very heart of early Christianity's theological position."[1] After all, if the Church had really replaced the Jews, how was it possible that they continued to prosper? Consequently, while maintaining its claim of superiority over Judaism, Christianity began to sever itself from its Jewish roots through the *adversos Judaeos* literature of the Early Church Fathers. According to Ruether, this literature was created "to affirm the identity of the Church, which could only be done by invalidating the identity of the Jews."[2]

Adversos Judaeos *Literature*

The literature of the Early Church invalidated the identity of the Jews, and it negated their claim to the Bible as well. One example

1. Rutgers, *Making Myths*, 56, 123.
2. Rosemary Radford Ruether, *Faith and Fratricide: The Theological Roots of Anti-Semitism* (Eugene, OR: Wipf and Stock, 1997), 181.

of the nullification of Jewish identity with Jewish Scripture is found in the Letter of Barnabas, written between 95 and 135 CE. The Letter states, "all the institutions of the Old Testament are theologically negated in order to set forth a polemic directed against Judaism's claim to sacred Scripture."[1] The widespread appearance of early Christian teachings against the Jews in letters, sermons, commentaries, apologies, and theological treatises testifies to the fact that "the synagogue posed an active threat to the church."[2] The growth of Christianity as a separate religion was facilitated by the development of anti-Jewish theology expressed in this literature, as "the Church sought to conquer its opponent by demonstrating with every possible evidence that Judaism was a dead and legalistic faith."[3]

The *adversos Judaeos* literature of the Early Church Fathers established the foundation for the replacement theology that continues to this day. Church Fathers such as Ignatius of Antioch (c. 50–c. 108 CE), Justin Martyr (c. 100–165), Clement of Alexandria (150–c. 215), Tertullian (160–225), Origen (184–253), Cyprian (200–258), Eusebius (c. 260–339), Gregory of Nyssa (335–395), Chrysostom (347–407), Jerome (c. 347–420), and Augustine (354–430) all wrote various kinds of literature and preached sermons against the Jews. This literature was motivated by the need to prove the superiority of Christianity over Judaism, and was inspired by Greek philosophy and the Greek allegorical method of interpreting the Hebrew Bible. Every one of these Early Church Fathers came from a Greco-Roman background and context.

The Allegorical Method of Interpretation and Replacement Theology

As has been said, the foundation of replacement theology is the allegorical interpretation of the Bible. This hermeneutical method was adopted from the Greek culture of the time, and

---

1. Henning Graf Reventlow, *History of Biblical Interpretation, Volume I: From the Old Testament to Origen* (trans. Leo G. Perdue; Atlanta, GA: Society of Biblical Literature, 2009), 120.

2. Paula Fredriksen, *Augustine and the Jews: A Christian Defense of Jews and Judaism* (New Haven, CT, and London: Yale University Press, 2010), xvii.

3. Wilson, *Our Father Abraham*, 92.

is as old as the first Christian seminary in Alexandria, Egypt, which, according to Jerome (347–420), was founded by Mark, the apostle. One of the Church Fathers listed above was Clement of Alexandria (150–c. 215), who was a prominent Greek scholar. Clement became head of the school in about 190 CE, and he combined Greek philosophy with Christian instruction. In so doing, Clement established the precedent that placed an emphasis on Greek philosophy rather than the Hebrew Bible as the foundation for the Christian faith. It is significant to note that this technique is in direct contradiction to the approach of the New Testament itself, which demonstrates its dependency on the Jewish Scriptures throughout. Therefore, the emphasis on Greek philosophy and method of interpretation at the first seminary in Alexandria was another step in the severance of Christianity from its Hebrew roots.

Origen (184–253) was another very influential Early Church Father who followed Clement as head of the seminary in Alexandria and continued to teach the allegorical method of interpretation of the Hebrew Bible. He taught his students that the Church had replaced the Jews in the plan of God, and that the Church had inherited the biblical blessings originally intended for the Jews, while the curses were still in effect for the Jews. By the time of Origen, the *adversos Judaeos* teaching of the Church had expanded on the first century claim of superiority to Judaism to include the invalidation of the identity of the Jews, their claim to their Scriptures, and any purpose for them in the plan of God. It would not be long before this emerging doctrine of replacement would provide the theological justification for persecution of Jews in every generation, even to this day.

Many of Origen's students became leading theologians at the same time that the Church was expanding throughout the Greco-Roman world, and they in turn trained future church leaders. One of Origen's students, Pamphilus, taught Eusebius (c. 260–339), who would become an advisor to Constantine the Great, the Roman emperor from 306 to 337. Constantine made Christianity the official religion of the Roman Empire. Under the influence of Eusebius, Constantine adopted Origen's interpretation of the Hebrew Bible with its emphasis on how the Church has replaced Judaism. As a result, replacement theology has been entrenched in the doctrine of much of the Church ever since.

Adversos Judaeos *Material and the Charge of "Christ-Killers"*

Chrysostom (347–407), Jerome (c. 347–420), and Augustine (354–430) perpetuated the anti-Judaism and the doctrine of replacement handed down by those who came before them. Perhaps the best known case of the use of *adversos Judaeos* material is the series of eight sermons preached by Chrysostom in Antioch in 386–388 CE. In those sermons, Chrysostom used crude and offensive anti-Jewish rhetoric to emphasize his point that because the Jews killed Christ, they have been rejected by God. He cited the destruction of Jerusalem in 70 CE as evidence of their divine punishment.

The charge against the Jews as "Christ-killers" has been used in every generation since Chrysostom to simultaneously justify anti-Judaism and persecution of the Jews and explain why the Jews suffer that persecution. However, a close reading of the Christian Scriptures clearly contradicts this accusation. The Gospel accounts record that it was a select group of leaders from the Sadduceean sect of Judaism who encouraged Pilate to execute Jesus. It is obvious from the overall biblical context that the Jews calling for Jesus' death were a small minority in comparison to the number of Jews who followed Jesus throughout his ministry. So, it is quite erroneous to label all Jews as "Christ-killers." It is interesting to note that the Jewish identity of the original followers of Jesus – and therefore the Jewish identity of the inhabitants of Israel 2,000 years ago – is often ignored or denied by modern Christians who argue against the right of the Jews to reestablish themselves in their ancient homeland.

The leaders of the Sadducees who wanted Jesus killed sought to remove him because they felt their positions and the security of the Jews were threatened by his popularity with the people. John 11:48-50 reveals their reasoning thus: "If we let him alone like this, everyone will believe in him, and the Romans will come and take away both our place and nation." These leaders were worried about losing their positions of authority, but as subjects under Roman rule, they did not have the authority to kill Jesus. They also had no authority to kill him according to their own legal system, because Jesus had done nothing that deserved death according to Jewish law. That is why they had to appeal to Pilate, the Roman governor of Judea, who did have the authority and the motivation to put someone to death who was perceived as a threat to the stability and success of his governorship. It was in Pilate's best interest to have Jesus out of the way; Pilate was the one who gave the order for Jesus to be killed; and Jesus was executed by the Roman method of crucifixion. Indeed, Jesus himself did not assign responsibility for his death to either Jewish or Roman authority. Instead, he said, "No one can take my life from me. I sacrifice it voluntarily." (John 18:6).

From Chrysostom to Now

Like Chrysostom, Jerome also maintained a very hostile, classic *adversos Judaeos* understanding of Christian identity – an understanding that Augustine attempted to counteract by asserting that Christian identity was bound historically and textually to Jewish identity. However, according to Paula Fredriksen, references to Jews in Augustine's sermons "range from mildly positive . . . to hardly inviting to downright insulting."[1] Fredriksen's goal is to present Augustine's position on the Jews as positive in contrast to earlier Church Fathers in general, and Jerome in particular. But even she points out that "a glance at the subject index under *Jew* or *Judaism* in any volume of Augustine's sermons reveals the familiar themes of *adversus* [*sic*] *Judaeos* invective such as: Jews are blind, hard-hearted, fleshly, stubborn, and prideful; they murdered Christ; they are exiles; they carry the church's books; and they are saved only by conversion."[2] These same invectives were handed down generation after generation, and were the cause of, and justification for, violent persecution of Jews in every generation.

The epidemic of medieval anti-Semitic sentiment and its accompanying violence is well documented,[3] as is the fact that the Reformation period began with anti-Judaism well-entrenched in the Church, evidenced in part by the writings of Martin Luther.[4]

---

1. Fredriksen, *Augustine and the Jews*, 310-11.

2. *ibid.*, 311.

3. See Joshua Trachtenberg, *The Devil and the Jews: The Medieval Conception of the Jew and Its Relation to Modern Anti-Semitism* (Philadelphia, PA: Jewish Publication Society, 1983); Leon Poliakov, *The History of Anti-Semitism, Volume I: From the Time of Christ to the Court Jews* (Philadelphia, PA: University of Pennsylvania Press, 2003), 42-169; James Parkes, *The Jew in the Medieval Community: A Study of His Political and Economic Situation* (London: The Soncino Press, 1938), 42-4, 59-89.

4. See Martin Luther, *In That Jesus Christ was Born a Jew* in *Luther's Works: Volume 45, The Christian in Society II* (ed. Walther I. Brandt;

As a former Augustinian monk, Luther did not abandon the *adversos Judaeos* diatribes of Augustine. Instead, he included and expanded upon them in his writings.[1] Luther's works then formed the foundation for subsequent German theologians, who, beginning in the eighteenth century, became extremely influential in the field of biblical scholarship worldwide.

Because of their pervasive influence on biblical scholarship, German scholars have also played a leading and influential role in anti-Semitic critique of the book of Esther.[2] Following the lead of German scholars, anti-Semitic critiques of Esther became prominent in British scholarship by the late nineteenth century and then in American scholarship by the beginning of the twentieth century. Anti-Jewish interpretations resulting from this scholarship are still felt, as the erroneous perception of the character of Esther and the actions of the Jews of Persia derived from the Greek versions of the story continue to have an effect on Christian perceptions of modern day Jews, which, in turn, influence beliefs concerning the actions of the State of Israel in the context of the Arab-Israeli conflict.

In the nineteenth century, the methods of critical study of the biblical text, known as "higher criticism" and "lower criticism," reached their zenith, primarily due to the influence of German scholars such as Julius Wellhausen (1844–1918). Wellhausen is the author of *Prolegomena to the History of Ancient Israel*, which was first published in 1878 under the title *History of Israel*. The main thesis of the book is that "the Mosaic history is not the starting point for the history of ancient Israel, but for the history of Judaism."[3] Wellhausen believed that the Pentateuch and historical books of the Hebrew

---

Philadelphia, PA: Muhlenberg Press, 1962); Martin Luther, *Against the Sabbatarians: Letter to a Good Friend, 1538* in *Luther's Works: Volume 47, The Christian in Society IV* (ed. Franklin Sherman; Philadelphia, PA: Fortress Press, 1971); and Martin Luther, *On the Jews and Their Lies, 1543* in *Luther's Works: Volume 47, The Christian in Society IV* (ed. Franklin Sherman; Philadelphia, PA: Fortress Press, 1971).

1. See Luther, *On the Jews and Their Lies.*
2. As Esther scholar Lewis Bayles Paton points out, "the book of Esther early became objects of [the] attack" of the "higher criticism" of the last two to three centuries of German scholarship. See Lewis Bayles Paton, *The International Critical Commentary: A Critical and Exegetical Commentary on the Book of Esther* (Edinburgh: T and T Clark, 1908), 111-18, for a discussion of "modern" critical Esther scholarship.
3. Julius Wellhausen, *Prolegomena to the History of Ancient Israel* (Eugene, OR: Wipf and Stock Publishers, 2003), v.

Bible were late creations and the result of multiple sources, and that the law did not reach its present form until after the Israelites were in exile. These premises provided an essential foundation for the academic deconstruction of the biblical history of the Jews, as well as biblical authority for the Mosaic Law. As a result of Wellhausen's work, Torah came to represent the "dead" and "legalistic" form of Judaism as it is commonly viewed in Christian belief, rather than being recognized as a revelation of divine law through the writings of Moses. After deconstructing the relationship between the Jews and their biblical history and law by defining what is written in the Bible as the beginning of Judaism, Wellhausen then proceeded to define Judaism as "a mere empty chasm over which one springs from the Old Testament to the New."[1]

By the twentieth century, the combination of centuries of anti-Semitic biblical scholarship represented by the work of Wellhausen and ecclesiastical anti-Judaism rooted in Luther's *adversos Judaeos* diatribes provided the theological justification used by Adolf Hitler and German theologians for the attempted annihilation of the Jews through the Holocaust.

Significant Features of Christian Anti-Judaism

The *adversos Judaeos* literature of the Early Church Fathers has remained effective long after the first few centuries of the Christian era, as evidenced by the brief historical survey above and by the continued acceptance of significant features of Christian anti-Judaism. These features helped to define Christian identity historically, and they are still doing so today. A brief summary of significant features of Christian anti-Judaism in the work of four different scholars will contribute to a more complete definition of the term and will illustrate how anti-Jewish theology helps to define Christian identity.

Jules Isaac addresses the Christian roots of anti-Semitism by identifying three themes of what he calls "the teaching of contempt." The first of these themes is that the dispersion of the Jews was a divine punishment for the crucifixion of Jesus; the second is that at the time of Jesus, Judaism was only a form of legalism; and the third is that the Jews are guilty of deicide.[2]

---

1. *ibid.*, 1.
2. Jules Isaac, *The Teaching of Contempt: Christian Roots of Anti-Semitism*

Charlotte Klein provides a thematic and chronological survey of scholarship – most of which is German – concerning theological views of Jewish religion after the Exile. The summary of the view of the authors surveyed is that between the Exile and the beginning of Christianity, Judaism was in a state of decadence, its faith was externalized, Judaism had failed, and the destruction of the Temple was a just punishment. Furthermore, Torah and its observance were condemned, and the Jews were judged guilty of the death of Jesus.[1]

Katharina von Kellenbach proposes "that the distorted representation of Judaism in Christianity is governed by three rules of formation." The first is that Judaism is the antithesis of Christian beliefs and values, the second casts Israel into the role of scapegoat, and the third "accounts for Christianity's continuity with Israel's past by reducing Judaism to the status of a prologue of Christianity."[2]

Rosemary Ruether presents an excellent survey of the *adversos Judaeos* writings of the Church Fathers in the third chapter of *Faith and Fratricide*. On page 117, she refers to these works as a "continuous tradition of Christological and anti-Judaic midrashim." These compositions emphasize the rejection of the Jews and the election of the Gentiles, as well as the inferiority and spiritual fulfillment of the Jewish law, cult, and scriptural interpretation. In chapter five, she identifies three dualisms that "shaped early Christian self-understanding" and "make Judaism their negative side."[3] These dualisms are the schism of judgment and promise, the schism of particularism and universalism, and the schism of letter and spirit.[4]

The following discussion will illuminate how these same characteristics of anti-Jewish theology feature prominently in the replacement theology of Palestinian Christians and a growing number of Evangelicals. This theology not only defines their Christian identity, but determines the position they take in relation to the Arab-Israeli conflict as well.

(New York: Holt, Rinehart and Winston, 1964).

1. Charlotte Klein, *Anti-Judaism in Christian Theology* (Philadelphia, PA: Fortress Press, 1978).
2. Katharina Von Kellenbach, *Anti-Judaism in Feminist Religious Writings* (Atlanta, GA: Scholars Press, 1994), 40-51.
3. Ruether, *Faith and Fratricide,* 228-9.
4. *ibid.*, 117-65, 226-45.

Anti-Jewish Theology at the Heart
of Christian Anti-Zionism

In recent years, these features of Christian anti-Judaism have been adapted for the purpose of powering a new movement that is targeting a specific audience: American Evangelicals, who have historically supported Israel's right to exist as a Jewish State. This Christian anti-Zionist crusade is spear-headed by Palestinian Christians, promoted by leaders in the United States, and justified through a customized replacement theology that has its roots in historic anti-Jewish theology. Rather than taking an approach to the Bible that leads to an understanding of God's purposes for Israel and the Jews, this campaign employs the allegorical method of interpretation used throughout Church history to replace the Jewish people in those purposes. The replacement theology that results from this hermeneutical method, in combination with elements of the anti-Jewish dogma outlined above, is joined to a Palestinian liberation theology to produce a virulent form of Christian anti-Zionism that demonizes and delegitimizes the State of Israel.

Palestinian Liberation Theology and Naim Ateek

Liberation theology began as a political movement within the Roman Catholic Church in Latin America in the 1950s and 1960s. It is based on a re-interpretation of Christian faith in relation to liberation from unjust economic, political, or social conditions. Naim Ateek, a Palestinian Anglican priest, adapted this theology in order to develop a Palestinian Christian theology in his doctoral dissertation titled "Toward a Strategy for the Episcopal Church in Israel with Special Focus on the Political Situation: Analysis and Prospect," which was submitted August 1, 1982, at San Francisco Theological Seminary. The result was a customized liberation theology that identifies Palestinians as the poor, disenfranchised victims of powerful Israeli oppressors. Ateek's theology is articulated further in his subsequent book, *Justice, and Only Justice: A Palestinian Theology of Liberation.*[1]

---

1. Naim Ateek, *Justice and Only Justice: A Palestinian Theology of Liberation* (Maryknoll, NY: Orbis Books, 1991).

The third chapter of Ateek's dissertation "sets out an introduction to a Palestinian Christian Theology," which "sheds theological light from a Palestinian Christian's view on Nationalism and Zionism."[1] In addition to being addressed to the Christian community in Israel and the Jewish community in general, Ateek seeks to address "the wider Christian community especially in the West and particularly those who believe in the literal inerrancy of the Bible."[2] Ateek's difficulty with Christians who take the Bible literally in relation to Israel is clarified by a subsequent statement when he says, "After the creation of the State [Israel], and largely due to some Jewish and Christian interpretations, the Old Testament's Jewish [Zionist] character became so visible that it has become repugnant to Palestinian Christians."[3] As a result, "there are certain passages in the Old Testament whose theological presuppositions and at times assertions, need not be affirmed by the Christian today. . . . [T]hese passages need not impose particular doctrinal views or obligations on the contemporary Christian."[4] In other words, according to Ateek, because the Old Testament's Jewish character is repugnant to Palestinian Christians, it does not have to be read literally and its theology and claims do not need to be taken seriously. This is the message he seeks to impress upon a Western Christian audience.

In 1989, Ateek implemented one of the goals behind the writing of his dissertation through the convening of an ad-hoc committee of ten clergy and lay people in Jerusalem. This meeting resulted in the founding of the Sabeel Ecumenical Liberation Theology Center in Jerusalem, which seeks "to pursue ways of finding answers to ongoing theological questions about the sanctity of life, justice, and peace."[5] In March 1990, Sabeel hosted an international conference that put Palestinian liberation theology in the context of other liberation theologies from around the world. Since then, International Friends of Sabeel chapters have been founded in

---

1. Naim Ateek, "Toward a Stategy for the Episcopal Church in Israel with Special Focus on the Political Situation: Analysis and Prospect" (San Francisco Theological Seminary, August 1 1982), 2.
2. *ibid.*, 176-7.
3. *ibid.*, 180.
4. *ibid.*, 184.
5. "Vision," *Sabeel Ecumenical Liberation Theology Center, 2010,* accessed on 21 March 2015: http://www.sabeel.org/vision.php.

Australia, Scandinavia, the United Kingdom, Ireland, Canada, and the United States for the purpose of providing support for Sabeel's work in education and resistance against the Israeli "occupation."

A statement from Sabeel's website illustrates the particular focus of this form of liberation theology, as well as the organization's intent to promote "international awareness" and to encourage Christians worldwide to stand with the Palestinian people. The "Palestinian Liberation Theology" section of "Our Story" states:

> By learning from Jesus – his life under occupation and his response to injustice – this theology hopes to connect the true meaning of Christian faith with the daily lives of all those who suffer under occupation, violence, discrimination, and human rights violations. Additionally, this blossoming theological effort promotes a more accurate international awareness of the current political situation and encourages Christians from around the world to work for justice and to stand in solidarity with the Palestinian people.[1]

In comparison to the biblical text, Ateek's theology places a disproportionate emphasis on peace and justice, while manipulating Jesus' Sermon on the Mount to support his interpretation. In addition, Ateek leaves out much of the rest of the Bible when it does not fit into his customized theology. In particular, any reference to Israel as a nation and/or the prophesied restoration of Israel is ignored or interpreted as a reference to the Church. As a result, this theology is faulty, biased, and powered by a political agenda.

Because Israel and Zionism are portrayed as the root of all evil for the Palestinians, this theological position inevitably results in an anti-Israel position. Israel is not only falsely portrayed as an evil state, but Christians who support Israel are falsely portrayed as a dangerous threat to peace in the Middle East as well. Within the framework of Ateek's theology, the only acceptable Christian position is to work for the liberation of the poor and oppressed Palestinians from the Israeli "occupation." This theological position naturally leads to taking a stand against Israel, as demonstrated by the anti-Zionist teaching materials of the Presbyterian Church (USA) and its decision to divest from

---

1. "Our Story," *Sabeel Ecumenical Liberation Theology Center, 2010,* accessed on 14 September 2014: http://www.sabeel.org/ourstory.php.

companies that do business with Israel.[1] Ironically enough, this stance also works against the prospect of a two-state solution, which Palestinians purport to want. After all, if Palestinians had their own state, they would no longer be able to claim the status of "poor and oppressed," and their liberation theology would no longer be applicable. But in spite of this irony, every proponent of the pro-Palestinian/anti-Israel theology surveyed below adheres to this customized liberation theology in combination with Palestinian replacement theology.

Palestinian Proponents of Christian Anti-Zionism

Bethlehem Bible College

According to its website, Bethlehem Bible College (BBC) is an interdenominational Christian college located in Bethlehem, "the very site where Jesus was born."[2] It was founded in 1979 by local Arab pastors under the leadership of Bishara Awad to provide theological education and training for Christian leaders in the local church. It also "aims to strengthen and revive the Christian church and support the local Christians in the Holy land."[3] BBC claims to "be committed to the great truths and abiding fundamentals of the Christian faith," and it affirms the National Association of Evangelicals' Statement of Faith.[4]

However, Bethlehem Bible College's website does not mention its role as sponsor of the biennial "Christ at the Checkpoint" conferences, nor the replacement theology that is promoted

---

1. Naim Ateek's liberation theology has informed the work of the Israel Palestine Mission Network (IPMN) of the Presbyterian Church (USA), which published a blatantly anti-Zionist educational tool titled *Zionism Unsettled: A Congregational Study Guide* in January 2014. The IPMN committee also played a very influential role in resolutions passed at this church's General Assembly in June 2014, which included divesting from companies that do business with Israel, and questioning the viability of the two-state solution in favor of a one-state solution that would result in the establishment of a Palestinian state through the destruction of the State of Israel.
2. "About Us," *Bethlehem Bible College,* accessed on 14 September 2014: http://www.bethbc.org/welcome/about-us.
3. *ibid.*
4. "Beliefs," *Bethlehem Bible College,* accessed on 14 September 2014: http://www.bethbc.org/welcome/aboutus/beliefs.

at those conferences and by those associated with BBC. It also does not reference a recent video its media department produced that is blatantly anti-Israel and anti-American. Before going into more detail about the "Christ at the Checkpoint" conferences or the individuals associated with these conferences who espouse a Palestinian replacement theology, a brief analysis of the recent video, *Bethlehem Voices on Gaza*, will reveal what BBC is truly all about.

Bethlehem Voices on Gaza *(2014)*

The video, *Bethlehem Voices on Gaza*, was produced by Bethlehem Bible College's media department and posted on YouTube on August 8, 2014. It was made in the midst of the Hamas-Israeli conflict of July-August 2014 and purports to "interview people on the streets of Bethlehem regarding the war in Gaza."[1] It includes a thirty-five-second introduction by Rev. Alex Awad, followed by six minutes and twenty seconds of statements from twelve unidentified people. Alex Awad is the brother of Dr. Bishara Awad, President Emeritus and the inspiration behind the founding of BBC. He is also the Dean of Students and a full-time instructor at BBC, a chartered member of the BBC Board of Directors, and the Senior Pastor of East Jerusalem Baptist Church.

Awad, the only person to appear who is identified, introduces the video with a greeting of love in the name of the Lord Jesus Christ that is followed by a plea for prayers, help, and love for the suffering Palestinian church. The video is obviously directed at an American audience, as evidenced by each of the speakers who follow Awad. All twelve speakers, who for some reason remain unidentified, perpetuate an anti-Israel, and sometimes anti-American, narrative through an absence of historical or political context and factual error. All of them address their comments directly to Americans, and appeal for US intervention in the Hamas-Israeli conflict.

In light of the fact that this video was obviously made for an American audience, the anti-American animosity expressed by several of those who speak comes as quite a surprise, particularly

---

1. Alex Awad, "Bethlehem Voices on Gaza," *YouTube*, 8 August 2014, accessed on 14 September 2014: https://www.youtube.com/watch?v=5s7nq6B6KJQ.

in light of the fact that the speakers are requesting support from that Christian American audience. Surprise becomes incredulity when one learns that the anti-American propaganda being directed at an American audience is partially funded by American donations through an American organization registered as a 501(c)(3) non-profit.

There are two men in particular who make blatantly false statements concerning actions taken by the US in the Middle East. One of them refers to an American policy that resulted in the destruction of "a lot of cities and nations like Iraq, Syria and Palestine." The US did invade Iraq in 2003, but it did not destroy cities in Syria and "Palestine" in the context of that war. This man's statement not only reveals an ignorance of recent history on his part, but also demonstrates an egregious anti-American agenda on the part of BBC, who produced this video and most certainly knows better.

A second man says, "This destruction [referring to Gaza] is American-made and handed to Israelis." Again, this statement shows a lack of knowledge of the realities concerning the American administration's position in relation to this conflict. Contrary to the implication that America was in support of Israel's actions in Gaza, President Obama's opposition to this campaign was evidenced by his repeated and consistent pressure on Prime Minister Netanyahu for an immediate ceasefire. This reality is documented in an article published in *The Times of Israel* on July 28, 2014.[1] Even if the man speaking in the video is not aware of the tenuous relationship between the Israeli prime minister and the American administration, the producers of the video at BBC certainly know.

While anti-American remarks are limited to just a few of the speakers in the video, every one of them perpetuates anti-Israel propaganda. One of the most frequent accusations, common to most, if not all, of the comments, is the insinuation that the so-called Israeli "attacks" in Gaza were unprovoked and arbitrary and that Israel was targeting civilians. This allegation ignores the fact that terrorists fired over 11,000 rockets into Israel between

---

1. Ilan Ben Zion, Lazar Berman and Marissa Newman, "4 soldiers killed in mortar attack, as PM says Gaza op goes on, vows to counter tunnels," *The Times of Israel*, 28 July 2014, accessed on 14 September 2014: http://www.timesofisrael.com/day-21-obama-calls-netanyahu-urges-immediate-unconditional-ceasefire-in-hamas-conflict/.

the time Israel withdrew from Gaza in 2005 and the beginning of Operation Protective Edge on July 8, 2014. In addition to the 11,000, more than 4,480 rockets were aimed at Israeli citizens in July and August in the midst of the conflict.

The Israeli military campaign in the summer of 2014 was conducted for the purpose of putting an end to the rocket attacks on Israeli citizens, cities, and towns. It was an operation carried out in response to assaults initiated by Hamas, and, therefore, was not unprovoked. At the conclusion of the campaign, "The IDF said it had struck nearly 4,762 terror targets — most of them rocket-launching sites, nearly 1,000 of them command and control centers, about 240 Izz ad-Din al-Qassam Brigades buildings, nearly 200 weapons storage and manufacturing facilities, nearly 150 terror training compounds and 1,535 additional terror sites."[1] In stark contrast to the intentional targeting of civilians by Hamas, and in direct contradiction to the false allegation that Israel singled out civilians during Operation Protective Edge, these numbers demonstrate that Israel took aim at strategic military sites for the purpose of reducing Hamas' ability to target Israeli civilians.

The propaganda that accuses Israel of targeting civilians also flies in the face of well-documented facts about the identity of those killed during Operation Protective Edge. According to an article published on the website of the Committee for Accuracy in Middle East Reporting in America, the "fatalities are disproportionately [compared to the overall population] among young males, which corresponds with the characteristics of combatants." In addition, "only about 12 percent of the total fatalities are female, though females make up half the population."[2] If the IDF was targeting civilians, one would think the number of women killed would be far greater than 12 percent. And one would also expect to see comparable numbers of men of all ages among the casualties. But the

---

1. Yifa Yaacov, "After 29 Days: Operation Protective Edge by the Numbers," *The Times of Israel*, 5 August 2014, accessed on 19 March 2015: http://www.timesofisrael.com/after-29-days-operation-protective-edge-by-the-numbers/.

2. Steven Stotsky, "Reporting of Casualties in Gaza," *Committee for Accuracy in Middle East Reporting in America*, 14 July 2014, accessed on 14 September 2014: http://www.camera.org/index.asp?x_context=55&x_article=2762.

numbers show that the vast majority of men killed were the age of combatants, which is further indication of Israel's intent to target military sites.

And finally, the second speaker makes an outrageous statement when he says, "as you know, we have been under occupation for sixty-five years." First of all, the comments he makes were supposed to be in reference to what was currently happening in Gaza. Gaza is not "under occupation," unless this man considers Hamas to be an occupying force. There have not been any Jews in Gaza, much less any IDF forces, since Israel withdrew unilaterally in 2005. Furthermore, the West Bank is not "under occupation" either, and certainly has not been for "sixty-five years" – at least not by Israel. Prior to Israel gaining this territory after the 1967 war, the West Bank – so named because it was the west bank of the Jordan River in relation to the country of Jordan – was *illegally* occupied by Jordan. Israel captured the territory from Jordan after it won a defensive war against Egypt, Syria, and Jordan, all of whom attacked with the goal of destroying the Jewish State. Following the 1967 war, the UN passed Resolution 242, which identifies the West Bank as *administered* territory, whose ownership is disputed.[1] The final status of this territory will – according to this resolution – be determined in some future peace agreement between Israel and the Palestinians. But until then, the West Bank is *disputed* territory, not *occupied* territory.

By including remarks that promote such erroneous material in the video they produced, the media center of Bethlehem Bible College and Alex Awad, dean and full-time professor at this institute of higher learning, demonstrate either an ignorance of the facts, or an intent to ignore the facts. Equally disturbing is the fact that this video employs egregious anti-Israel and anti-American propaganda in an effort to raise support from co-religionists in the United States. Indeed, by producing a video filled with such factual error and lack of historical or political context, Awad and BBC demonstrate their intent to capitalize on their status as the "poor and oppressed" victims of Israeli (and American) aggression. In the process, they reveal a base animosity to the Jewish State that can only be explained by the anti-Jewish/anti-Israeli theology revealed during the "Christ at the Checkpoint" conferences they host in Bethlehem.

---

1. "UN Security Council: The Meaning of Resolution 242," *Jewish Virtual Library*, accessed on 14 September 2014: http://www. jewishvirtuallibrary.org/jsource/UN/meaning_of_242.html.

"Christ at the Checkpoint"

The "Christ at the Checkpoint" (CATC) conference is hosted every two years by Bethlehem Bible College. The first CATC conference was held in Bethlehem in 2010, with subsequent conferences in 2012 and 2014. The name of these conferences, as well as the logo – which depicts a church behind the security barrier built by Israel to prevent suicide bombers from targeting Israeli civilians – demonstrates the focus of these meetings. In fact, Article 9 of the CATC manifesto states: "For Palestinian Christians, the occupation is the core issue of the conflict." Through their connection of the checkpoints, the security barrier, and the "occupation" with the significance of Bethlehem for Christians, the message is clear: If Jesus lived in Bethlehem today, he would have to go through checkpoints just like the Palestinians do. The imagery also suggests that either the Israelis are trying to stop Mary and Joseph from entering the city before the birth of Jesus, or that they are trying to keep the infant Jesus trapped in the city. This message, as well as the content presented, reveals the anti-Jewish and anti-Israel perspective promoted at these conferences. Through content and imagery, the CATC conferences perpetuate the millennia-old Christian doctrine that the Jews are an obstacle to God's purposes.

In addition to perpetuating this anti-Jewish doctrine, the leaders of CATC adhere to a Palestinian replacement theology, in which Palestinians replace Jews as the indigenous people of the Holy Land, and Jesus and the early Christians were all Palestinians. The logical conclusion of this theology is that the Jewish State of Israel does not have a legitimate right to exist. Because Evangelical leaders participate in these conferences, CATC plays an influential role in the targeting of Evangelicals with this message of Christian anti-Zionism.

American Proponents of Christian Anti-Zionism

The theological/political movement spear-headed by Naim Ateek, Sabeel, Bethlehem Bible College, and "Christ at the Checkpoint" has already been accepted by the majority of mainline denominational churches in the United States. The current concern is how it is now being promoted in American Evangelical churches and para-church organizations that have traditionally supported Israel's right to exist and its right to self-defense. The following discussion will look at specific organizations, leaders, and media that promote an anti-Israel message – cloaked in the guise of a Christian pursuit of peace and justice – specifically intended to encourage Evangelical Christians to abandon their support for Israel and stand in solidarity with Palestinian Arabs. This anti-Zionist narrative is powered by a combination of the same anti-Jewish arguments used historically to define Christian identity, and the new customized liberation/replacement theologies. The following examples of current leaders in this movement are not exhaustive, but they are highly representative. The features of this particular form of Christian anti-Judaism/anti-Zionism are relevant regardless of who promotes them. This is because the demonization and delegitimization of Jews and the State of Israel will continue in the Christian world as long as those who identify as Christians continue to adhere to the same errant theologies discussed in this chapter.

The Telos Group

The Telos Group is one of the primary engines driving the anti-Zionist movement in the Evangelical Christian world. Although it operates under the guise of being pro-Israeli, pro-Palestinian, and pro-peace, this organization and its followers are actually moving Evangelicals towards an anti-Israel position in relation to the Arab-Israeli conflict through a combination of replacement and liberation theology, and the demonization and delegitimization of Jews and the State of Israel. The organization is headquartered in Washington DC and was co-founded in 2009 by California-born lawyer of Palestinian Christian descent, Gregory Khalil, and Evangelical Christian and former State Department employee, Todd Deatherage. According to the Telos Group website, both of these men have impressive accomplishments.[1] However, none of their training or work experience includes theological education, in spite of the fact that they are leading an organization whose stated mission is to "strengthen the capacity of American faith communities – and especially American Evangelicals – to help positively transform the Israeli-Palestinian conflict."[2] As they

---

1. "The Telos Team," *The Telos Group*, accessed on 14 September 2014: http://www.telosgroup.org/about/staff.
2. "Mission + Vision," *The Telos Group*, accessed on 14 September 2014: http://www.telosgroup.org/about/mission.

pursue this goal, they are offering theological instruction without any previous preparation that qualifies them for this role. In light of this reality, thoughtful Christians should question the theological perspective that supports their anti-Zionist position.

The group organizes local training seminars and national gatherings to educate Evangelicals about the conflict and brings selected Israeli and Palestinian leaders to the US for speaking tours. Perhaps most significantly, Telos invites strategic leaders in the American church to participate in all-expenses-paid educational pilgrimages to the Holy Land, on which tour participants are presented with a one-sided narrative that portrays Palestinians as victims and Israelis as oppressors. However, core issues of the conflict, such as Palestinian refusal to recognize Israel as a Jewish State and the use of terrorism against Israeli citizens, are ignored. This biased narrative is not surprising in light of the speakers Evangelical leaders meet when they participate in Telos' tours.

REV. MITRI RAHEB

Telos pilgrimage participants meet with leading Palestinian speakers such as Rev. Mitri Raheb, the pastor of the Evangelical Lutheran Christmas Church in Bethlehem. Raheb has a long history of anti-Israel activism, and has been criticized by NGO Monitor and the Simon Wiesenthal Center due to "his efforts to delegitimize the Jewish State's existence." According to the Wiesenthal Center:

> In speeches given to various religious symposia and church summits (including the infamous 2004 US Presbyterian assembly that approved a boycott and divestment campaign against Israel), Raheb promoted a "Palestinian theology" that purports that Jews are not the Chosen People and therefore have no right to the Holy Land.[1]

When he spoke at the "Christ at the Checkpoint" conference in Bethlehem in 2010, Raheb used a racial theory to support his belief that Jews are not the true people of the Land of Israel.

---

1. Benjamin Weinthal, "Israel Slams Award to Anti-Semitic Pastor," *Jerusalem Post*, 9 February 2014, accessed on 14 September 2014: http://www.jpost.com/International/Israel-slams-award-to-anti-Semitic-pastor.

He claims that the Palestinians are the indigenous people of the land, and that Jesus was a Palestinian. He said:

> Israel represents Rome of the Bible, not the people of the land. And this is not only because I'm a Palestinian. I'm sure if we were to do a DNA test between David, who was a Bethlehemite, and Jesus, born in Bethlehem, and Mitri, born just across the street from where Jesus was born, I'm sure the DNA will show that there is a trace. While, if you put King David, Jesus and Netanyahu, you will get nothing, because Netanyahu comes from an East European tribe who converted to Judaism in the Middle Ages.[1]

This statement provides a vivid example of how Palestinian Christians delegitimize Jews and, by extension, the existence of the Jewish State of Israel. It also demonstrates Palestinian replacement theology, in which Palestinians have replaced Jews as the indigenous people of the Land, and Jesus and the early Christians are identified as Palestinians. The logical outworking of this theology is the belief that the Jewish State of Israel does not have a right to exist.

The idea that Jews of European descent are not really Jewish is an old anti-Semitic fabrication used to delegitimize the connection between modern Jews, their Israelite ancestors, and their historic ties to the Land of Israel. This fraudulent theory has been debunked by recent genetic studies. In his book, *Legacy: A Genetic History of the Jewish People*, Dr. Harry Ostrer, Professor of Pathology and Genetics at Albert Einstein College of Medicine and Director of Genetic and Genomic Laboratories at Montefiore Medical Center, summarized his and other work in genetics of the last twenty years.[2] He not only concluded that all major Jewish groups share a common Middle Eastern origin, but he also refuted the belief that there was any large-scale genetic contribution from European tribes. But Raheb ignores such data in order to cling to his racial theory that Jews are not the true people of the Land of Israel, which in turn supports his Palestinian replacement theology, in which Palestinians have replaced Jews as the indigenous people of the Land.

---

1. Mitri Raheb, *Christ at the Checkpoint*, accessed on 14 September 2014: http://www.christatthecheckpoint.com/lectures/Mitri_Raheb.pdf.
2. Harry Ostrer, *Legacy: A Genetic History of the Jewish People* (Oxford: Oxford Press, 2012).

ARCHBISHOP ELIAS CHACOUR

Telos tour participants are also exposed to Archbishop Elias Chacour, who resigned his position as the Melkite Catholic Bishop of Galilee in January 2014 in the shadow of charges of sexual harassment, mismanagement, and disputes with priests. Chacour is the vice president of Sabeel Ecumenical Liberation Theology Center, the organization founded by Naim Ateek mentioned above. As was said, Sabeel's theology advocates for the liberation of Palestinians from Israeli "occupation" in the name of working for justice and peace. Because Ateek also believes that the Church has replaced the Jews in the purposes of God, the continued existence of any form of Jewish sovereignty represents an affront to both his and Chacour's replacement theology.[1] In other words, because the Church has replaced the Jews, Jews have no right to have a sovereign state of their own. This belief is consistent with one of the root themes Jules Isaac addresses in his "teaching of contempt," which is that the dispersion of the Jews was a divine punishment for the crucifixion of Jesus. For Palestinian Christian theologians like Chacour, the regathering of the Jewish people in their ancient homeland is a direct affront to their belief that the Jews' dispersion was evidence of their guilt in relation to the charge of deicide. According to this teaching of contempt, the existence of a Jewish State in the Land of Israel is illegitimate.

Chacour plays a prominent role in an anti-Israel movie, *The Stones Cry Out*, produced by Italian filmmaker Yasmine Perni in 2013. In this movie, Chacour tells his personal story of displacement and expulsion from his boyhood home of Kafr Bir'im in the Upper Galilee. Chacour's story is tragic and the people who lived in this town did suffer as a result of Israeli policy. However, what Chacour is unable to acknowledge is that the expulsion of Palestinians from Kafr Bir'im happened in the context of a war that was initiated by surrounding Arab nations for the purpose of destroying the newly established Jewish State. In that context, Palestinians were viewed as possible allies with their fellow Arabs. Because of Kafr Bir'im's proximity to the Lebanese border, and the frequent occurrence of cross-border infiltration, the need to remove the villagers was

---

1. *Sabeel Ecumenical Liberation Theology Center,* accessed on 14 September 2014: http://www.sabeel.org/index.php.

a strategic consequence of Israel's war of self-defense. It was not, as Chacour alleges, simply the result of a Jewish desire to "get rid" of as many Palestinians as possible.

In the context of telling this story, Chacour descends into classic anti-Israel polemic when he comments that he finds it surprising that "they [the Jews] made others endure what they had endured." In so doing, Chacour is suggesting that Israelis are the new Nazis; an association that obviously demonizes Israelis and delegitimizes the State of Israel. However, there is absolutely no equivalency between the removal of residents from a village for strategic purposes in a war of self-defense and the systematic annihilation of six million Jews by the Nazis simply because they were Jewish. The removal of Palestinians from Kafr Bir'im was a tragedy for those involved, but it certainly cannot be compared to the Holocaust.

In attempting to assign any kind of moral equivalency between what happened to the residents of Kafr Bir'im and what happened to the Jews during the Holocaust, Chacour exemplifies the anti-Israel narrative promoted by the Telos Group. A more accurate reference to Nazis in the context of the Arab-Israeli conflict would point out that it was the Palestinian nationalist leader, Haj Amin al-Husseini, who collaborated with the Nazis during World War II, asked Adolf Hitler for help in making Palestine *Judenrein*,[1] and was indicted as a war criminal at Nuremberg. But the speakers who work with the Telos Group only present one-sided accounts of the conflict that leave out a multitude of facts. As a result, there is little chance that listeners who are uninformed about the history and context of the conflict will come away with anything but a conviction that to be truly Christian, one must support the Palestinians and oppose Israel.

MEMBERS OF THE TELOS PRESIDENTIAL ADVISORY COUNCIL

In 2013, Telos formed the Telos Presidential Advisory Council. According to their website, this council is "a diverse panel of 20 policymakers and opinion shapers who have been assembled to

---

1. *Judenrein* is a German term meaning "free of Jews." Haj Amin al-Husseini wanted Hitler's help in making Palestine *Judenrein* in his day, and the current Palestinian President, Mahmoud Abbas, has declared that a future Palestinian state will be *Judenrein* as well.

share their insight into the sectors of faith, politics, and policy."[1] While these twenty people may be diverse in terms of occupation, they are not diverse when it comes to their position on the Arab-Israeli conflict. One of the members of the council, Salam Al-Marayati, is a founder and current President of the Muslim Public Affairs Council.[2] He has a long-term history of defending terrorist groups and acts of terrorism as "legitimate resistance." His hostile view of Israel is evident in a statement made on September 11, 2001, concerning the attacks on the Twin Towers and the Pentagon. He said:

> If we're going to look at suspects, we should look to the groups that benefit the most from these kinds of incidents, and I think we should put the state of Israel on the suspect list because I think this diverts attention from what's happening in the Palestinian territories so that they can go on with their aggression and occupation and apartheid policies.[3]

Another member of the Telos Presidential Advisory Council is Lynne Hybels, a co-founder of Willow Creek Community Church in Chicago, Illinois. She is a well-known speaker in this new movement within the Evangelical world and was one of the speakers at the "Christ at the Checkpoint" conference in Bethlehem in 2012. While she and her church will be discussed in more detail below, it is sufficient to note at this point that according to Dexter Van Zile, Christian Media Analyst for the Committee for Accuracy in Middle East Reporting in America (CAMERA), Willow Creek Church is a "bastion of anti-Zionism in the Evangelical community."[4] With people like Salam Al-Marayati and Lynne Hybels on their Presidential Advisory Council, it is difficult to imagine how the Telos Group can continue to assert that they are pro-Israel.

1. "News," *The Telos Group*, accessed on 14 September 2014: http://www. telosgroup.org/news/P10.
2. Salam al-Marayati, "Apologists or Extremists," *The Investigative Project on Terrorism*, 24 March 2010, accessed on 14 September 2014: http://www.investigativeproject.org/profile/114.
3. *ibid.*
4. Dexter Van Zile, "Book Promoted by Willow Creek Church Leaves Readers Ill-Prepared for Peacemaking," *Committee for Accuracy in Middle East Reporting in America*, 28 October 2013, accessed on 14 September 2014: http://www.camera.org/index.asp?x_context=55&x_ article=2575.

In summary, the Telos Group targets strategic Evangelical leaders and provides them with all-expenses-paid pilgrimages, during which they are exposed to speakers with a long history of anti-Israel activism. The message these leaders hear openly condemns Israel and presents a narrative that portrays Palestinians as victims and Israelis as oppressors. In particular, the storyline demonstrates features of the two-thousand-year-old anti-Jewish theology outlined by Isaac, Klein, von Kellenbach, and Ruether. These features include the "Christ-killer" charge, the rejection of the Jews as the historic people of the Bible and the Land, and the election of the Gentiles – in this case, the Palestinians – as the true people of the Land. Of specific concern is the fact that Judaism – or in this case, the existence of a Jewish State – is understood to be the antithesis of Christian beliefs and values. In keeping with the logical conclusion of these anti-Jewish features, the Telos narrative emphasizes the necessity of standing in solidarity with the Palestinians because of the need to see them "liberated" from Israeli "oppression." Pilgrimage participants then use their influence with Evangelicals to promote a Christian anti-Zionist position based on a storyline that has its foundations in a Palestinian replacement and liberation theology, and the demonization and delegitimization of Jews and the Jewish State.

Cameron Strang

An excellent example of the influence of the Telos Group can be seen in an article written in 2014 by Cameron Strang, the publisher of *Relevant*, a popular magazine among millennial Evangelicals who consider themselves "moderate" or "progressive" in relation to theology and social issues. When *Relevant* was first published in 2003, it was quite supportive of Israel, as demonstrated by a pro-Israel article published in December 2005 titled "Israel: Why You Should Care." But since then, Strang, along with other young Evangelical leaders, has been an invited guest on one of Telos' all-expenses-paid pilgrimages to the Holy Land. After participating in the Telos tour, Strang and his magazine took a sharp turn away from support of Israel, as demonstrated by his article in the March/April 2014 issue of *Relevant*. The feature article, titled "Blessed are the Peace Makers," addresses the action the author believes the Church must take to work for peace in relation to the Arab-Israeli conflict. In addition to input from Palestinians who advocate for peace, this piece includes like-minded quotes from Todd Deatherage, the co-founder of Telos. By the end of the article, Strang is able to conclude that "many are beginning to believe it is possible to be authentically pro-Israeli, pro-Palestinian and pro-peace."

However, another of his concluding statements displays the very one-sided approach of this piece, thereby revealing the false nature of the claim of these self-identified "pro-peace" people to be both pro-Israeli and pro-Palestinian. Strang writes:

> To remain a democratic state that is Jewish in character and majority, Israelis must find a way to acknowledge Palestinian demands for sovereignty in a portion of the historic land of Israel. And in order for Palestinians to achieve dignity and freedom, they must be either be allowed to create their own state in a portion of historic Palestine or be given equal civil and political rights in Israel.

This statement exhibits how those who profess to be "pro-Israeli, pro-Palestinian and pro-peace" place all the responsibility for a successful peace process on the Jewish State. As Strang articulates so clearly, Israel "must find a way to acknowledge Palestinian demands" and Palestinians "must be allowed to create . . . or be given." At no point in the article does this author assign responsibility to the Palestinians for anything. According to his definition of what it means for the Jewish State to remain a democratic state, Israel must do all the giving. This assertion completely ignores the history of Israel's repeated attempts to negotiate for peace, as well as the history of Palestinian refusal of those attempts. By ignoring relevant historical context, Strang – along with all those he quotes – not only contradicts his claim to be both pro-Palestinian and pro-Israeli, but also demonizes Israel in the process. Furthermore, by falsely portraying Israel as the sole source of the problem, this author demonstrates the continuing effect of Naim Ateek's liberation theology, which requires Christians to work for the liberation of the oppressed Palestinians from the Israeli "occupation." This theological position results in an anti-Israel position that is dependent on a complete omission of the political and historical context of the Palestinian-Israeli conflict, as well as a blindness concerning disingenuous Palestinian demands for sovereignty.

PALESTINIAN DEMANDS FOR SOVEREIGNTY

In his *Relevant* article, Strang also writes, "Israelis must find a way to acknowledge Palestinian demands for sovereignty in a portion of the historic land of Israel." This statement implies that Palestinian demands for sovereignty are sincere, and that Israel has never recognized those demands, attempted to reach an agreement, or given up land for peace. The attempt to place all the responsibility for peace on Israel, while not holding the Palestinians responsible for anything, fails to take into account any of the history of Israel's repeated attempts to make peace, including its unilateral withdrawal from Gaza in 2005. The following survey of the political and historical context of this conflict will reveal that, in contrast to the false perception perpetuated by Strang and the Telos Group, the Palestinian demands for sovereignty are disingenuous, as multiple opportunities for sovereignty have been refused in favor of continuing Arab efforts to annihilate the Jewish State.

THE POLITICAL AND HISTORICAL CONTEXT OF THE CONFLICT

The 1949 Armistice Lines

On November 29, 1947, the UN General Assembly voted to partition Palestine into two states, one Jewish and the other Arab. The UN partition plan (UN Resolution 181)[1] divided the British Mandate so that each state would have a majority of its own population, although a few Jewish settlements would fall within the proposed Arab state while hundreds of thousands of Palestinian Arabs would become part of the proposed Jewish state. However, the Palestinian Arabs and the surrounding Arab states rejected the UN plan on the grounds that the General Assembly vote was an international betrayal that allotted too much territory to the Jews. As a result, the Palestinian Arab state envisioned by UN Resolution 181 was never established. Instead of accepting an opportunity for sovereignty under a two-state solution, the Arabs attempted to destroy the new State of Israel with the intent of establishing a Palestinian state that encompassed all the territory.

---

1. "United Nations General Assembly Resolution 181," *The Avalon Project at Yale Law School*, 29 November 1947, accessed on 14 September 2014: http://avalon.law.yale.edu/20th_century/res181.asp.

On May 15, 1948, the British evacuated Palestine, and the State of Israel was born. The neighboring Arab states of Egypt, Syria, Jordan, and Iraq immediately invaded Israel, claiming that they sought to "save" Palestine from the Zionists. The war between Israel and the Arab states ended with the signing of armistice agreements in 1949. The territory known as Palestine prior to 1948 was divided into three parts, and the boundaries between them are known as the 1949 armistice lines (the "Green Line"). Israel got control of much of the territory that is currently part of the State, Jordan occupied East Jerusalem and the hill country of Judea and Samaria (the "West Bank"), and Egypt took control of the coastal plain around the city of Gaza (the "Gaza Strip"). At this point, Jordan and Egypt could have enabled the founding of a Palestinian state in the territories under their control, which are the current disputed territories. However, they did not, choosing instead to use the Palestinian people as pawns in the ongoing propaganda war against Israel.

The Three No's of Khartoum

Another opportunity for the creation of a Palestinian state came in 1967, after Israel defeated the armies of Egypt, Jordan, and Syria in what is known as the Six Day War. This was a defensive war, fought in spite of multiple Israeli attempts to convince its neighbors to negotiate a peace settlement in response to years of terrorist attacks by Arabs from Jordan, the Gaza Strip, and Lebanon, shelling of the Galilee from the Golan Heights by Syria, and threatening rhetoric from President Nassar of Egypt. The position of all the countries surrounding Israel was made explicitly clear by Nasser on May 27, 1967, when he said, "Our basic objective will be the destruction of Israel. The Arab people want to fight."[1]

After just six days of war, Israeli forces had captured the Sinai and Gaza Strip from Egypt, the Golan Heights from Syria, and the West Bank from Jordan. Israel also took possession of East Jerusalem, which, along with the West Bank, had been illegally occupied by Jordan. After winning against what looked like impossible odds, the Israelis – as well as many others – had hopes that the Arabs would finally be ready to talk peace.

---

1. "The Six-Day War: Background and Overview," *Jewish Virtual Library*, accessed on 14 September 2014: http://www.jewishvirtuallibrary.org/jsource/History/67_War.html.

Indeed, the *Christian Century*, a magazine not known for its Zionist sympathies, wrote on June 21, 1967:

Israel's astounding military repulsion of threats from its Arab neighbors – whatever else may be said of it – has added a new, important, and potentially healthful dimension to the 20-year-old conflict between the two sides. Until now the Arab states have shouted a recalcitrant "Never" to all proposals that the quarrels between them and Israel be negotiated. They have refused to recognize Israel's legitimacy as a state, have denied it innocent use of the Suez Canal, have precluded any settlement of the Arab refugee problems by refusing to enter into diplomatic relations with Israel and have constantly threatened to annihilate Israel at a time of their own choosing. Until now the situation was one that kept Israel under constant pressure. Now that Israel has penetrated deeply into and controls vast areas of Egypt, Jordan and Syria, the situation is reversed. The Arab states are under pressure, and their "Never" does not have the permanence it appeared to have a month ago. Now men who refused to talk must talk.

But just three weeks after the end of the war, hostilities began again as the Soviet Union initiated a massive resupply of arms to Egypt and Syria, prompting Nasser of Egypt to declare that he was preparing to continue the battle against Israel. Then, from 29 August to 1 September of 1967, the leaders of thirteen Arab states met in Khartoum, Sudan, and pledged to continue their struggle against Israel. The agreed-upon conditions were very specific: there would be *no* peace with Israel, *no* negotiations with Israel, and *no* recognition of Israel. These are the infamous "three no's of Khartoum."[1] The adoption of this stance in favor of maintaining the effort to destroy Israel represents another missed opportunity for the creation of a Palestinian state.

United Nations Resolution 242

Following the Six Day War of June 1967 and the three no's of Khartoum, the United Nations Security Council adopted Resolution 242 on November 22, 1967, for the purpose of

---

1. "The 3 No's of Khartoum," *Committee for Accuracy in Middle East Reporting in America*, accessed on 14 September 2014: http://www.sixdaywar.org/content/khartoum.asp.

establishing the principles that were to guide the negotiations for an Arab-Israeli peace settlement.[1] In short, Israel would withdraw from land won in the war in exchange for peace with its neighbors. This "land for peace" formula has been at the root of all attempts at negotiations ever since. However, this UN resolution was passed three months *after* thirteen Arab states had agreed on the three no's of Khartoum. Therefore, it is not surprising that all subsequent attempts on Israel's part to negotiate land for peace have consistently been met with Palestinian rejections of all offers of sovereignty. But in his article, Strang ignores all relevant political and historical context in favor of lending credibility to disingenuous Palestinian demands for sovereignty while he demonizes Israel as the party responsible for the lack of peace.

Camp David Accords, 1978-1979

One notable exception to the failure of negotiations since the adoption of UN Resolution 242 in 1967 is the signing of the peace treaty between Anwar Sadat of Egypt and Menachem Begin of Israel in 1979, in which Israel withdrew from the Sinai Peninsula in exchange for Egypt, making the Sinai a demilitarized zone. The framework of the treaty was negotiated when the two leaders met at Camp David in 1978, but ultimately this accord was the result of direct negotiations between the two nations, initiated by President Sadat's visit to Jerusalem to meet with Prime Minister Begin and speak to the Israeli Knesset. This was an unprecedented move that infuriated most of the rest of the Arab world, but as a result of this treaty, Egypt got the Sinai back and Israel was able to live in peace with one of its neighbors.

Full diplomatic relations were established between Israel and Egypt in 1982, making Egypt the only Arab state to officially recognize Israel until 1994, when Jordan did as well. The fact that Israel continues to have diplomatic relations with Egypt and Jordan demonstrates that Israel is ready, willing, and able to reach an agreement for peace when dealing with a party that engages in serious negotiations. However, as the examples of Egypt and Jordan show, successful negotiations with Israel include the acknowledgment of Israel's right to exist. The refusal on the part

1. "UN Security Council: Resolutions on Israel/Middle East," *Jewish Virtual Library*, accessed on 14 September 2014: http://www. jewishvirtuallibrary.org/jsource/UN/sctoc.html.

of the Palestinians to acknowledge Israel's right to exist – choosing instead to continue to wage jihad for the purpose of liberating all of "Palestine" – is the reason there have been no successful negotiations of land for peace between Israel and the Palestinians.

The Camp David Summit of 2000
and the Clinton Parameters

At the Camp David Summit in the summer of 2000, Israel's Prime Minister Ehud Barak offered the Palestinians sovereignty over 95 percent of Judea and Samaria (the West Bank) and 100 percent of Gaza. He proposed a division of Jerusalem that would include Arab neighborhoods inside the present boundaries of Jerusalem as part of the future Palestinian state. The proposal would have also made Arab areas outside of Jerusalem part of a new Arab city of Al-Quds. Israeli land would be exchanged for territory in the West Bank remaining under Israeli control. Jerusalem's Old City would be divided and the Arabs would have religious sovereignty over the Temple Mount. This was an unprecedented offer of land and sovereignty on the part of the Israelis. However, Palestinian Authority Chairman Yassar Arafat refused and made no counter-offer.

Following the failure of the Camp David Summit, President Bill Clinton presented a peace plan that came to be known as "the Clinton parameters." Clinton's plan proposed a Palestinian state comprising between 94 percent and 96 percent of the West Bank and the entire Gaza Strip; Israeli annexation of settlements in blocks; Palestinian sovereignty over Arab areas in East Jerusalem; Israeli sovereignty over Jewish areas in West Jerusalem, including the Western Wall; Palestinian sovereignty over its own airspace; and the return of refugees to the Palestinian state. Land swaps were part of this proposal as well. The fact that this was an excellent offer of sovereignty for the Palestinians is evidenced by a warning the Saudi Arabian Ambassador to the US, Prince Bandar bin Sultan, gave to Yassar Arafat. He said, "I hope you remember, sir, what I told you. If we lose this opportunity, it is not going to be a tragedy. This is going to be a crime." Bandar later told *The New Yorker*'s Elsa Walsh, "It broke my heart that Arafat did not take that offer."[1]

---

1. Gilead Ini, "Bandar's Legacy," *Committee for Accuracy in Middle East Reporting in America*, 21 July 2005, accessed on 14 September 2014: http://blog.camera.org/archives/2005/07/bandars_legacy.html.

Israel's Ehud Barak accepted the Clinton plan. But just as he had with Barak's offer at the Camp David Summit, Arafat refused it. Instead of accepting such an exceptional opportunity for sovereignty, endorsed by the Saudi Arabian ambassador, Arafat gave orders to initiate a violent campaign of terror against Israel, known as the Second Intifada.[1] This intifada began in September 2000 and resulted in the deaths of more than 1,000 Israelis by 2005. Arafat's refusal of such an extraordinary offer of sovereignty combined with his instigation of the Second Intifada makes it exceptionally clear that the Palestinians are much more interested in attacking Israel than in accepting land for peace. This historic reality makes Strang's insinuation that Israel alone is responsible for the lack of peace especially egregious.

The Example of Gaza

In its continued quest of peace in exchange for land, the State of Israel forcibly removed all of its citizens from Gaza in August 2005. Jewish homes, greenhouses, and infrastructure were left intact. But rather than taking advantage of what they had been given and building upon it to develop a thriving economy in their own sovereign territory, the Arabs dismantled everything left by the Jews and used whatever they could as raw material for rockets designed to kill the same people who had provided them with the resources and opportunity to do so. Instead of using this opportunity to establish an independent state dedicated to improving the lives of its citizens, Hamas turned Gaza into a launching pad from which over 11,000 rockets were fired into Israel prior to the beginning of Operation Protective Edge on July 8, 2014.

This behavior is consistent with the position of Hamas' leaders, who do not recognize Israel's right to exist, refuse to negotiate with Israel, and continue to call for the end of "the Zionist project in Palestine."[2] As Osama Hamden, a Hamas representative, said

---

1. JPost.com Staff, "Suha Arafat Admits Husband Premeditated Intifada," *The Jerusalem Post*, 29 December 2012, accessed on 14 September 2014: http://www.jpost.com/Middle-East/Suha-Arafat-admits-husband-premeditated-Intifada.
2. Ricki Hollander, "The Facts About Hamas," *Committee for Accuracy in Middle East Reporting in America*, 24 April 2014, accessed on 20 September 2014: http://www.camera.org/index.asp?x_context=7&x_issue=11&x_article=1618.

at a press conference for Hamas Al Aqsa TV in December 2008, "Our goal is to liberate all of Palestine, from the river to the sea, from Rosh Hanikra to Umm Al-Rashrash [Eilat]." The fact that Hamas is also concerned with the territory known as the West Bank (included in the land between the river and the sea) is evident in a statement made by Hamas co-founder Mahmoud al-Zahar, June 15 2010, on Future TV, Lebanon. In a video clip translated by the Middle East Media Research Institute (MEMRI),[1] he said:

> We demand the liberation of the West Bank, and the establishment of a state in the West Bank and Gaza, with Jerusalem as its capital – but without recognizing [Israel]. This is the key – without recognizing the Israeli enemy on a single inch of land. . . . This is our plan for this stage – to liberate the West Bank and Gaza, without recognizing Israel's right to a single inch of land, and without giving up the Right of Return for a single Palestinian refugee. Our plan for this stage is to liberate any inch of Palestinian land, and to establish a state on it. Our ultimate plan is [to have] Palestine in its entirety.[2]

This statement makes it abundantly clear that Hamas has no interest in a two-state solution, for Gaza, the West Bank, or any combination thereof. In fact, as is evident from this quote, their ultimate goal is "Palestine in its entirety," which obviously means the elimination of the Jewish State. Unfortunately, this position is not unique to Hamas. Fatah, the majority faction of the PA and the current governing body in the West Bank, shares the goal of the destruction of the Jewish State with Hamas. In a statement on Hezbollah TV on April 2 2014 and in a video posted to YouTube on April 20 2014, which was translated by Palestinian Media Watch, Fatah Central Committee member Tawfiq Tirawi made statements such as

> The two-state solution does not exist. . . . We must return to the option of one Palestine from the [Jordan] River to the [Mediterranean] Sea. . . . The homeland . . . is . . . all of Palestine . . . which is represented by [the] Gaza [Strip] and the [West] Bank, by Palestine – all of Palestine, from its

---

1. "About Memri," *The Middle East Media Research Institute*, accessed on 20 September 2014: http://www.memri.org/about-memri.html.
2. "Video Clip," *The Middle East Media Research Institute*, accessed on 20 September 2014: http://www.memri.org/clip/en/0/0/0/0/0/0/2527. html.

[Jordan] River to its [Mediterranean] Sea. This is our goal; this is the lantern that lights our way; these are our principles in the Fatah Movement: Palestine – [the] Gaza [Strip] is part of it; the [West] Bank is part of it; and it is Haifa, Jaffa, Acre, and it is all of Palestine, which will be an independent state for us, Allah willing.[1]

In light of this history of how time after time Israel has sought peace with its neighbors, only to be attacked again and again, it is unconscionable that Strang attempts to persuade the readers of *Relevant* that Israel "must find a way to acknowledge Palestinian demands" for there to be peace. In order to presume that there is something else Israel can do to make peace – other than voluntarily cease to exist – and in order to believe that Palestinian leaders want peace, one must either be ignorant of history, or have made a willful decision to disregard that history. Indeed, the omission of all historical context in the promotion of the Palestinian narrative is indicative of a profound bias on the part of Strang and the Telos Group. It would appear that this prejudice is the logical result of their adherence to Palestinian liberation and replacement theology. In any case, by placing all the responsibility for peace on Israel while expecting nothing in return from the Palestinians, Strang makes a reprehensible contribution to the delegitimization of the Jewish State in the Christian press.

THE RWANDAN GENOCIDE

In his article, Strang compares the Arab-Israeli conflict to the Rwandan genocide. This happens to be an appropriate comparison, but not in the way the author intended. It appears Strang's intent was to perpetuate the well-worn trope that Israel is guilty of attempted genocide. However, once again, some historical and political context reveals that it is actually the Palestinian leaders who routinely incite and train their people towards the desired goal of the annihilation of the Jews. Indeed, the tactics of the Palestinians are easily recognized by those who lived through the genocide in Rwanda.

---

1. Itamar Marcus and Nan Jacques Zilberdik, "Fatah Leader Calls for Israel's Destruction," *Palestinian Media Watch*, 29 April 2014, accessed on 20 September 2014: http://www.palwatch.org/main. aspx?fi=157&doc_id=11319.

In 2009, at the United Nations Durban II conference in Geneva – a follow-up to the blatantly anti-Semitic and anti-Israel Durban I "Conference against Racism, Racial Discrimination, Xenophobia and Related Intolerance" – a group of Rwandan diplomats and scholars expressed concern about the demonization of Jews and Israel to Dr. Charles Asher Small, the Director of the Institute for the Study of Global Antisemitism and Policy.[1] In his article of April 19 2014 in *The Times of Israel*, titled "On Cockroaches, Apes and Genocide," Small validated those concerns by documenting how the tactics used today against Israel and the Jews are the same as those used by Hutu extremists against the Tutsis in Rwanda, and are the same as those used by the Nazis against the Jews preceding the Holocaust.[2] A few examples from the Human Rights Watch (HRW) report, *Propaganda and Practice*, will illustrate the parallels between Hutu propaganda and Palestinian propaganda.[3]

According to the HRW report, "[Hutu] propagandists stressed that Tutsi were foreign to the area and had stolen Rwanda from its rightful inhabitants, and that the ruthless conquerors had ground the Hutu under their heel in a repressive and bloody regime." Just as the Hutu propagandists claimed that Tutsi were foreigners who had stolen the land and oppressed the rightful owners of the land, so too the Palestinians claim that they are the historic inhabitants of the land and that the Israelis are foreign occupiers and oppressors. In an insightful article titled "Why the Palestinians Refuse to Recognize Israel as a Jewish State" published by the Gatestone Institute on February 3, 2014, Ali Salim points out that in spite of the fact that "every Muslim knows that the Jews in Israel are the descendants of the ancient Hebrew nation known as the Israelites," "high-ranking PA figures claim that the Jews do not have religious or historical claims to the Holy Land" and that "the Jews took the land by force."[4] As Salim demonstrates,

---

1. Gerald M. Steinberg, "Analyzing the Durban II Conference," *Jerusalem Center for Public Affairs*, 4 March 2010, accessed on 20 September 2014: http://jcpa.org/article/analyzing-the-durban-ii-conference/.
2. Charles Asher Small, "On Cockroaches, Apes and Genocide," *The Times of Israel*, 19 April 2014, accessed on 20 September 2014: http://blogs.timesofisrael.com/cockroaches-apes-and-genocide/.
3. "Propaganda and Practice," *Human Rights Watch*, 8 August 2014, accessed on 20 September 2014: http://www.hrw.org/reports/1999/rwanda/Geno1-3-10.htm.
4. Ali Salim, "Why the Palestinians Refuse to Recognize Israel as a Jewish State," *Gatestone Institute*, 3 February 2014, accessed

"The real reason for their refusal to recognize Israel as a Jewish country . . . is . . . so that it might be destroyed." As can be seen, both Hutu and Palestinian propagandists have promoted a false claim for the purpose of inciting their followers to annihilate "the other."

The Hutus compared the Tutsi to cockroaches in propaganda that said, "A cockroach gives birth to another cockroach. . . . The history of Rwanda shows us clearly that a Tutsi stays always exactly the same, that he has never changed. The malice, the evil are just as we knew them in the history of our country."[1] Just as the Tutsi were compared to cockroaches that are perpetually evil, so too Jews/Israelis are dehumanized and identified as animals who are the enemies of Muslims and the Palestinian people. This analogy is clearly demonstrated in "Case Study: Portraying Jews as Apes and Pigs," published by the Palestinian Media Watch (PMW).[2] The widespread nature of this teaching is illustrated through such examples as a teacher at Al-Aqsa Mosque school teaching students that Jews who visit the Temple Mount are "monkeys and pigs," girls on PA TV stating that Jews are "barbaric monkeys, wretched pigs," and the moderator at a Fatah ceremony declaring that "Our war with the descendants of the apes and pigs [i.e. Jews] is a war of religion."

The Hutu propagandists also "insisted that not just the freedom and prosperity of Hutu were at risk but their very lives . . . charging that the Tutsi had prepared a war that would leave no survivors."[3] Based on the false claim that the enemy's objective was extermination, Hutu leaders exhorted their audiences to "rise up . . . really rise up." Underlying much of the propaganda was the image of the Hutu as the innocent victim of aggression by Tutsi conquerors. Authorities used lies, exaggeration, and rumors about the local situation to make the general propaganda against Tutsi more immediate and frightening. The parallels between Hutu propaganda and Palestinian propaganda are glaring. Just as the Hutu claimed to be innocent victims who were in danger

---

on 20 September 2014: http://www.gatestoneinstitute.org/4151/palestinians-recognition-israel-jewish-state.

1. "Propaganda and Practice," *Human Rights Watch*.
2. "Case Study: Portraying Jews as Apes and Pigs," *Palestinian Media Watch*, accessed on 20 September 2014: http://www.palwatch.org/main.aspx?fi=786.
3. "Propaganda and Practice," *Human Rights Watch*.

of being annihilated by the Tutsi, so too the Palestinians claim to be innocent victims of attempted genocide at the hand of Israelis. And just as Hutu leaders exhorted their audiences to "rise up," so too Palestinian leaders encourage their followers to rise up in jihad to wipe out Israelis from the land.[1]

As Small points out in "On Cockroaches, Apes and Genocide," genocide begins with "words that dehumanise; ideas that incite. . . . In Nazi Germany, the decimation of two thirds of Europe's Jews was the culmination of a process of state-sanctioned incitement which began with the dehumanization of the Jewish People." Indeed, these same tactics are used today by Palestinian leaders as they incite their followers towards the annihilation of Jews and the Jewish State. Palestinian Media Watch maintains an ongoing account of current examples of Palestinian dehumanization and demonization of Jews/Israelis that demonstrates how this strategy enables state-sponsored incitement of genocide.[2]

Small makes the observation that, "The lesson of the Holocaust was not learned in time to prevent the genocide in Rwanda." He then questions if the lesson of Rwanda will be learned in time to stop the next attempted genocide of the Jews. While this remains to be seen, one thing is certain: people who are fed a steady diet of incitement for jihad cannot be expected to suddenly live at peace no matter what Israel may or may not offer for the sake of that peace. Palestinian President Mahmoud Abbas has made two things abundantly clear: first, a Palestinian state will never

---

1. Palestinian leaders' consistent encouragement of jihad for the purpose of "liberating" the Land from the Jews is based on principles found in Articles 11-15 of the Hamas Charter and Articles 3, 4, 5, 7, 9, 12, 17, and 19 of Fatah's Constitution. As Article 19 of Fatah's Constitution states, "the Palestinian Arab People's armed revolution is a decisive factor in the liberation fight and in uprooting the Zionist existence, and this struggle will not cease unless the Zionist state is demolished and Palestine is completely liberated." To read the entire Hamas Charter, visit http://www.thejerusalemfund.org/www.thejerusalemfund.org/carryover/documents/charter.html?chocaid=397. To read the entire Fatah Constitution, visit https://www.mythsandfacts.org/conflict/statute-treaties/FATEH_Constitution.pdf.

2. "Jews/Israelis are Evil," *Palestinian Media Watch*, "published shortly after a ceasefire was reached between Israel and Hamas, concluding the 2014 Gaza war," accessed on 20 September 2014: http://www.palwatch.org/main.aspx?fi=762.

recognize Israel's right to exist as a Jewish state,[1] and second, the efforts of jihad will not stop until Israel ceases to exist.[2] These two realities are in themselves quite remarkable when considered in the overall context of the Arab-Israeli conflict. While demanding their own sovereign state – which must be *Judenrein* – the Palestinians, and the twenty-two member nations of the Arab League, refuse to acknowledge the legitimacy of just one Jewish state – even though the Israeli population is made up of approximately 20 percent Arab citizens who have the same rights as its Jewish citizens.

Contrary to Strang's confident belief – a belief he holds in common with the Telos Group – Israel's acknowledgment of Palestinian demands for sovereignty in a portion of the Land of Israel is not some magic bullet that will bring peace. Indeed, Israel has already demonstrated its willingness to live in peace next to a sovereign Palestinian state in Gaza. But through their actions, Palestinian leaders in Gaza and the West Bank have consistently demonstrated their lack of genuine interest in obtaining sovereignty as opposed to the priority they place on waging jihad against Israel for the purpose of eliminating the Jewish State.

Lynne Hybels and
Willow Creek Community Church

Lynne Hybels, member of the Telos Presidential Advisory Council and co-founder of the Willow Creek Community Church, has become an extremely effective advocate for the pro-Palestinian cause. She speaks frequently at Evangelical events in the US and was a featured speaker at the "Christ at the Checkpoint" conference in Bethlehem in 2012 as well. She brings a compassionate and motherly dimension to the narrative as she speaks about her meetings with Israeli and Palestinian mothers

---

1. Jodi Rudoren and Mochael R. Gordon, "As Kerry Visits Jordan, Abbas Holds His Ground," 7 March 2014, accessed on 21 March 2015: http://www.nytimes.com/2014/03/08/world/middleeast/secretary-of-state-john-kerry.html?_r=1.

2. Itamar Marcus and Nan Jacques Zilberdik, "PA TV broadcasts 19 times in 3 days Abbas' implicit call for violence in Jerusalem," 28 October 2014, accessed on 21 March 2015: http://www.palwatch.org/main.aspx?fi=157&doc_id=12915.

who have lost children in the conflict. However, the overriding motivation behind this empathetic approach appears to be her intent to neutralize Evangelical support of Israel by emphasizing the need for the Jewish State to make continual concessions to those who are intent on its annihilation.

In addition to the potency of her emotional appeals, Hybels is an effective voice for the Christian Palestinian movement simply because of the extensive reach of the Willow Creek Church. Located in Chicago, Illinois, the church boasts seven campuses that are each a fully functioning church within themselves.[1] But beyond the influence the church wields in seven different locations around Chicago, it also runs an international organization, the Willow Creek Association (WCA). According to its website, the WCA "exists to help local churches thrive." It "serves pioneering pastors and leaders around the world by curating inspirational leadership, intentional skill development, and experiences. Each year, the WCA serves more than 18,000 churches in 90 countries with vision, training, and resources."[2] This makes Willow Creek – and by extension, Lynne Hybels – one of the most influential voices among Evangelicals today. And Hybels uses this position to advocate in favor of the pro-Palestinian narrative, which, by definition, is anti-Israel.

Gary Burge

Willow Creek Church also hosts the preaching of Dr. Gary Burge, an ordained minister with the Presbyterian Church USA (PCUSA) and Professor of New Testament at Wheaton College in Chicago, Illinois. The church promotes Burge's book about Israel and the Palestinians titled *Whose Land? Whose Promise? What Christians are Not Being Told about Israel and the Palestinians*. This volume is highly acclaimed by Presbyterians, Methodists, Lutherans, and the Reform Church in America, and has also been endorsed by various academics and the editor of *Christianity Today* as a credible source of information about the Palestinian-Israeli conflict. However, the book is actually an excellent example of

---

1. "About Willow," *Willow Creek Community Church*, accessed on 20 September 2014: http://www.willowcreek.org/aboutwillow/one-church-multiple-locations.
2. *ibid.*

very bad scholarship and, as a result, presents the reader with a decidedly pro-Palestinian, anti-Israel narrative that is based on Burge's own replacement theology.[1]

The first edition was published in 2003 by Pilgrim Press, the publishing company of the United Church of Christ. According to Van Zile of CAMERA, "the book is a compendium of factual errors, misstatements, omissions and distortions that portray the modern state of Israel in an inaccurate manner."[2] Furthermore, this text is "marred with a number of factual misstatements that undermined the credibility of the text and its author."[3] However, the author's credibility is not all that is undermined by the significant extent of error present in this work. The credibility of Wheaton College, the Evangelical Christian institution where Burge teaches – which prides itself on being "a rigorous academic community that takes seriously the life of the mind"[4] – is also undermined if they continue to endorse, or even tolerate, his deficient scholarship.

As a result of Van Zile's articles and advocacy on the subject, Pilgrim Press agreed to publish a second edition in which all the errors would be corrected.[5] However, the "new and revised" edition, published in 2013, still includes a number of falsehoods, some of which were not previously identified in the first edition.

1. Dexter Van Zile, "Book Promoted by Willow Creek Church Leaves Readers Ill-Prepared for Peacemaking," *Committee for Accuracy in Middle East Reporting in America,* accessed 20 September 2014: http://www.camera.org/index.asp?x_context=55&x_article=2575.
2. Dexter Van Zile, "Mainline Churches Embrace Burge's False Narrative," *Committee for Accuracy in Middle East Reporting in America,* 23 August 2007, accessed on 20 September 2014: http://www.camera.org/index.asp?x_context=2&x_outlet=118&x_article=1356. See this article for extensive documentation of the errors in Gary Burge's work.
3. Dexter Van Zile, "Gary Burge's Missed Opportunity," *Committee for Accuracy in Middle East Reporting in America,* 31 December 2013, accessed on 20 September 2014: http://www.camera.org/index.asp?x_context=55&x_article=2615.
4. "Community Covenant," *Wheaton College,* accessed on 20 September 2014: http://www.wheaton.edu/About-Wheaton/Community-Covenant.
5. All the articles written by Dexter Van Zile on this subject can be found on the Committee for Accuracy in Middle East Reporting in America website at http://www.camera.org/index.asp?x_context=55&x_auth=55.

It also includes new errors. The end result is that Burge has given his readers a new text that continues to encourage Christian contempt and hostility towards the Jewish State. Most alarming in light of the theological concerns of this book is the fact that Burge "portrays Jewish sovereignty in the land of Israel as a violation of Christian theology. Invoking passages from the New Testament Book of Hebrews, which speaks of God's promises to Abraham as becoming 'obsolete' and 'vanishing away,' Burge writes that Christians inherit the promises to Abraham (including the land) by virtue of their faith in Christ."[1] This is a dramatic demonstration of Burge's own form of replacement theology, in which Christians have replaced Jews as the recipients of the promises made in the Abrahamic covenant.

In addition to developing a theological argument to inspire his Evangelical students to abandon their support for Israel in favor of the Palestinians, Burge has had a significant effect on anti-Israel actions taken by his denomination, the Presbyterian Church USA. His writings had a noteworthy effect on the Presbyterian Church's 2014 General Assembly decision to divest from three companies that do business with Israel. In addition, his work was included in the seventh chapter, titled "Evangelicals and Christian Zionism," of the PCUSA's anti-Israel study guide, *Zionism Unsettled: A Congregational Study Guide,* published in January 2014. This seventy-six-page booklet is still available from the Israel/Palestine Mission Network – a group affiliated with the PCUSA – but it was removed from the PCUSA website in the summer of 2014 due to the controversy it incited. The message of chapter seven is that the Land of Israel is irrelevant to God's redemptive plan. According to Burge, there is no need for an earthly "kingdom" for the Jews because the Kingdom of God as established by Jesus "fulfills" the promises made to Abraham – promises that included possession of the Land.

Burge's use of the term "fulfills" demonstrates that, since he wrote *Whose Land? Whose Promise?,* he has revised his replacement theology. Speaking at the "Christ at the Checkpoint" conference in Bethlehem in March 2014, he explained that replacement theology as understood by the Church historically is in error. He then described how the covenant God made with Abraham – including the promise of a specific piece of land – has been "fulfilled" as opposed to

1. Van Zile, "Mainline Churches Embrace Burge's False Narrative."

having been "replaced."[1] By using this new term, Burge apparently hopes to distance himself from the negative history associated with Christian replacement theology. However, the consequences of Burge's effort to justify any attempt to delegitimize the Jews in any way are just as drastic as the ones realized by the historic theology he is attempting to revise. Whether God's promises and purposes for the Jewish people are believed to be *fulfilled* or *replaced*, the end result is the same. The Jews – and the land promised them in the Abrahamic covenant – are no longer of any relevance or importance to the purposes of God. This theological position raises what should be an obvious question, but it is one Burge does not seem to have considered. If God's promises and purposes for the Jewish people and the Land of Israel – given in the context of what the Bible refers to as an "everlasting covenant" – can be replaced or fulfilled, then what hope can Burge or anyone who believes this fallacious doctrine have that the promises they depend on – those found in the New Testament – are any more trustworthy?

Documentaries

In recent years, three documentaries have been produced that incorporate replacement and/or fulfillment theology such as that promoted by Gary Burge. The first of these films, *With God on Our Side*, was produced by Porter Speakman, released by Rooftop Productions in 2010, and endorsed by Tony Campolo.[2] While it purports to be concerned about promoting reconciliation between Jews and Palestinians, the message of the film is actually a very thinly disguised attack on what Speakman believes to be "the theology of Christian Zionism." The result is a blatantly biased pro-Palestinian narrative that ignores facts and context in order to promote what Speakman calls "a Biblical alternative" to Christian Zionism. This alternative to Christian Zionism is justified by fulfillment theology and delegitimizes Christian Zionism along with the existence of the State of Israel.

---

1. "CATC 2014 'Dialogue on Replacement Theology': Gary Burge & Daniel Juster," *Christ at the Checkpoint 2014*, accessed on 20 September 2014: http://vimeo.com/89570014.
2. Dexter Van Zile, "The Mis-Education of a Young Evangelical," *New English Review*, October 2011, accessed on 20 September 2014: http://www.newenglishreview.org/Dexter_Van_Zile/The_Mis-Education_of_a_Young_Evangelical/.

A second documentary, *Little Town of Bethlehem*, was produced by Mart Green in 2010 under the direction of Sami Awad of the Holy Land Trust, a pro-Palestinian organization headquartered in Bethlehem that helps organize the "Christ at the Checkpoint" conferences. This film features the efforts of three men – a Palestinian Christian, a Palestinian Muslim, and an Israeli Jew – to work for peace by following the example of Martin Luther King, Jr. and Mahatma Gandhi. However, as in the case of *With God on Our Side*, essential facts and context for understanding the Palestinian-Israeli conflict are omitted, and a pro-Palestinian/anti-Israeli narrative is promoted with the help of erroneous theology.[1] This film and *With God on Our Side* have been shown to Evangelical students on a number of Christian campuses, such as Wheaton College in Illinois and Oral Roberts University in Oklahoma.

The third, aforementioned, film, *The Stones Cry Out*, was produced in 2013 by Italian filmmaker Yasmine Perni. Using the testimony of Palestinian leaders such as Mitri Raheb and Elias Chacour, it tells the same kind of story as the two previous documentaries, and was made with the same target audience in mind: Evangelical Christians. The underlying theme is that Christian support of Israel is theologically erroneous and detrimental to any potential for peace in the Middle East.[2] The rationale behind this message is the belief that the Palestinians are the indigenous people of the Land and the true descendants of Jesus and the first disciples. The Jews play no role in the purposes of God, and are portrayed as being synonymous with the Romans. Just as the Romans oppressed the Early Church, so too the Jews allegedly oppress Palestinian Christians. Accordingly, the only appropriate Christian position in relation to the Arab-Israeli conflict is to stand in solidarity with the Palestinian "victims" in opposition to Israel, the "oppressor." All three of these films demonstrate a dependency on a

1. Jim Fletcher, "Bethlehem Like You Haven't Seen It Before," *The Balfour Post*, 13 May 2013, accessed on 20 September 2014: http://balfourpost. com/bethlehem-like-you-havent-seen-it-before/.
2. Tricia Miller, "'The Stones Cry Out' Misrepresents Plight of Palestinian Christians," *Committee for Accuracy in Middle East Reporting in America*, 11 February 2014, accessed on 20 September 2014: http://www.camera.org/index.asp?x_context=55&x_ article=2650.

combination of Palestinian liberation theology and replacement/ fulfillment theology, and promote a pro-Palestinian narrative that delegitimizes and demonizes the Jewish State.

The marketing of these documentaries to an Evangelical audience is an obvious attempt to erode support for Israel and build support for the Palestinians by convincing Evangelicals that the current Christian community in the Holy Land springs from the original occupants of the Land. According to this narrative, the Palestinian church is descended from the original followers of Jesus, and Jesus and his disciples were Palestinian, not Jewish. In this way, Palestinian theology is used to teach a political doctrine that is decidedly anti-Jewish and anti-Israel. Ultimately however, this theology is anti-Christian as well. By denying the biblically attested connection between Jews and the Land, the everlasting covenant God established with the nation of Israel, and the Jewishness of Jesus and his original followers, Palestinian Christians effectively rewrite the Scriptures they claim as sacred.

MICHEL SABBAH AND THE KAIROS DOCUMENT

Michel Sabbah, the Archbishop and Latin Patriarch of Jerusalem from 1987 to 2008, is one of the featured speakers in *The Stones Cry Out*. In December 2009, Sabbah helped promote the Palestinian Kairos Document at an international conference in Bethlehem together with Archbishop Attalah Hanna, Rev. Mitri Raheb, Rev. Naim Ateek, and Father Jamal Khader. The Kairos Document was named after a statement published in South Africa in 1985 for the obvious purpose of comparing Israel to that apartheid regime. It begins with these words:

> This document is the Christian Palestinians' word to the world about what is happening in Palestine. It is written at this time when we wanted to see the Glory of the grace of God in this land and in the sufferings of its people. In this spirit the document requests the international community to stand by the Palestinian people who have faced oppression, displacement, suffering and clear apartheid for more than six decades. The suffering continues while the international community silently looks on at the occupying State, Israel.[1]

---

1. "Home," *Kairos Palestine*, accessed on 20 September 2014: http:// www.kairospalestine.ps/.

This succinct summary of the Christian Palestinian narrative places the responsibility for Palestinian suffering on Israel, the "occupying State." Here again, the impact and use of Ateek's liberation theology is clearly seen. Furthermore, under the pretense of advocating for the rights of the Palestinian people, this document reveals the belief that Jewish sovereignty is contrary to God's plan for the Christian people of "Palestine." In other words, the rights of Christian Palestinians have superseded the historical right of Jews to live in their ancient homeland. The Kairos Document is so dishonest and discriminatory that in 2010, the Central Conference of American Rabbis (CCAR) declared the statement "supersessionist" and "anti-Semitic." While the rabbis acknowledged that the document "paints a compelling picture of the reality of Palestinians living under Israeli rule," they emphasized that "it ignores the reality of Israelis forced to flee for their lives into bomb shelters, or in fear of being blown up while eating in a restaurant, celebrating a Passover Seder or dancing at a Bar Mitzvah Celebration."[1]

HANAN ASHRAWI, MEMBER OF THE PALESTINIAN LIBERATION ORGANIZATION

The Stones Cry Out makes extensive use of testimony from Hanan Ashrawi, who is a member of the Executive Committee of the Palestinian Liberation Organization (PLO) and the daughter of Daoud Mikhail, one of the founders of the PLO. She was an important leader during the First Intifada, served as the official spokesperson for the Palestinian Delegation to the Middle East peace process, and has been elected numerous times to the Palestinian Legislative Council. She has been considered a peacemaker and a brilliant spokeswoman for her cause by people such as Archbishop Desmond Tutu and Madeleine Albright. However, the means she uses to promote the Palestinian narrative are anything but peaceful or brilliant because in the process of doing so, she rewrites Jewish history and delegitimizes Zionism as a Jewish movement to establish a nation in their historic homeland.

---

1. "Resolution Adopted by the CCAR," *Central Conference of American Rabbis*, accessed on 20 September 2014: http://ccarnet. org/rabbis-speak/resolutions/2010/ccar-resolution-2009-kairos-document/.

As David Harris says in his September 2012 *Huffington Post* article titled "Hanan Ashrawi is to Truth what Smoking is to Health,"

> [Ashwari's] line of Palestinian argumentation is of a piece with other efforts to delegitimize Jewish history. In other words, the Palestinian strategy, of which Ashrawi has been an integral part, is essentially to try to eliminate any grounds for Jewish self-determination and nationhood.[1]

As was mentioned previously, the denial of the right of Jews to self-determination – which includes the right to establish a nation in their historic home – is not only anti-Zionist, but is anti-Semitic as well in that the delegitimization of Zionism is racially based.

In *The Stones Cry Out*, Ashrawi expressed concern that "Christians are leaving the Holy Land," and her belief that it would be a tragedy if some day there were no Christians left in the birthplace of Christianity. However, the facts reveal that this is a disingenuous concern, and in reality, is evidence of her attempt to rewrite history in the making. According to a CAMERA article of June 20, 2013,

> The Statistical Abstract of Israel reports that in 1949, there were approximately 34,000 Christians living in Israel. This figure was not broken down by ethnicity, but the vast majority of these people were Arab Christians. At the end of 2011, there were approximately 125,000 Arab Christians living in Israel.[2]

As this article points out, "The population of Arab Christians in Israel has increased *268 percent* since 1949." This remarkable growth in the Israeli Christian population stands in stark contrast to other countries in the Middle East, where Christians continue to flee due to pogroms, forced marriages and conversions, destruction of property, and fear of death. Contrary to Ashrawi's

---

1. David Harris, "Hanan Ashrawi is to Truth what Smoking is to Health," *The World Post*, 2 September 2012, accessed on 20 September 2014: http://www.huffingtonpost.com/david-harris/hanan-ashrawi-is-to-truth_b_1851044.html.
2. Dexter Van Zile, "*Sojourners* Portrays Israel at Center of Christian Crisis in Middle East," *Committee for Accuracy in Middle East Reporting in America*, 20 June 2013, accessed on 20 September 2014: http://www.camera.org/index.asp?x_context=55&x_article=2490.

attempts to rewrite both past history and history in the making, Jews and Christians have been, and continue to be, forced from their homes in Muslim-majority countries. And yet she – as well as the other participants in *The Stones Cry Out* – refuses to acknowledge this reality, along with the fact that the Christian population is not only growing, but is welcome in the Jewish State of Israel.

Conclusions

The preceding analysis of anti-Israel documentaries and the statements and activities of particular organizations and individuals has revealed the doctrine at the heart of Christian anti-Zionism. This present-day crusade is informed and justified by the combination of a customized liberation theology and a replacement/fulfillment theology that has its roots in the same anti-Jewish arguments used historically to define Christian identity. The statements and activities of Bethlehem Bible College, the Telos Group, and individuals such as Mitri Raheb, Elias Chacour, Cameron Strang, Lynne Hybels, Gary Burge, Michel Sabbah, and Hanan Ashrawi, combined with the narratives presented in all three documentaries, demonstrate adherence to these tailor-made Palestinian theologies.

Through conferences, tours, publications, and media, the liberation theology of Naim Ateek – with its identification of Palestinian Christians as the poor, disenfranchised victims of powerful Israeli "oppressors," and replacement/fulfillment theology – which incorporates significant features of historic Christian anti-Judaism, are being introduced to an American Christian audience that, for the most part, has little or no understanding of the historical context of the erroneous theologies involved, or the realities of the Arab-Israeli conflict. As a result, the image of Israelis as illegitimate "occupiers" is perpetrated through false dogma that purports that the Jews – and the land promised them in the Abrahamic covenant – are no longer of any relevance or importance to the purposes of God.

Through its inaccurate portrayal of the actions Israel takes to protect the lives of its citizens, this movement reveals the similarity of its beliefs with historic anti-Semitic interpretations of the character of Esther and the actions of the Jews of Persia based on the Greek versions of the story. By omitting essential historical context, Israelis are portrayed as vengeful and bloodthirsty "occupiers," rather than being understood as a people who have to defend themselves repeatedly against those who intend to murder them. In so doing, this pro-Palestinian campaign reveals its complete lack of understanding of Hebrew Esther's emphasis on the right to self-defense when threatened with annihilation. The lethal mix of errant theologies and lack of theological and historical context produces a virulent form of Christian anti-Zionism that delegitimizes and demonizes Israel. As a result, the danger facing the Jewish State, and all Jews around the world, is greatly intensified.

FINAL CONCLUSIONS

This book has used an academic approach to demonstrate the relationship between the story of Esther, historic anti-Judaism, and the contested legitimacy of the State of Israel. For that purpose, the majority of this volume has been devoted to discussions of the message of the Hebrew text, the reality of the danger of annihilation revealed by all three versions of Esther, and the unbroken history of anti-Judaism/Semitism from the ancient world to the present as revealed through the history of interpretation of Esther. The message of the text – that humans have the responsibility and right to protect themselves against those who would murder – is profoundly relevant to current controversy over the existence and actions of the Jewish State. And because the story of Esther reveals much about the anti-Judaism/Semitism that was yet to come, it is also quite pertinent to the history of Christian anti-Judaism and replacement theology.

As has been said, the continued presence of Jews and the fact that Judaism continued to flourish in Late Antiquity represented a threat to the evolving Christian identity and "raised disconcerting questions that stuck at the very heart of early Christianity's theological position."[1] In response to those "disconcerting questions," the Early Church developed its anti-Jewish stance. Unfortunately, this phenomenon did not end in the first centuries of the Christian era, but is alive and well today in the form of Christian anti-Zionism. Just as the flourishing of Judaism in Late Antiquity raised difficult questions in relation to the Church's belief that Christians had replaced Jews in the purposes of God, so too the existence of the State of Israel

---

1. Leonard V. Rutgers, *Making Myths: Jews in Early Christian Identity Formation* (Leuven: Peeters, 2009), 56, 123.

presents a challenge to the replacement/fulfillment theology at the heart of Christian anti-Zionism. After all, if the Jews – and the land promised to them in the Abrahamic covenant – are no longer of any relevance or importance to the purposes of God, how can the establishment, survival, and prosperity of the Jewish State be explained theologically? The answer is that it can't. In order to justify a faulty theological construct, Israel's right to exist must be delegitimized, its actions to defend itself against enemies intent on its destruction must be demonized, and its people must be dehumanized.

The study of Esther and historic anti-Jewish theology provides a helpful context for identifying the theological and historical errors that form the foundation of the anti-Jewish/Israel message that Palestinian Christians are promoting with the help of prominent Evangelical leaders in the United States. This book was written in order to expose the flawed narrative Palestinian leaders are foisting on an unsuspecting American audience, and to provide that audience with helpful material with which to counter the deceptive message being thrust at it. This work is not intended to discourage Christians from understanding, and being sympathetic to, the plight of Palestinian Christians. Rather, its objective is to provide Evangelical Christians with theological and historical information that explains why they should maintain their position of support for the State of Israel in the face of the anti-Israel propaganda promoted by Christian anti-Zionism.

Because this anti-Zionist crusade is rooted in the same fallacious doctrine that fed German anti-Judaism/Semitism and provided the theological justification for the Holocaust, a statement that German pastor Martin Niemöller made is particularly relevant. Niemöller (1892–1984) was a prominent, but controversial, Protestant pastor who spent the last seven years of Nazi rule in concentration camps because of his outspoken, public opposition to Hitler. Speaking in Göttingen, he said:

> Hatred of the Jews is a deep, dark secret, totally different from the hate between nations, which is usually not directed against a suffering individual. And it is also totally different from the hate against foreigners. The Jew is not hated as a foreigner, he is hated as a Jew, and this hate cannot be explained. Because for too long the church went along with practicing or tolerating anti-Semitism instead of fighting

it. . . . The church bears the heaviest burden of guilt because it was aware of what it was doing when it did nothing. Anti-Semitism is anti-Christendom, so an anti-Semitic church is an anti-Christian church, and as such the most acute threat to the church as a church.[1]

As Niemöller pointed out, the German church was guilty of anti-Semitism in the context of the Holocaust, and it knew what it was doing when it did nothing to oppose it. This confession of guilt presents a clarion call to today's Church in the context of the Arab-Israeli conflict, which is driven by the intent to annihilate the Jewish State. Niemöller's judgment against the church in Germany means that the church in America must know what it is doing in relation to its position on Israel, must not be guilty of anti-Semitism, and must not be guilty of doing nothing to oppose it.

In light of the spiritual and historic legacy of the Holocaust, and in consideration of the horrific consequences of 2,000 years of anti-Jewish theology, Christians have a moral obligation to maintain their position of support for Israel and to oppose ideologies that call for its destruction. The message of Hebrew Esther – which expresses a timeless issue of justice concerning "the fundamental responsibility and universal right of self-protection against those who would murder"[2] – must be understood in relation to Israel's legitimate right to exist and defend itself as a Jewish State. Any other stance will result in an anti-Semitic Church, which, as Niemöller revealed, is an anti-Christian Church. An anti-Semitic Church not only represents "the most acute threat to the church as a church," but, as history so clearly demonstrates, constitutes a very real threat to the safety of Jews as well.

---

1. Sibylle Sarah Niemoeller, *Crowns, Crosses, and Stars: My Youth in Prussia, Surviving Hitler, and a Life Beyond* (West Lafayette, IN: Purdue University Press, 2012), 267-8.

2. Marvin A. Sweeney, "Absence of G-d and Human Responsibility in the Book of Esther," in *Reading the Hebrew Bible for a New Millennium* (ed. Wonil Kim, Deborah Ellens, Michael Floyd, and Marvin A. Sweeney; Harrisburg, PA: Trinity Press International, 2000), 264-75.

BIBLIOGRAPHY

Alexander, Philip S. "3 Maccabees, Hanukkah and Purim." Pages 321-39 in *Biblical Hebrews, Biblical Texts: Essays in Memory of Michael P. Weitzman.* Edited by Ada Rapoport-Albert and Gillian Greenberg. London: Sheffield Academic Press, 2001.

Allen, L. and T. Laniak. *New International Biblical Commentary: Ezra, Nehemiah, Esther.* Peabody, MA: Hendrickson Publishers, 2003.

Anderson, Bernhard W. "The Place of the Book of Esther in the Christian Bible." Pages 130-41 in *Studies in the Book of Esther.* Edited by Carey A. Moore. New York: KTAV Publishing House, 1982.

Ateek, Naim S. "Toward a Strategy for the Episcopal Church in Israel with Special Focus on the Political Situation: Analysis and Prospect." San Francisco Theological Seminary, 1982.

———. *Justice and Only Justice: A Palestinian Theology of Liberation.* Maryknoll, NY: Orbis Books, 1991.

Augustine. *City of God.* Book 18, chapter 43 in *Nicene and Post-Nicene Fathers, Volume 2: Augustine: City of God, Christian Doctrine.* Edited by Philip Schaff, DD, LLD. Hendrickson Publishers, 1994.

Avidov, Avi. *Not Reckoned among Nations: The Origin of the so-called "Jewish Question" in Roman Antiquity.* Tübingen: Mohr Siebeck, 2009.

Barclay, John M.G. *Jews in the Mediterranean Diaspora: From Alexander to Trajan (323 BCE–117 CE).* Berkeley, CA: University of California Press, 1996.

Bar-Kochva, Bezalel. *The Image of the Jews in Greek Literature: The Hellenistic Period.* Berkeley and Los Angeles, CA: University of California Press, 2010.

Bartlett, J.R. *I Maccabees.* Sheffield: Sheffield Academic Press, 1998.

Bechtel, Carol M. *Interpretation: A Bible Commentary for Teaching and Preaching: Esther.* Louisville, KY: John Knox Press, 2002.

Bellis, Alice Ogden. *Helpmates, Harlots, Heroes: Women's Stories in the Hebrew Bible.* Louisville, KY: Westminster/John Knox Press, 1994.

Berg, Sandra Beth. *The Book of Esther: Motifs, Themes and Structure.* Society of Biblical Literature, 1979.

Berlin, Adele. *The JPS Bible Commentary: Esther.* Philadelphia, PA: The Jewish Publication Society, 2001/5761.

Berman, Joshua A. "Hadassah Bat Abihail: The Evolution from Object to Subject in the Character of Esther." *JBL* 120/4 (2001): 647-69.

Berquist, Jon L. *Judaism in Persia's Shadow: A Social and Historical Approach.* Eugene, OR: Wipf and Stock, 2003.Bickerman, Elias J. "The Colophon of the Greek Book of Esther." Pages 529-52 in *Studies in the Book of Esther.* Edited by Carey A. Moore. New York: KTAV Publishing House, 1982.

———. "Notes on the Greek Book of Esther." Pages 488-520 in *Studies in the Book of Esther.* Edited by Carey A. Moore. New York: KTAV Publishing House, 1982.

———. *The Jews in the Greek Age.* Cambridge and London: Harvard University Press, 1988.

Black, Jeremy, Andrew George, and Nicholas Postgate, eds. *A Concise Dictionary of Akkadian.* Wiesbaden: Harrassowitz Verlag, 2000.

Briant, Pierre. *From Cyrus to Alexander: A History of the Persian Empire.* Winona Lake, IN: Eisenbrauns, 2002.

Briggs, Sheila. "Images of Women and Jews in Nineteenth and Twentieth Century German Theology." Pages 226-59 in *Immaculate and Powerful: The Female in Sacred Image and Social Reality.* Edited by Clarissa W. Atkinson, Constance H. Buchanan, and Margaret R. Miles. Boston, MA: Beacon Press, 1985.

Bronner, Leila Leah. "Esther Revisited: An Aggadic Approach." Pages 176-97 in *A Feminist Companion to Esther, Judith and Susanna.* Edited by Athalya Brenner. Sheffield: Sheffield Academic Press, 1995.

———. "Reclaiming Esther: From Sex Object to Sage." *Jewish Bible Quarterly* 26/1 (1998): 3-10.

Brown, Francis. *The Brown-Driver-Briggs Hebrew and English Lexicon.* Peabody, MA: Hendrickson Publishers, 2000.

Budde, Karl. *Geschichte der althebräischen Literatur.* Leipzig, 1906.

Burns, Joshua Ezra. "The Special Purim and the Reception of the Book of Esther in the Hellenistic and Early Roman Eras." *Journal for the Study of Judaism* XXXVII: 1 (2006): 1-34.

Bush, Frederic W. *Word Biblical Commentary: Ruth/Esther.* Thomas Nelson Publishers, 1996.

Butting, Klara. "Esther: A New Interpretation of the Joseph Story in the Fight Against Anti-Semitism and Sexism." Pages 239-48 in *Ruth and Esther: A Feminist Companion to the Bible.* Edited by Athalya Brenner. Sheffield: Sheffield Academic Press, 1999.

Carruthers, Jo. *Esther Through the Centuries.* Oxford: Blackwell Publishing, 2008.

Chrysostom. Homily V: Chapter 4 in *Nicene and Post-Nicene Fathers: Volume 10; Chrysostom: Homilies on the Gospel of Saint Matthew.* Edited by Philip Schaff, DD, LLD. Hendrickson Publishers, 1994.

———. Homily VIII: Chapter 9 in *Nicene and Post-Nicene Fathers, Volume 14; Chrysostom: Homilies on the Gospel of Saint John and the Epistle to the Hebrews*. Edited by Philip Schaff, DD, LLD. Hendrickson Publishers, 1994.

Clement of Alexandria. *The Stromata*. Chapter XXII in *Ante-Nicene Fathers, Volume 2: Fathers of the Second Century: Hermas, Tatian, Athenagoras, Theophilus, and Clement of Alexandria*. Edited by Alexander Roberts, DD, and James Donaldson, LLD. Hendrickson Publishers, 1994.

Clines, David J.A. *The Esther Scroll: The Story of the Story*. Sheffield: JSOT Press, 1984.

———. *The New Century Bible Commentary: Ezra, Nehemiah, Esther*. Grand Rapids, MI: Wm. B. Eerdmans Publishing Co, 1984.

Collins, John J. *Between Athens and Jerusalem: Jewish Identity in the Hellenistic Diaspora*. Grand Rapids, MI: Eerdmans, 2000.

———. *Jewish Cult and Hellenistic Culture: Essays on the Jewish Encounter with Hellenism and Roman Rule*. Leiden: Brill, 2005.

Conzelmann, Hans. *Gentiles, Jews, Christians: Polemics and Apologetics in the Greco-Roman Era*. Translated by M. Eugene Boring. Minneapolis, MN: Fortress Press, 1992.

Cornill, Carl. *Introduction to the Canonical Books of the Old Testament*. Translated by G.H. Box, MA. New York: G.P. Putnam's Sons, 1907.

Curtis, John E., and Nigel Tallis, eds. *Forgotten Empire: The World of Ancient Persia*. Berkeley, CA: University of California Press, 2005.

Davies, W.D., and Louis Finkelstein, eds. *The Cambridge History of Judaism, Volume One: The Persian Period*. Cambridge: Cambridge University Press, 1984.

Day, Linda. *Three Faces of A Queen: Characterization in the Books of Esther*. Sheffield: Sheffield Academic Press, 1995.

———. *Abingdon Old Testament Commentaries: Esther*. Nashville, TN: Abingdon Press, 2005.

deSilva, David A. *Introducing the Apocrypha: Message, Context, and Significance*. Grand Rapids, MI: Baker Academic, 2002.

De Troyer, Kristin. "An Oriental Beauty Parlor: An Analysis of Esther 2.8-18 in the Hebrew, the Septuagint and the Second Greek Text." Pages 47-70 in *A Feminist Companion to Esther, Judith and Susanna*. Edited by Athalya Brenner. Sheffield: Sheffield Academic Press, 1995.

———. *The End of the Alpha Text of Esther: Translation and Narrative Technique in MT 8:1-17, LXX 8:1-17, and AT 7:14-41*. Atlanta, GA: Society of Biblical Literature, 2000.

———. *Rewriting the Sacred Text: What the Old Greek Texts Tell Us About the Literary Growth of the Bible*. Atlanta, GA: Society of Biblical Literature, 2003.

Diodorus. *Bibliotheca Historica*. Quoted in Menahem Stern. *Greek and Latin Authors on Jews and Judaism: Volume I, From Herodotus to Plutarch*. Jerusalem: The Israel Academy of Sciences and Humanities, 1976.

Eissfeldt, Otto. *Einleitung in das Alte Testament*. Tübingen: Mohr, 1964.

Even-Shoshan, Abraham. *A New Concordance of the Bible*. Jerusalem: Kiryat Sefer Publishing House, 1996.

Feldman, Louis H. *Studies in Josephus' Rewritten Bible*. Atlanta, GA: Society of Biblical Literature, 1998.

Fox, Michael V. *Character and Ideology in the Book of Esther*. Columbia, SC: University of South Carolina, 1991.

———. *The Redaction of the Books of Esther*. Atlanta, GA: Scholars Press, 1991.

———. "Three Esthers." Pages 50-60 in *The Book of Esther in Modern Research*. Edited by Sidnie White Crawford and Leonard J. Greenspoon. London: T and T Clark, 2003.

Fredriksen, Paula. *Augustine and the Jews: A Christian Defense of Jews and Judaism*. New Haven, CT, and London: Yale University Press, 2010.

Fröhlich, Ida. *Time and Times and Half a Time: Historical Consciousness in the Jewish Literature of the Persian and Hellenistic Eras*. Sheffield: Sheffield Academic Press, 1996.

Gambetti, Sandra. *The Alexandrian Riots of 38 C.E. and the Persecution of the Jews: A Historical Reconstruction*. Leiden: Brill, 2009.

———. "Ptolemies." Pages 1117-21 in *The Eerdmans Dictionary of Early Judaism*. Edited by John J. Collins and Daniel C. Harlow. Grand Rapids, MI: Eerdmans Publishing Company, 2010.

Gerleman, Gillis. *Biblischer Kommentar Altes Testament: Esther*. Neukirchen-Vluyn: Neukirchener Verlag Des Erziehungsvereins GMBH, 1973.

Gevaryahu, Haim M.I. "Esther is a Story of Jewish Defense Not a Story of Jewish Revenge." *Jewish Bible Quarterly* 21/1 (1993): 3-12.

Gordis, Robert. "Religion, Wisdom and History in the Book of Esther-A New Solution to an Ancient Crux." *JBL* 100/3 (1981): 359-88.

Grabbe, Lester L. *An Introduction to Second Temple Judaism: History and Religion of the Jews in the Time of Nehemiah, The Maccabees, Hillel and Jesus*. London: T and T Clark, 2010.

Greenstein, Edward L. "A Jewish Reading of Esther." Pages 225-243 in *Judaic Perspectives on Ancient Israel*. Edited by Jacob Neusner, Baruch A. Levine, and Ernest S. Frerichs. Philadelphia, PA: Fortress Press, 1987.

Grossfeld, Bernard. *The Two Targums of Esther: Edited, with Apparatus and Notes*. Collegeville, MN: The Liturgical Press, 1991.

Hadas, Moses, ed. *The Complete Works of Tacitus*. New York: Random House, 1942.

———, ed. *Aristeas to Philocrates (Letter of Aristeas)*. New York: Harper and Brothers, 1951.

Hadas-Lebel, Mireille. *Jerusalem Against Rome*. Leuven: Peeters, 2006.

Hanhart, Robert, ed. *Esther: Septuaginta*. Göttingen: Vandenhoeck and Ruprecht, 1983.

Harkabi, Yehoshafat. "On Arab Antisemitism Once More." Pages 227-239 in *Antisemitism Through the Ages*. Edited by Shmuel Almog. Oxford: Pergamon Press, 1988.

Harper, Prudence O., Joan Aruz and Francoise Tallon, eds. *The Royal City of Susa: Ancient Near Eastern Treasures in the Louvre*. New York: The Metropolitan Museum of Art, 1992.

Haupt, Paul. "Critical Notes on Esther." Pages 1-79 in *Studies in the Book of Esther*. Edited by Carey A. Moore. New York: KTAV Publishing House, 1982.

Hecataeus. Preserved in Diodorus. *Bibliotheca Historica*. Quoted in Menahem Stern. *Greek and Latin Authors on Jews and Judaism: Volume I, From Herodotus to Plutarch*. Jerusalem: The Israel Academy of Sciences and Humanities, 1976.

Heltzer, Michael. *The Province of Judah and Jews in Persian Times (Some Connected Questions of the Persian Empire)*. Tel Aviv: Archaeological Center Publication, 2008.

Hempel, Johannes. *Das Ethos des Alten Testaments*, 2nd ed. Berlin: Töpelmann, 1964.

Hengel, Martin. "The Septuagint as a Collection of Writings Claimed by Christians: Justin and the Church Fathers before Origen." Pages 39-83 in *Jews and Christians: The Parting of the Ways, A.D. 70 to 135*. Edited by James D.G. Dunn. Grand Rapids, MI: Eerdmans Publishing Company, 1999.

Herodotus. *The Histories*. Translated by Robin Waterfield. Oxford: Oxford University Press, 1998.

Hölbl, Günther. *A History of the Ptolemaic Empire*. Translated by Tina Saavedra. London and New York: Routledge, 2001.

Horowitz, Elliot. *Reckless Rites: Purim and the Legacy of Jewish Violence*. Princeton, NJ: Princeton University Press, 2006.

Irenaeus. *Against Heresies*. Chapter XXI:2 in *Ante-Nicene Fathers, Volume 1: The Apostolic Fathers, Justin Martyr, Irenaeus*. Edited by Alexander Roberts, DD, and James Donaldson, LLD. Hendrickson Publishers, 1994.

Isaac, Jules. *The Teaching of Contempt: Christian Roots of Anti-Semitism*. New York: Holt, Rinehart and Winston, 1964.

Jobes, Karen H. *The Alpha Text of Esther: Its Character and Relationship to the Masoretic Text*. Atlanta, GA: Scholars Press, 1996.

Johnson, Sara Raup. *Historical Fictions and Hellenistic Jewish Identity: Third Maccabees in Its Cultural Context*. Berkeley and Los Angeles, CA: University of California Press, 2004.

Josephus. *Contra Apion*. From *The New Complete Works of Josephus*. Translated by William Whiston. Grand Rapids, MI: Kregel Publications, 1999.

———. *Jewish Antiquities*. From *The New Complete Works of Josephus*. Translated by William Whiston. Grand Rapids, MI: Kregel Publications, 1999.

Klein, Charlotte. *Anti-Judaism in Christian Theology*. Philadelphia, PA: Fortress Press, 1978.

Koehler, Ludwig and Walter Baumgartner. *The Hebrew and Aramaic Lexicon of the Old Testament*. Leiden: Brill, 2001.

Kuhl, Curt. *The Old Testament: Its Origins and Composition*. Translated by C.T.M. Herriot. Edinburgh and London: Oliver and Boyd, 1961.

Kuhrt, Amelie. *The Ancient Near East c. 3000–330 BC, Volume Two*. London: Routledge, 1995.

Levenson, Jon D. "The Scroll of Esther in Ecumenical Perspective." *Journal of Ecumenical Studies* XIII (1976): 440-51.

———. *Esther: A Commentary*. Louisville, KY: Westminster John Knox, 1997.

Lubitch, Rivkah. "A Feminist's Look at Esther." *Judaism: A Quarterly Journal of Jewish Life and Thought* 42.4 (Fall 1993): 438-46.

Luther, Martin. *In That Jesus Christ was Born a Jew*. In *Luther's Works: Volume 45, The Christian in Society II*. Edited by Walther I. Brandt. Philadelphia, PA: Muhlenberg Press, 1962.

———. *Table Talk XXIV*. In *Luther's Works: Volume 54, Table Talk*. Edited by Theodore G. Tappert. Philadelphia, PA: Fortress Press, 1967.

———. *Against the Sabbatarians: Letter to a Good Friend, 1538*. In *Luther's Works: Volume 47, the Christian in Society IV*. Edited by Franklin Sherman. Philadelphia, PA: Fortress Press, 1971.

———. *On the Jews and Their Lies, 1543*. In *Luther's Works: Volume 47, The Christian in Society IV*. Edited by Franklin Sherman. Philadelphia, PA: Fortress Press, 1971.

Martyr, Justin. *Dialogue with Trypho, Apology*, and *Justin's Hortatory Address to the Greeks*. In *Ante-Nicene Fathers, Volume 1: The Apostolic Fathers, Justin Martyr, Irenaeus*. Edited by Alexander Roberts, DD, and James Donaldson, LLD. Hendrickson Publishers, 1994.

Mason, Steve. *Josephus, Judea, and Christian Origins: Methods and Categories*. Peabody, MA: Hendrickson Publishers, 2009.

Millard, A.R. "The Persian Names in Esther and the Reliability of the Hebrew Text." *JBL* 96/4 (1977): 481-8.

Moore, Carey A. *The Anchor Bible: Esther*. New York: Doubleday, 1971.

———. "On the Origins of the LXX Additions to the Book of Esther." *Journal of Biblical Literature* 92:3 (1973): 382-93.

———. "Archaeology and the Book of Esther." Pages 369-86 in *Studies in the Book of Esther*. Edited by Carey A. Moore. New York: KTAV Publishing House, 1982.

———, ed. *Studies in the Book of Esther*. New York: KTAV Publishing House, 1982.

Nickelsburg, George W.E. *Jewish Literature between the Bible and the Mishnah*. Minneapolis, MN: Fortress Press, 2005.

Niemoeller, Sibylle Sarah. *Crowns, Crosses, and Stars: My Youth in Prussia, Surviving Hitler, and a Life Beyond*. West Lafayette, IN: Purdue University Press, 2012.

Olmstead, A.T. *History of the Persian Empire*. Chicago, IL: University of Chicago Press, 1948.Parkes, James. *The Jew in the Medieval Community: A Study of His Political and Economic Situation*. London: The Soncino Press, 1938.

———. *The Conflict of the Church and the Synagogue: A Study in the Origins of Antisemitism*. New York: Atheneum, 1969.

Paton, Lewis Bayles. *The International Critical Commentary: A Critical and Exegetical Commentary on the Book of Esther*. Edinburgh: T and T Clark, 1908.

Perry, Marvin and Frederick M. Schweitzer. *Antisemitism: Myth and Hate from Antiquity to the Present*. New York: Palgrave Macmillan, 2002.

Philo. *Flaccus*. From *The Works of Philo: Complete and Unabridged, New Updated Version*. Translated by C.D. Yonge. Peabody, MA: Hendrickson Publishers, 1993.———. *On the Embassy to Gaius*. From *The Works of Philo: Complete and Unabridged, New Updated Version*. Translated by C.D. Yonge. Peabody, MA: Hendrickson Publishers, 1993.

———. *On the Life of Moses, II*. Chapters V-VII in *The Works of Philo: Complete and Unabridged, New Updated Version*. Translated by C.D. Yonge. Peabody, MA: Hendrickson Publishers, 1993.

Poliakov, Leon. *The History of Anti-Semitism, Volume I: From the Time of Christ to the Court Jews*. Philadelphia, PA: University of Pennsylvania Press, 2003.

Reventlow, Henning Graf. *History of Biblical Interpretation, Volume I: From the Old Testament to Origen*. Translated by Leo G. Perdue. Atlanta, GA: Society of Biblical Literature, 2009.

Ruether, Rosemary Radford. *Sexism and God-Talk: Toward a Feminist Theology*. Boston, MA: Beacon Press, 1983.

———. *Faith and Fratricide: The Theological Roots of Anti-Semitism*. Eugene, OR: Wipf and Stock, 1997.

Rutgers, Leonard V. *Making Myths: Jews in Early Christian Identity Formation*. Leuven: Peeters, 2009.

Sack, Ronald H. *Cuneiform Documents from the Chaldean and Persian Periods*. London: Associated University Presses, 1994.

Sandgren, Leo Duprée. *Vines Intertwined: A History of Jews and Christians from the Babylonian Exile to the Advent of Islam*. Peabody, MA: Hendrickson Publishers, 2010.

Schäfer, Peter. *Judeophobia: Attitudes toward the Jews in the Ancient World*. Cambridge, MA: Harvard University Press, 1997.

Segal, Eliezer. *The Babylonian Esther Midrash: A Critical Commentary, Volume 2*. Atlanta, GA: Scholars Press, 1994.

Smallwood, E. Mary. *The Jews under Roman Rule: From Pompey to Diocletian*. Leiden: Brill, 1976.

Stern, Menachem. *Greek and Latin Authors on Jews and Judaism: Volume I, From Herodotus to Plutarch*. Jerusalem: The Israel Academy of Sciences and Humanities, 1976.

——. *Greek and Latin Authors on Jews and Judaism: Volume II, From Tacitus to Simplicius.* Jerusalem: The Israel Academy of Sciences and Humanities, 1980.

Sweeney, Marvin A. "Absence of G-d and Human Responsibility in the Book of Esther." Pages 264-275 in *Reading the Hebrew Bible for a New Millenium.* Edited by Wonil Kim, Deborah Ellens, Michael Floyd, and Marvin A. Sweeney. Harrisburg, PA: Trinity Press International, 2000.

Talmon, Shemaryahu. "Wisdom in the Book of Esther." *VT* 13 (1963): 419-55.

Tcherikover, Victor. "The Ideology of the Letter of Aristeas." *The Harvard Theological Review* L1 (1958): 59-85.

——. *Hellenistic Civilization and the Jews.* Grand Rapids, MI: Baker Academic, 1999.Tec, Nechama. "Jewish Resistance: Facts, Omissions and Distortions." Nechama Tec: Assigned to the United States Holocaust Memorial Council, 1997. Third Printing, September 2001.

Thackeray, H. St. J. *The Letter of Aristeas.* London: Macmillan and Co., 1904.

Theophrastus, *De Pietate.* Quoted in Menahem Stern. *Greek and Latin Authors on Jews and Judaism: Volume I, From Herodotus to Plutarch.* Jerusalem: The Israel Academy of Sciences and Humanities, 1976.

Trachtenberg, Joshua. *The Devil and the Jews: The Medieval Conception of the Jew and Its Relation to Modern Anti-Semitism.* Philadelphia, PA: Jewish Publication Society, 1983.

Van der Horst, Pieter W. *Philo's Flaccus: The First Pogrom, Introduction, Translation and Commentary.* Atlanta, GA: Society of Biblical Literature, 2003.

VanderKam, James C. *An Introduction to Early Judaism.* Grand Rapids, MI: Eerdmans, 2001.

Von Kellenbach, Katharina. *Anti-Judaism in Feminist Religious Writings.* Atlanta, GA: Scholars Press, 1994.

Walfish, Barry D. "Kosher Adultery? The Mordecai-Esther-Ahasuerus Triangle in Talmudic, Medieval and Sixteenth Exegesis." Pages 111-136 in *The Book of Esther in Modern Research.* Edited by Sidnie White Crawford and Leonard J. Greenspoon. London: T and T Clark International, 2003.

Wasserstein, Abraham, and David J. Wasserstein. *The Legend of the Septuagint from Classical Antiquity to Today.* Cambridge: Cambridge University Press, 2006.

Wellhausen, Julius. *Prolegomena to the History of Ancient Israel.* Eugene, OR: Wipf and Stock Publishers, 2003.

Whiston, William. *The New Complete Works of Josephus.* Grand Rapids, MI: Kregel Publications, 1999.

White, Sidnie Ann. "Esther: A Feminine Model for Jewish Diaspora." Pages 161-177 in *Gender and Difference in Ancient Israel.* Edited by Peggy L. Day. Minneapolis, MN: Fortress Press, 1989.

Williams, Margaret., ed. *The Jews among the Greeks and Romans: A Diasporan Sourcebook.* Baltimore, MD: Johns Hopkins University Press, 1998.

Wilson, Marvin R. *Our Father Abraham: Jewish Roots of the Christian Faith.* Grand Rapids, MI: Eerdmans Publishing Company, 1989.

Wistrich, Robert S. *A Lethal Obsession: Anti-Semitism from Antiquity to the Global Jihad.* New York: Random House, 2010.

Yamauchi, Edwin. "Mordecai, the Persepolis Tablets and the Susa Excavations." *Vetus Testamentum* XLII, 2 (1992): 272-5.

———. *Persia and the Bible.* Grand Rapids, MI: Baker Books, 1996.

Yonge, C.D. *The Works of Philo: Complete and Unabridged, New Updated Version.* Peabody, MA: Hendrickson Publishers, 1993.

Web Sources

"About Memri." *The Middle East Media Research Institute.* Accessed on 20 September 2014: http://www.memri.org/about-memri.html.

"About Us." *Bethlehem Bible College.* Accessed on 14 September 2014: http://www.bethbc.org/welcome/about-us.

"About Willow." *Willow Creek Community Church.* Accessed on 20 September 2014: http://www.willowcreek.org/aboutwillow/one-church-multiple-locations.

Al-Marayati, Salam. "Apologists or Extremists." *The Investigative Project on Terrorism,* 24 March 2010. Accessed on 14 September 2014: http://www.investigativeproject.org/profile/114.

Awad, Alex. "Bethlehem Voices on Gaza." *YouTube.* 8 August 2014. Accessed on 14 September 2014: https://www.youtube.com/watch?v=5s7nq6B6KJQ.

Ben Zion, Ilan, Lazar Berman and Marissa Newman. "4 soldiers killed in mortar attack, as PM says Gaza op goes on, vows to counter tunnels." *The Times of Israel.* 28 July 2014. Accessed on 14 September 2014: http://www.timesofisrael.com/day-21-obama-calls-netanyahu-urges-immediate-unconditional-ceasefire-in-hamas-conflict/.

"Case Study: Portraying Jews as "Apes and Pigs." *Palestinian Media Watch.* Accessed on 20 September 2014: http://www.palwatch.org/main.aspx?fi=786.

"CATC 2014 'Dialogue on Replacement Theology': Gary Burge & Daniel Juster." *Christ at the Checkpoint 2014.* Accessed on 20 September 2014: http://vimeo.com/89570014.

"Community Covenant." *Wheaton College.* Accessed on 20 September 2014: http://www.wheaton.edu/About-Wheaton/Community-Covenant.

Fletcher, Jim. "Bethlehem Like You Haven't Seen It Before." *The Balfour Post.* 13 May 2013. Accessed on 20 September 2014: http://balfourpost.com/bethlehem-like-you-havent-seen-it-before/.

Harris, David. "Hanan Ashrawi is to Truth what Smoking is to Health." *The World Post.* 2 September 2012. Accessed on 20 September 2014: http://www.huffingtonpost.com/david-harris/hanan-ashrawi-is-to-truth_b_1851044.html.

Hollander, Ricki. "The Facts About Hamas." *Committee for Accuracy in Middle East Reporting in America.* 24 April 2014. Accessed on 20 September 2014: http://www.camera.org/index.asp?x_context=7&x_issue=11&x_article=1618.

"Home." *Kairos Palestine.* Accessed on 20 September 2014: http://www.kairospalestine.ps/.

Ini, Gilead. "Bandar's Legacy." *Committee for Accuracy in Middle East Reporting in America.* 21 July 2005. Accessed on 14 September 2014: http://blog.camera.org/archives/2005/07/bandars_legacy.html.

"Jews/Israelis are Evil." *Palestinian Media Watch* Accessed on 20 September 2014: http://www.palwatch.org/main.aspx?fi=762.

JPost.com Staff. "Suha Arafat Admits Husband Premeditated Intifada." *The Jerusalem Post.* 29 December 2012. Accessed on 14 September 2014: http://www.jpost.com/Middle-East/Suha-Arafat-admits-husband-premeditated-Intifada.

Marcus, Itamar and Nan Jacques Zilberdik. "Fatah Leader Calls for Israel's Destruction." *Palestinian Media Watch.* 29 April 2014. Accessed on 20 September 2014: http://www.palwatch.org/main.aspx?fi=157&doc_id=11319.

———. "PA TV broadcasts 19 times in 3 days Abbas' implicit call for violence in Jerusalem." *Palestinian Media Watch.* 28 October 2014. Accessed on 21 March 2015: http://www.palwatch.org/main.aspx?fi=157&doc_id=12915.

Miller, Tricia. "'The Stones Cry Out' Misrepresents Plight of Palestinian Christians." *Committee for Accuracy in Middle East Reporting in America.* 11 February 2014. Accessed on 20 September 2014: http://www.camera.org/index.asp?x_context=55&x_article=2650.

"Mission + Vision." *The Telos Group.* Accessed on 14 September 2014: http://www.telosgroup.org/about/mission.

"News." *The Telos Group.* Accessed on 14 September 2014: http://www.telosgroup.org/news/P10.

"Our Story." *Sabeel Ecumenical Liberation Theology Center, 2010.* Accessed on 14 September 2014: http://www.sabeel.org/ourstory.php.

"Propaganda and Practice." *Human Rights Watch.* 8 August 2014. Accessed on 20 September 2014: http://www.hrw.org/reports/1999/rwanda/Geno1-3-10.htm.

Raheb, Mitri. *Christ at the Checkpoint.* Accessed on 14 September 2014: http://www.christatthecheckpoint.com/lectures/Mitri_Raheb.pdf.

"Resolution Adopted by the CCAR." *Central Conference of American Rabbis.* Accessed on 20 September 2014: http://ccarnet.org/rabbis-speak/resolutions/2010/ccar-resolution-2009-kairos-document/.

Rudoren, Jodi and Mochael R. Gordon. "As Kerry Visits Jordan, Abbas Holds His Ground." *The New York Times.* 7 March 2014. Accessed on 21 March 2015: http://www.nytimes.com/2014/03/08/world/middleeast/secretary-of-state-john-kerry.html?_r=1.

Sabeel Ecumenical Liberation Theology Center. Accessed on 14 September 2014: http://www.sabeel.org/index.php.

Salim, Ali. "Why the Palestinians Refuse to Recognize Israel as a Jewish State." *Gatestone Institute.* 3 February 2014. Accessed on 20 September 2014: http://www.gatestoneinstitute.org/4151/palestinians-recognition-israel-jewish-state.

"The Six-Day War: Background and Overview." *Jewish Virtual Library.* Accessed on 14 September 2014: http://www.jewishvirtuallibrary.org/jsource/History/67_War.html.

Small, Charles Asher. "On Cockroaches, Apes and Genocide." *The Times of Israel.* 19 April 2014. Accessed on 20 September 2014: http://blogs.timesofisrael.com/cockroaches-apes-and-genocide/.

Steinberg, Gerald M. "Analyzing the Durban II Conference." *Jerusalem Center for Public Affairs.* 4 March 2010. Accessed on 20 September 2014: http://jcpa.org/article/analyzing-the-durban-ii-conference/.

Stotsky, Steven. "Reporting of Casualties in Gaza." *Committee for Accuracy in Middle East Reporting in America.* 14 July 2014. Accessed on 14 September 2014: http://www.camera.org/index.asp?x_context=55&x_article=2762.

"The Telos Team." *The Telos Group.* Accessed on 14 September 2014: http://www.telosgroup.org/about/staff.

"The 3 No's of Khartoum." *Committee for Accuracy in Middle East Reporting in America.* Accessed on 14 September 2014: http://www.sixdaywar.org/content/khartoum.asp.

"United Nations General Assembly Resolution 181." *The Avalon Project at Yale Law School.* 29 November 1947. Accessed on 14 September 2014: http://www.yale.edu/lawweb/avalon/un/res181.html.

"UN Security Council: Resolutions on Israel/Middle East." *Jewish Virtual Library.* Accessed on 14 September 2014: http://www.jewishvirtuallibrary.org/jsource/UN/sctoc.html.

"UN Security Council: The Meaning of Resolution 242." *Jewish Virtual Library.* Accessed on 14 September 2014: http://www.jewishvirtuallibrary.org/jsource/UN/meaning_of_242.html.

Van Zile, Dexter. "Mainline Churches Embrace Burge's False Narrative." *Committee for Accuracy in Middle East Reporting in America.* 23 August 2007. Accessed on 20 September 2014: http://www.camera.org/index.asp?x_context=2&x_outlet=118&x_article=1356.

———. "The Mis-Education of a Young Evangelical." *New English Review.* October 2011. Accessed on 20 September 2014: http://www.newenglishreview.org/Dexter_Van_Zile/The_Mis-Education_of_a_Young_Evangelical/.

———. "*Sojourners* Portrays Israel at Center of Christian Crisis in Middle East." *Committee for Accuracy in Middle East Reporting in America.* 20 June 2013. Accessed on 20 September 2014: http://www.camera.org/index.asp?x_context=55&x_article=2490.

———. "Book Promoted by Willow Creek Church Leaves Readers Ill-Prepared for Peacemaking." *Committee for Accuracy in Middle East Reporting in America.* 28 October 2013. Accessed on 14 September 2014: http://www.camera.org/index.asp?x_context=55&x_article=2575.

———. "Gary Burge's Missed Opportunity." *Committee for Accuracy in Middle East Reporting in America.* 31 December 2013. Accessed on 20 September 2014: http://www.camera.org/index.asp?x_context=55&x_article=2615.

"Video Clip." *The Middle East Media Research Institute.* Accessed on 20 September 2014: http://www.memri.org/clip/en/0/0/0/0/0/0/2527.html.

"Vision." *Sabeel Ecumenical Liberation Theology Center.* Accessed on 21 March 2015: http://www.sabeel.org/vision.php.

Weinthal, Benjamin. "Israel Slams Award to Anti-Semitic Pastor." *Jerusalem Post.* 9 February 2012. Accessed on 14 September 2014: http://www.jpost.com/International/Israel-slams-award-to-anti-Semitic-pastor.

INDEX

CPSIA information can be obtained at www.ICGtesting.com
Printed in the USA
BVOW08s0253090415

395368BV00002B/20/P